IFRS™
and
US
GAAP

A Comprehensive Comparison

IFRS™
and
US
GAAP

A Comprehensive Comparison

Steven E. Shamrock

WILEY

John Wiley & Sons, Inc.

For general information on our other products and services, or technical support, please contact our Customer Care Department within the United States at 800-762-2974, outside the United States at 317-572-3993 or fax 317-572-4002.

Wiley also publishes its books in a variety of electronic formats. Some content that appears in print may not be available in electronic books.

For more information about Wiley products, visit our website at http://www.wiley.com.

Library of Congress Cataloging-in-Publication Data:

ISBN 978-1-118-14430-5 (book); ISBN 978-1-118-22573-8 (ebk); ISBN 978-1-118-23906-3 (ebk); ISBN 978-1-118-26371-6 (ebk)

Printed in the United States of America.

10 9 8 7 6 5 4 3 2 1

CONTENTS

ABOUT THE AUTHOR

Steven E. Shamrock is and has been a practicing accounting professional for twenty-two years, ten of those years as a controller. During his career, Steven has led accounting teams in both large, multinational public companies and smaller, entrepreneurial enterprises. He has used IFRS simultaneously with US GAAP for eight years. He is a frequent speaker at AICPA and IFRS Foundation events. Steven was a member of the AICPA Special Advisory Group for the creation of the AICPA's IFRS Certificate Program. Steven has also taught IFRS to executives in both the United States and the United Kingdom. He has been a contributing author to other Wiley publications. His motivation for writing this book is to further the competent use of IFRS by US accounting professionals to empower them in the world of two pervasive accounting standards. US accountants need to know both standards given the large foreign ownership of US companies.

Steven is a native of Cleveland, Ohio, but has resided in Naperville, Illinois, a suburb of Chicago, Illinois, for most of the past ten years with his wife Lisa, and twin sons, Pete and Luke. Steven wishes to thank his wife and sons for their unyielding support during the writing of this book. He also wishes to thank his father, Edward, also an accountant, and his mother, Tina for their positive support.

Steven is a CPA, has a bachelor's degree in Accounting from John Carroll University in Cleveland, Ohio, and an MBA in Economics from DePaul University in Chicago, Illinois. He also is a Certified Management Accountant, as issued by the Institute of Management Accountants in Montvale, New Jersey.

INTRODUCTION

Much has been made of the convergence of IFRS and US GAAP. In every corner of the country, from Washington to Wall Street, from boardrooms to business schools, the past decade has produced a deluge of information that has inundated the media, trade publications, seminars, and CPE courses with opinions of every shape, form, and point of view. This is not a bad thing. The adoption of IFRS from the tried-and-true US GAAP is both an important and formidable task. Information, debate, and education are essential to this decision.

This book has an accompanying Web site, www.wiley.com/go/shamrockifrsgaap, that contains Excel spreadsheets that illustrate some of the concepts in the book and provide templates for modeling your own organization's IFRS/US GAAP differences.

However, one could say that adopting IFRS will be less of a decision and more of a process. In 2008, the Gross Domestic Product of countries using IFRS exceeded those that do not, by hundreds of billions of dollars. This includes the United States. Moreover, the ubiquity of IFRS (used or slated to be used in over 117 countries) indicates a near future where providers of capital will insist on receiving financial information using IFRS. Why? Markets dislike uncertainty—uncertainty comes with incomparability. When the volume of business that capital providers do for clients that use IFRS exceeds that of US GAAP, capitalism will dictate standardization in the qualification for financing as a cost-saving measure. This is inevitable. It is much less believable that all the countries who have recently adopted IFRS will suddenly switch to US GAAP.

CPA exams already have IFRS questions. Universities now include it in their curriculums. The signs are bold. The time to learn about IFRS is now.

For all the differences between the two standards, they are roughly 85% identical in core accounting concepts. This assessment does not include the myriad of interpretations that are part of the US GAAP Codification. However, more often than not, these interpretations provide guidance on a very narrow type of transaction.

What do the two have in common? Fortunately, these include most important and seminal characteristics.

The qualitative characteristics and elements of accounting (e.g., assets, liabilities, neutrality, representational faithfulness) are, for all intents and purposes, identical. In other words, the semantics are the same. This provides a robust and easily adopted framework for learning about IFRS.

That said, however, the old "20/80" rule is applicable. More specifically, 20% of things result in 80% of the problems! So the adoption of IFRS cannot be taken lightly.

Perhaps the most pervasive difference is in the application of the standards. As mentioned earlier, US GAAP has become rule-based. Practitioners, auditors, and regulators have grown accustomed to searching diligently for the most specific paragraph in a standard to validate accounting treatment. This is not wrong, only different from IFRS.

The philosophy of IFRS can be construed as to have standards that are flexible enough to accommodate unforeseen economic transactions, yet specific enough to prevent misrepresentation of economic events. Some would argue that there are holes in this approach, that US GAAP is matured and has a large body of interpretation that increases comparability. But another view of this state is that the rules have become so narrow as to decrease comparability. Consider the analogy of a square peg in a round hole. Conversely, IFRS continually refers back to the *IFRS Framework* (similar to the US GAAP *Concepts*

Statements). In fact, the *Framework* is authoritative. US GAAP *Concepts Statements* are not. This strident adherence to principles in using IFRS puts the onus on practitioners and auditors to account for and report transactions based on the economic reality, not a series of increasingly restrictive interpretations. In a world of increasingly diverse transactions, this will serve to *increase* comparability. It can allow investors to see the economic impact of the unique mix of transactions that an entity is comprised of.

This flexibility does come with a transition cost. Many of the debates about accounting treatment that would have once occurred in EITF meetings and the like will now transpire among the controller, CFO, CEO, and staff, including operational team members. Using IFRS often entails really understanding an entity's operations, objectives, and processes. This means that as IFRS becomes part of the US accountant tool set, there will be more time spent on accounting and reporting. However, less time will be spent researching, which will balance the workload.

Certainly systems, processes, and tools will need to change. However, accountants are used to projects. The adoption of IFRS is, in fact, a project. Traditional project management tools will work well.

The time is now to embrace IFRS, when the US accounting community can help shape its direction. Many multinational companies already prepare "statutory" financial information using IFRS for local governments. Having a single standard will reduce cost and complexity for these enterprises. So there is an immediate, practical benefit of using IFRS.

Some say that IFRS would only benefit large companies. And certainly, in terms of scale, that is true. However, as IFRS becomes more pervasive, the bank officers that provide loans to private businesses will have begun to use IFRS. It is plausible that they may become more accustomed to IFRS. Thus, small businesses that are conversant with IFRS will benefit by having a wider pool of loan providers. Smaller companies are usually less complex than larger ones. As complexity of businesses decreases, so do the differences between IFRS and US GAAP. Thus the cost will not be as great.

In the final analysis, cash is cash, and timing is everything. No matter what rules and principles are used to measure the performance of an entity, the ability to consistently generate cash is a major factor in success. Lastly, timing is everything. At one time or another, everything that ends up as comprehensive income in IFRS will also be part of comprehensive income under US GAAP. This does not mean timing is unimportant. On the contrary, if it were not, companies would not spend endless efforts on meeting their quarterly numbers. However, understanding that the basis of both US GAAP and IFRS is measuring the timing, amount, and risk of cash flow removes a layer of mystery from IFRS.

IFRS and US GAAP are about measuring the success or failure of an entity. This is something that people of any language or culture can understand.

1 STANDARD SETTING

Just as the Financial Accounting Standards Board (FASB) creates and maintains US GAAP Codification, the International Accounting Standards Board (IASB) does the same for International Financial Reporting Standards (IFRS™). Both are overseen by a group of trustees. The FASB reports to the Financial Accounting Foundation. The IASB is accountable in the first instance to the International Accounting Standards Committee (IASC). Both have interpretive bodies. The FASB has the Emerging Issues Task Force (EITF) in addition to many nonauthoritative bodies such as the American Institute of Certified Public Accountants (AICPA). The IASB/IASC have the International Financial Reporting Interpretations Committee (IFRIC).

Where the standard-setting apparatus diverges is with the role of the Securities and Exchange Commission (SEC) with regard to US GAAP. The SEC delegates its day-to-day rule-making authority to the FASB. The SEC also can supersede US GAAP for public companies. Regulations S-X and S-K define the form and content of financial statement reports, as well as disclosures that are not required under the US GAAP Codification.

Since IFRS is not owned by any one country, the IASB is the top-level authoritative body for IFRS standards. In 2008, recognizing the potential shortcomings of not having a rule-making oversight body such as the SEC, the IASC formed the Monitoring Board (MB). The MB's role is to provide an extra layer of independence from political influence. The need to protect the IASB from the political winds was underscored when in 2008, David Tweedie, chairman of the IASB at the time, temporarily suspended parts of the IFRS statements regarding classification of the fair market value effects on financial instruments. This directive allowed companies to take the large losses from the 2008 global financial crisis out of net income and into comprehensive income. The public fallout was swift and severe. Critics of IFRS pointed to this as an example of the highly political nature of the IFRS standard-setting process as a result of the multinational mix of board members.

However, what these critics did not mention is that the US GAAP has for decades been shaped by corporate lobbying via the exposure draft process. The most egregious example is the number of years and slow evolution of the accounting for pension and postretirement benefits. It took 17 years for the US GAAP to require companies to reflect in their financial statements the full value of these liabilities. Early comments on the first statement brought laments of doom and gloom as companies would become insolvent overnight. This did not happen. The investor community regularly adjusts the financial statements they are analyzing for off-balance-sheet items. Analysis also typically adds future minimum lease payments that are disclosed for operating leases to the liabilities of an entity when assessing financial condition.

Both bodies employ rigorous process in forming standards. Both have position papers, exposure drafts, and specific instructions and the timing of transition from prior standards. In fact, the two bodies have been jointly developing standards since the 2002 Norwalk Agreement, which creates a roadmap to convergence. The broad outline of the plan is that the two boards converge standards where they have mutual interests. Its objective does not include the synchronization of every standard.

The Norwalk Agreement has been prolific. The two boards have produced many joint standards. However, despite these efforts, jointly issued statements, while substantially identical, still have persistent, if not pervasive, differences. Recent standards have included sections that detail the differences between the two statements.

The governance of the IASB also includes a constitution that establishes the overall objectives of IFRS, the integrity of the standard-setting process, funding of the board, and consultations that are required as part of the process. The constitution is reviewed every five years, and the most recent update was in 2009. The board takes a vote to decide which issues are on the standard-setting agenda. Conversely, the FASB chairman decides on issues to undertake after consultation.

INTERPRETATIONS

Both the IASB and FASB provide interpretations of their standards. The FASB, primarily via the EITF, issues many more interpretations than IFRS. The number since the founding of the FASB in 1972 easily reaches into the hundreds. These together with other bodies, including SEC FRM updates, FASB staff positions, and AICPA Statements of Position likely add at least 200. In contrast, IFRS has only 17 active interpretations and a few amendments. Some prior IFRS interpretations (perhaps a dozen) have been subsumed into updated or new standards. It should be noted, however, that when a standard is reconsidered, the IASB, as a matter of process, attempts to incorporate the interpretations (IFRICs) in the main standard. The number of interpretations is still orders of magnitudes less than US GAAP.

While the FASB ratifies interpretations and does reject considering matters, the IFRIC routinely rejects issuing interpretations. Instead, it issues a monthly update that summarizes the interpretations sought by the user community and usually points out paragraphs of existing standards that the board feels provides adequate guidance with which to account for the matters in question. This approach is indicative of the principle-based nature of IFRS. When the IFRIC identifies an issue where there is an obvious gap in guidance or strong possibility of divergence in practice, the matter is placed on the agenda. Additionally, each year the IASB sets an IFRS improvements agenda that is sourced from constituent requests. The improvements typically result in statement amendments.

STATEMENT NUMBERING

In 2008, the FASB released the US GAAP Codification. The Codification summarized and organized into topics the substance of all prior standards such as Statements on Financial Accounting Standards (SFAS), EITFs, AICPA Statements of Position, and standard updates. Updates to the Codification are announced and put into a temporary section of the Codification until they are inserted into the proper sections as they become effective. The topics are numbered as follows.

IFRS uses sequential numbers as the FASB did prior to the Codification. There are two "sets" of IFRS standards. The first begin with IAS which stands for International Accounting Standards. These statements originated before the IASB came into existence and standard setting fell completely on the IASC. In 2000, when the IASB was founded, subsequent statements began with IFRS (and still do).

Similar to the change management of the US GAAP Codification, when standards are changed, the statement retains its number and title, but has a date appended to it to distinguish between prior versions. This convention means that there still are, and will continue to be IASs in effect. However, when a standard is fundamentally rewritten, or a new subject matter is undertaken, the statement begins with IFRS (with the former IAS number standard retired).

Currently there are 29 IASs, 13 IFRSs, 16 IFRICs, and 11 SICs.

2 THE FRAMEWORK

The most significant difference between US GAAP and IFRS for a practitioner is the role that the underlying concepts play in day-to-day accounting and reporting. In simple terms, effective practice of US GAAP compels the user to find the best paragraph that fits a transaction or balance. Under IFRS, users are expected to apply the principles in a way that faithfully represents economic reality.

A visual representation could be envisioning US GAAP as a great wall of cubbies in which one finds the one that best fits the transaction at hand and places it in that space. Following this depiction, IFRS is more like an orderly shelf of jars which are taken out as needed, and the contents of those containers combined to create the best mixture that faithfully represents the transaction.

This is not to say that US GAAP does not aim to create financial statements that faithfully represent the combination of transactions that an entity is made up of. The two standards just take different paths to the same destination.

In order to use IFRS effectively, it helps to understand the different political environments under which the statements are designed and interpreted. The Securities and Exchange Commission alone has the statutory responsibility to promulgate accounting rules in the United States. While the SEC has delegated most of this authority to the Financial Accounting Standards Board, the commission can and does supplement accounting rules of public companies. Because the SEC's commissioner is appointed by the president of the United States, it is influenced by politics, specifically the politics of the United States.

Conversely, the International Accounting Standards Board has no equivalent authority, but must answer to users and investors in over 100 countries. This diffusion of influence gives the IASB the freedom to hew statements close to the theory because using the objective platform of *The Framework* is an effective way for the IASB to eliminate the perception of favoritism.

This is not to say that the IASB does not need to heed the concerns of its constituents. The European Union (EU), for example, has created the European Financial Reporting Advisory Group (EFRAG) to endorse IFRS standards. The EU was able to effect changes favorable to EU countries in 2003 when IFRS was adopted for those countries. A 2008 decision by the chairman of the IASB to allow companies in the EU to effectively defer losses regarding some financial instruments by allowing them to reclassify losses to Other Comprehensive Income (OCI) demonstrates how broad political issues can affect the IFRS.

The *IFRS Framework* is a stand-alone statement that defines the elements of financial statements and their qualitative characteristics. In summary, it provides a seminal description of assets, liabilities, equity, revenue, and income. The qualitative characteristics define the boundaries of these financial statement elements. It also considers the tensions and trade-offs between the characteristics. IAS 1 directs practitioners to use *The Framework* for accounting decisions if IFRS does not address otherwise.

The FASB, however, uses the *Concepts Statements* as the edifice upon which statements, interpretations, and updates are based. It is clear that preparers are not to use *Concepts Statements* to decide upon the presentation and accounting for a given transaction. Following is an excerpt from Statement of Financial Accounting Standards No. 6:

> *Statements of Financial Accounting Concepts do not establish standards prescribing accounting procedures or disclosure practices for particular items or events, which are issued by the Board as Statements of Financial Accounting Standards. Rather, Statements in this series describe concepts and relations that will underlie future financial accounting standards and practices and in due course serve as a basis for evaluating existing standards and practices.*

This body of knowledge is only used to provide a fabric from which standards are cut—by the standard setters. As a consequence, US GAAP is very prescriptive compared with IFRS.

This is not to say that uncommon transactions surface frequently for accountants using US GAAP, but these are usually "vanilla" issues, such as an up-front payment to a retail customer for setting up displays and shelves. More complex subjects are dealt with very differently in the two standards.

The IASB through its interpretative arm, the International Financial Reporting Interpretation Committee (IFRIC), often responds to requests for interpretations by pointing out certain paragraphs that should be used to address the accounting or reporting issue. In other words, the IFRIC often refuses to interpret.

Here is an example: A constituent submitted a request to determine if part of the Foreign Currency Translation Adjustments (FCTA) in equity should be recycled through profit and loss if either the absolute investment in an investee changed but not the relative ownership, or if the investment remained the same but the relative ownership in the investee changed. The IFRIC, through its periodic newsletter (issued several times per year) responded that judgment must be used to determine if there "has been a change in interest." The IFRIC refused to opine.

Conversely, the FASB responds to inquiries only through Accounting Standards Updates (ASU) that have been through due process. These are narrow and specific. One case (2011) concerned determining when a creditor had a "troubled debt" in order to apply the accounting for troubled debt restructuring. The guidance defined a specific mathematical test that must be applied to determine this.

The IASB is disciplined in always referring to *The Framework* and existing standards when creating official interpretations (IFRICs) or new standards. This practice is aimed at not creating divergence among accounting for similar transactions. The FASB and the SEC have and continue to diverge from the established body of US GAAP.

In 2011, the FASB rejected including potential voting rights when determining control of an investee (and thus the determination of whether to consolidate), even though IFRS does. The potential voting rights of an investor can be used to wield influence and even control over an investee even though the investor does not own a majority of the voting interests. The FASB disagreed and kept its condition that potential rights are not considered. This brings about a trend I will call *divergence*.

Since the Norwalk Agreement of 2002, the FASB and IASB have issued many joint statements that are in almost all respects identical. However, there are differences, and some statements note these in the appendices. After the converged standard is released, interpretations by the FASB and refusals to interpret by the IASB create divergences in practice and standard. An ASU issued in 2011 proposed to allow companies to not perform Step 1 of the Goodwill Impairment Test if it is more likely than not (greater than 50%) that the reporting unit is not impaired. This increases the tolerance for not performing the test. The existing standard, converged in 2003, allows an entity to effectively not perform Step 1 for a reporting unit if the fair value calculated in the last test exceeded carrying value "by a substantial margin," provided there were no significant changes to the reporting unit (e.g., restructuring, market upheaval). The proposed ASU lowers this threshold, and this creates a divergence from the converged standard.

One set of characteristics, perhaps more than any other pair, illustrates a key difference between US GAAP and IFRS. The pair is relevance versus reliability. Relevance means that the information matters to a user's decision based on the financial statements. Reliability is what the general meaning of the word is outside of the accounting realms. Reliable information can be independently verified and is materially accurate given all the information known at the financial statement date, or, in some cases, when the statements are issued.

While there are numerous instances where US GAAP and IFRS are very similar with regard to relevance and reliability, generally speaking, IFRS weighs relevance as more important that reliability as compared to US GAAP. The most prominent area indicative of this disparity is accrued liabilities. IFRS contains the term *constructive liability,* which is an obligation that an entity has no realistic alternative but to satisfy. Constructive liabilities can arise in the absence of contractual commitments and arise solely on expectations of "creditors" based on the past actions of the entity. While US GAAP employs this concept in the recognition of asset retirement and environmental obligations, IFRS uses constructive liabilities as a main pillar of recognition. Accruals for legal settlements are a significant area of difference.

Characterization is another facet where US GAAP and IFRS have differences. In accounting for financial instruments, some changes in the value of the instruments are recognized as income under US GAAP and OCI (in equity) for IFRS, and vice versa. A more significant difference is the full recognition of pension and postretirement benefits. Under US GAAP, the full value of net obligations (or assets) is recognized at the end of each fiscal year. The adjustment from book value is reflected in OCI. Under IFRS, the change in net obligations (or assets) is kept off the balance sheet and amortized into income (although this will change in 2013).

Basis of accounting is largely consistent between IFRS and US GAAP, except in certain instances of measurement. Both rely on historical cost and fair value as a core basis, although IFRS uses fair value more than US GAAP.

FINANCIAL ELEMENTS

IFRS and US GAAP have very similar definitions of financial elements. That said, however, as we'll see in this book, there is sometimes a conflict between the two standards as to whether the benefit from an economic resource is certain enough to account for it as an asset. One example is development costs. Under US GAAP, all research and development costs are expensed. IFRS requires capitalization of development costs when certain conditions are met.

Likewise for liabilities, there are multiple instances where IFRS requires accruals before US GAAP does. One such difference is for an onerous contract. Onerous contracts are ones where the future economic benefit of an irrevocable contract is less than the cost of fulfilling the contract. IFRS requires immediate recognition and subsequent adjustment of onerous contracts in earnings. US GAAP does not permit this on the grounds that the future effects are too unreliable to be useful or cost-beneficial.

Turning to the income statement, IFRS defines an element called *income* that encompasses both revenue and gains. US GAAP defines gains/loss separately from revenue (income from the main activities of the entity). However, IFRS includes revenues and gains within the income definition.

COMPARISONS OF DEFINITIONS

Assets

There are subtle, yet consequential, differences in the definitions of assets between the standards:

US GAAP: Assets are probable future economic benefits obtained or controlled by a particular entity as a result of past transactions or events.
IFRS: An asset is a resource controlled by the entity as a result of past events and from which future economic benefits are expected to flow to the entity.

Note that IFRS uses the term *expected.* While expected includes those things that are probable, expected opens the door to recognition of assets that are less certain. For example, IFRS allows entities to revalue assets (upward and downward). US GAAP specifically prohibits this. IFRS also requires reversal of impairments when economic conditions turn favorable, while US GAAP does not permit reversals.

Liabilities

US GAAP: Liabilities are probable future sacrifices of economic benefits arising from present obligations of a particular entity to transfer assets or provide services to other entities in the future as a result of past transactions or events.
IFRS: A liability is a present obligation of the entity arising from past events, the settlement of which is expected to result in an outflow from the entity of resources embodying economic benefits.

As is the case when comparing the definition of assets between IFRS and US GAAP, the US GAAP definition of liabilities uses *probable* versus *expected* in IFRS.

Equity

> *US GAAP:* Equity, or net assets, is the residual interest in the assets of an entity that remains after deducting its liabilities.
>
> *IFRS:* Equity is the residual interest in the assets of the entity after deducting all its liabilities.

While these definitions are identical, IFRS and US GAAP differ with regard to some forms of preferred stock. IFRS classifies these forms as liabilities, while US GAAP classifies all preferred stock between liabilities and equity. The classification of some stock-based compensation awards can also be present on the balance sheet differently.

Income Statement

Revenue

> *US GAAP:* Revenues are inflows or other enhancements of assets of an entity or settlements of its liabilities (or a combination of both) from delivering or producing goods, rendering services, or other activities that constitute the entity's ongoing major or central operations.
>
> *IFRS:* Revenues are inflows or enhancements of assets from sources other than stakeholders. Revenue arises in the course of the ordinary activities of an entity and is referred to by a variety of different names including sales, fees, interest, dividends, royalties, and rent.

IFRS takes a residual approach to revenue. While in most cases revenues under IFRS are the same for US GAAP (although the timing of recognition can differ in many cases), IFRS directs that grants of assets by governments can be recorded as revenue. This is usually not the case for US GAAP.

Expenses

> *US GAAP:* Expenses are outflows or other using up of assets or incurrences of liabilities (or a combination of both) from delivering or producing goods, rendering services, or carrying out other activities that constitute the entity's ongoing major or central operations.
>
> *IFRS:* Expenses are decreases in economic benefits during the accounting period in the form of outflows or depletions of assets or incurrences of liabilities that result in decreases in equity, other than those relating to distributions to equity participants. Expenses that arise in the course of the ordinary activities of the entity include, for example, cost of sales, wages, and depreciation. They usually take the form of an outflow or depletion of assets such as cash and cash equivalents, inventory, property, plant, and equipment.

Note that the IFRS definition begins with a general definition of expenses. This is because in theory IFRS does not distinguish between expense and losses (expenses incidental to main operations). However, the standards of both US GAAP and IFRS require a distinction between expenses and losses in financial statements.

Gains and Losses

IFRS and US GAAP agree that gains and losses are inflows and outflows that are incidental to the main operations of an entity.

Complete Set of Financial Statements

A complete set of financial statements includes a Statement of Financial Position (balance sheet), Statement of Income, Statement of Cash Flows, Statement of Shareholders' Equity, and a Statement of Comprehensive Income.

The Statement of Comprehensive Income begins with Net Income and includes effects from transactions that are presented as OCI. OCI includes **certain** gains and losses from financial instruments, foreign currency translation effects (not remeasurement effects), pension and postretirement gains and losses, effects of share-based compensation, and other items. The tax effect on these items is also included in OCI.

IFRS allows for the presentation of a single statement of comprehensive income rather than a separate Income Statement and Statement of Comprehensive Income. OCI cannot be shown as part of the Statement of Shareholders' Equity, unlike US GAAP.

US GAAP requires the same statements, although OCI is included in the Statement of Shareholders' Equity. This difference between the two standards demonstrates a philosophical split. IFRS takes a more inclusive approach to income, whereas US GAAP presents it more or less as information. Generally speaking, OCI includes impacts where the eventual cash outflows or inflows are subject to long-term factors. For instance, currency translation effects may never be realized if the entity monetizes the interest in an investee in a period where the exchange rate is materially different from the current period. Additionally, the fluctuation on currency values is largely outside of the control of the entity (although companies may employ hedges, the offsetting effects of which, if meeting certain requirements, are reflected in OCI). The remeasurement of a transaction, conversely, is included in income because of the relatively near-term probability realization into cash of the transaction.

CHAPTER SUMMARY

The theoretical bases of IFRS and US GAAP are very similar. However, the timing of recognition and basis of assets and liabilities at a given point in time varies and the volume and content of guidance is disparate.

IFRS requires preparers of financial statements to consider *The Framework* in almost all cases for a transaction or class of transactions. The guidance in a particular IFRS statement is not only principles-based, but can be used as an analogy for transactions outside the scope of that statement where the other transaction does not have specific guidance. IFRS also permits an entity to use the current pronouncements of another standard setter that has a similar framework in cases where specific guidance does not exist, provided the guidance of the other standard setter is not contrary to *The Framework*. There are few exceptions to *The Framework* in IFRS statements. Interpretations by the IFRIC are rare.

Conversely, preparers of US GAAP financial statements are prohibited from using the FASB Concept Statements for a particular transaction (although, obviously, the Codification does reflect the principles in the Concepts Statements). US GAAP contains many deviations from its framework. Statements are prescriptive, descriptive, and specific. Interpretations are frequent and narrow. In some cases, the Codification prohibits the use of a standard by analogy.

Both sets of standards have the goal of providing useful, relevant, and reliable information for a broad set of financial statement users. However, the approach each one takes can be very different. This difference requires different processes and decisions. This book attempts to provide practical, plainly described ways to deal with the differences.

3 PROPERTY, PLANT, AND EQUIPMENT

The predominant standard that defines the accounting and reporting for Property, Plant, and Equipment (PP&E) is IAS 16. US GAAP guidance for PP&E was formed from several standards issued over many years until they were combined in the Codification. However, except for the areas of software, oil and gas, and mining assets, IFRS and US GAAP use nearly identical criteria for capitalization. Impairment of PP&E is covered later in the book.

PP&E are assets with physical form that an entity uses to make a profit. An example is a metal-forming machine in a plant that produces automobiles. Internally developed software can qualify for capitalization (as well as purchased software). Under IFRS, software is reported under the intangible assets category. Under US GAAP, software is **not** presented as intangible.

PP&E is recognized at historical costs, with an exception for agricultural assets under IFRS. Costs of PP&E include all materials, labor, permits, and other costs directly attributed to bringing the asset into a condition where it is ready to be used. PP&E does not need to directly contribute profit, but can be used to support or enable profit-making activities to be carried out. Examples include office buildings, furniture, and computers.

PP&E costs can also include certain borrowing costs, such as interest and discount or premium amortization. Capitalization of borrowing costs is covered later in this chapter. Costs that are not includable include costs of plant startup, idle costs, and the like. Spares of critical parts are permitted to be capitalized as part of the asset cost, using professional judgment with regard to how likely it is to be needed. Parts that are expected to last less than one year are included in inventory under IFRS.

Example of PP&E capitalization

In 201X, Company A constructs a custom computerized numerical control bore machine to employ in its new marine division. The company used both contract labor as well as some line workers. The company took out a loan specifically to build the machine for 100,000 LCU (local currency units). The interest rate on the loan is 5 percent/year (simple interest). Parts and components cost 1,000,000 LCU.

The following table summarizes the cost capitalized:

Components and material	1,000,000
Contract labor	300,000
Dedicated internal labor*	100,000
Capitalizable interest**	2,500
Total costs to capitalize	1,402,500

  * *Internal labor can only be capitalized if it is directly attributable to the construction specifically systematically tracked. Generally speaking, indirect costs such as management time and utilities are not includable since the direct benefit is difficult to attribute to the project.*
 ** *Although capitalized borrowing costs will be covered more extensively later in the text, borrowing cost capitalization begins when construction substantially begins and ends when it is ready for operation. Idle time during the construction cannot be capitalized. In this example, the construction took six months, during which time the loan was fully outstanding. Therefore six months of interest were included.*

Derecognition of PP&E includes depreciation. Depreciation is the systematic allocation of cost of assets over accounting periods that reflect the economic consumption of the PP&E. Straight-line depreciation is required if there is no other systematic method that is appropriate. IFRS requires entities to assess the useful life of PP&E each reporting period and make prospective adjustments to depreciation for any changes (except for errors, which are discussed later in the book). US GAAP does not contain a requirement for the regular review of useful lives, but reserves this for when impairment triggers are deemed to have been met.

IFRS requires the use of the component approach. A component is a significant part of the asset that has a different useful life than the primary asset. Because of the difference in useful life, the component is depreciated separately. If more than one component has the same useful life, they can, under efficiency principles, be treated as one asset. However, as will be articulated in the next section, major repairs require derecognition of that component and capitalization of the replacement cost.

Other bases of depreciation include units of production, whereby depreciation is based on the inception-to-date production of the asset, compared to the total number of units expected to be produced.

Depreciation begins when the asset is put into service. In practice, entities generally begin depreciation at the beginning of a month, either the month after the asset is in service, or the month of. Whichever method is chosen, it must be applied consistently to promote comparability of the entities' financial results from period to period.

Depreciation does not cease if an asset is taken out of service. If the idle period is short, there is generally no need to assess a change in useful life. However, if the idle period is the result of a fundamental change in the economics of the business, it could be a trigger for impairment and change in useful life.

Example of depreciation

The CNC bore machine illustrated in the previous example is determined by the controller in consultation with the plant manager to have four components: (1) the metal housing, (2) the motor, (3) the cutting chuck and apparatus, and (4) the circuit board that acts as the interface to the software.

Useful life of the housing and solid parts, which includes the superstructure of the machine, has the longest life, estimated at 15 years. This was based on the fact that the housing can accommodate new motors, cutting tools, and circuit boards. In other words, it will survive product line changes, is durable, and will not need to be replaced soon. The motor is expected to last 5 years under expected operating conditions (e.g., usage hours, horsepower, load, and other factors. The motor may be replaced two, or even three times during the life of the machine. The cutting chuck is somewhat durable, but also subject to tooling upgrades in response to changing product lines. Lastly, the circuit board is assigned a useful life of 3 years. It is subject to changes anytime there is a software change. Because changes are not easily predictable, the controller and plant manager decide that 3 years is reasonable given the history of similar machinery.

Below is a schedule of the costs per component, annual and monthly depreciation.

			\multicolumn{2}{c}{Depreciation}
Component	*Cost*	*Life (yrs)*	*Per Year*	*Per Month*
Housing/solid pieces	782,500	15	52,167	4,347
Motor	500,000	5	100,000	8,333
Chuck	100,000	5	20,000	1,667
Circuit board	20,000	3	6,667	556
	1,402,500		178,834	14,903

MAINTENANCE AND REPAIRS

The useful life of an asset takes into account regular or routine expenditures for maintenance. In other words, the cost of maintaining the asset over its useful life is considered in its longevity. Maintenance expenses and small repairs are expensed as incurred.

However, if a repair is significant, and replaces one or more components, the depreciated cost of that component (its carrying value or net book value) is written down to zero and recognized as a depreciation expense in the income statement. The cost to replace the component is capitalized and depreciated over the useful life. Generally, the useful life of the component is not greater than that of the primary asset, unless the component can be readily converted to another use. Because of this, the useful life of the component can be different than the life of the replaced component.

Under US GAAP, the component approach is not defined, although it is not prohibited either. Major repairs are capitalized only if the utility of the asset is significantly extended (considering ongoing maintenance costs, as is the case with new capital assets). Otherwise, it is expensed. Entities typically employ a standard threshold or decision tree to determine expense versus capitalization. Usually accounting policies specify a minimum increase in useful life or output. IFRS also follows this method if an asset is substantially enhanced.

The different approaches to major repairs and to some extent the component approach can result in some material differences in depreciation and maintenance expenses, with IFRS tending to recognize more depreciation and US GAAP more maintenance expense.

Example of PP&E replacement

The following example illustrates the difference between IFRS and US GAAP in the case of a replacement of a major portion of an asset. Note that this example assumes that the replaced portion is a component. Only the cost of the replacement is shown, not the original cost.

PP&E Replacement
IFRS vs. US GAAP

Expenditure	10,000
Historical Cost	100,000
Accum. Depreciation*	60,000
Carrying Value	40,000

	Current Year			*Depreciation*							
Policy	*Gross cost*	*Acc. depr.*	*Maint. exp.*	*Year 2*	*Year 3*	*Year 4*	*Year 5*	*Year 6*	*Year 7*	*Total depr*	*Total expense*
IFRS****	10,000										
	(8,000)	4,800	0	7,800	7,800	7,800	7,800	7,800	7,800	46,800	50,000
US GAAP Entity A**	10,000			8,333	8,333	8,333	8,333	8,333	8,333	50,000	50,000
US GAAP Entity B***			10,000	6,667	6,667	6,667	6,667	6,667	6,667	40,000	50,000

   * *Assumption is that the useful life of all components were the same, and thus depreciation is identical under US GAAP.*
  ** *According to its policy, the entity decided to not derecognize the carrying value of the replaced item.*
 *** *According to its policy, the entity expensed the replacement.*
**** *Note that US GAAP does permit the replacement method but it is not widely used, but it is required for IFRS.*

The fact that IFRS requires that the carrying value of a replaced PP&E item is derecognized, even if estimated, and that under US GAAP the practice is discouraged, is indicative of a pervasive and persistent difference in the philosophy between the two standards. IFRS weights relevance of information more heavily than reliability, whereas US GAAP favors reliability. This does not mean that IFRS eschews reliability. IFRS includes reliability in its qualitative characteristics as defined in the *IFRS Framework*. However, the way the standards are written under IFRS compels management to, where relevance and reliability are in contention, provide more information rather than less, that is, record sooner.

DISPOSAL

IFRS and US GAAP are essentially identical to accounting for the disposal of PP&E. The carrying value of the asset(s) is (are) removed from the balance sheet, resulting in the difference between the proceeds received as a gain or loss on the sale of an asset. Gains and losses are not combined with revenue, but displayed as a separate caption on the income statement. Costs incurred directly to dispose of the PP&E are included in the gain or loss.

DISCLOSURES

More detailed disclosures are required for PP&E under IFRS than US GAAP. US GAAP specifies only total depreciation expense, balances by major class (e.g., equipment, land, etc.), total accumulated depreciation, and a description of the depreciation methods used by class.

IFRS requires all of the US GAAP requirements in addition to a reconciliation of balances, changes for additions (capital expenditures), acquisitions, depreciation, impairment losses, impairment reversals, revaluation changes (if the revaluation model is used), changes for foreign currency translation, and other changes that are significant to understanding the change in fixed assets.

Qualitative disclosures for IFRS include

1. The existence and amounts of restrictions on title, and property, plant, and equipment pledged as security for liabilities
2. The amount of expenditures recognized in the carrying amount of an item of property, plant, and equipment in the course of its construction
3. The amount of contractual commitments for the acquisition of property, plant, and equipment
4. If it is not disclosed separately in the statement of comprehensive income, the amount of compensation from third parties for items of property, plant, and equipment that were impaired, lost, or given up that is included in profit or loss

In accordance with IAS 8, an entity discloses the nature and effect of a change in an accounting estimate that has an effect on the current period or is expected to have an effect in subsequent periods. For property, plant, and equipment, such disclosure may arise from changes in estimates with respect to

1. Residual values
2. The estimated costs of dismantling, removing or restoring items of property, plant, and equipment
3. Useful lives
4. Depreciation methods

If items of property, plant, and equipment are stated at revalued amounts, the following shall be disclosed:

1. The effective date of the revaluation
2. Whether an independent valuer was involved
3. The methods and significant assumptions applied in estimating the items' fair values
4. The extent to which the items' fair values were determined directly by reference to observable prices in an active market, or recent market transactions on arm's-length terms, or were estimated using other valuation techniques
5. For each revalued class of property, plant, and equipment, the carrying amount that would have been recognized had the assets been carried under the cost model

6. The revaluation surplus, indicating the change for the period and any re-strictions on the distribution of the balance to shareholders

In accordance with IAS 36, an entity discloses information on impaired PP&E in addition to the information required by paragraph 73(e)(iv)-(vi).

Users of financial statements may also find the following information relevant to their needs:

1. The carrying amount of temporarily idle property, plant, and equipment
2. The gross carrying amount of any fully depreciated property, plant, and equipment that is still in use
3. The carrying amount of property, plant, and equipment retired from active use and not classified as held for sale in accordance with IFRS 5
4. When the cost model is used, the fair value of property, plant, and equipment when this is materially different from the carrying amount

Therefore, entities are encouraged to disclose these amounts.

For comparison, below are links to PP&E disclosure for two chemical companies, one IFRS (Akzo Nobel, NV) and one US GAAP (Dow Chemical).

Akzo Nobel (note 10):

http://report.akzonobel.com/2010/ar/servicepages/downloads/files/akzonobel_report10_entire.pdf

Dow Chemical (Note G):

www.dow.com/financial/pdfs/annual-report-2010.pdf

The effect of this greater detail is to decrease the materiality of changes in PP&E by requiring analysis by major class rather than in total. This would obviously require additional work or change in the collection of external reporting information.

4 INVENTORY

The accounting and reporting for inventory are very similar under IFRS and US GAAP. It has the same definition and in most cases the same basis. The costs of inventory sold is matched to revenues, and obsolete or slow-moving inventories are written down. However, IFRS requires inventories that are held for trading and used in agriculture to be carried at fair value.

INITIAL COST UPON RECOGNITION

Inventory is made of goods that are held for resale, or used to create goods held for resale (e.g., glue used in constructing furniture). Like property plant and equipment, inventory is generally initially recognized on a historical costs basis (there is some exception for trading and agricultural inventory under IFRS). All the costs, including allocation of certain overhead, to bring the inventory into salable condition must be capitalized to inventory.

Under both IFRS and US GAAP, production overhead is allocated to inventory based on normal capacity, which is the volume that a plant or facility can produce in a period (usually a year) based on the expected work schedule, staffing, and downtime (for repairs, holidays, experience, etc.). Any excess cost is expensed in the period incurred. Conversely, in periods production is higher than normal, allocated overhead is reduced so as to not overstate inventory. To summarize, significant variances as a result of production different from normal capacity is a one-way concept; excess overhead due to lower-than-normal production cannot be capitalized, but overhead allocation must be reduced if production is higher than normal capacity.

Inventory does not include storage of finished goods, administrative costs (whether allocated or not), or interest in the case of routinely, mass-produced goods. However, both IFRS and US GAAP permits capitalization of borrowing to inventory that is not mass produced (e.g., a large freightliner). Storage of work-in-process (WIP) is permitted to be part of inventory cost if storage is routinely needed as part of the production process.

By-Products

The production of goods often produces waste and by-products. If by-products have a market value and can and will be sold, if material, the cost of inventory must be allocated among the finished goods and by-products. This is usually done on relative sales values.

Net Realizable Value

Under both IFRS and US GAAP, inventory must be assessed each period for decreases in value. However, the standards differ with regard to the basis for the reduction and the "floor" down to which inventory can be carried.

Under US GAAP, inventory that has lost value is written down to market. The definition of market under US GAAP is as follows (per the Codification):

As used in the phrase lower of cost or market, the term market means current replacement cost (by purchase or by reproduction, as the case may be) provided that it meets both of the following conditions:

a. Market shall not exceed the net realizable value
b. Market shall not be less than net realizable value reduced by an allowance for an approximately normal profit margin.

Net realizable value (NRV) is defined in US GAAP (per the Master Glossary) as

Estimated selling price in the ordinary course of business less reasonably predictable costs of completion and disposal.

Under US GAAP, the resulting cost of the reduction in inventory value must produce a normal profit margin when sold. This is done by defining boundaries for the carrying value. US GAAP requires inventory to be carried at the lower of cost or market, but market cannot be greater than NRV, nor can it be less than NRV less a normal profit margin. So an entity cannot realize profit by marking up inventory, nor can it write down inventory excessively, presumably to make future results trend upward.

Under IFRS, inventory is written down to lower of cost or NRV, and market is not in the equation.

IAS 2

9   Inventories shall be measured at the lower of cost and net realizable value.

IAS 2, *Inventories*, defines NRV as follows:

Net realizable value is the estimated selling price in the ordinary course of business less the estimated costs of completion and the estimated costs necessary to make the sale.

While the definition of NRV is the same under both standards, IFRS has a single target for carrying value when the value of inventory diminishes to below what an entity paid for it.

This difference in the basis and floor of inventory carrying value is illustrated in the table below.

Inventory Write-down

SKU#	Hist. cost/ unit	NRV	Repl cost (market)	Normal profit margin	NRV less NPM	New carrying value	US GAAP Basis		IFRS	
2010100	50.00	40.00	34.00	10%	36.00	36.00	NRV less NPM		40.00	NRV
2010101	125.00	115.00	120.00	20%	92.00	115.00	NRV		115.00	NRV
2010102	80.00	75.00	65.00	25%	56.25	65.00	Market		75.00	NRV

Under IFRS write-downs of inventory can be reversed when market conditions improve. Under US GAAP, write-downs can be reversed only if it is within the same fiscal year. This disparity with regard to write-down reversals is indicative of IFRS leaning more towards relevance than reliability. In fact, PP&E and financial instrument impairments can be restored under IFRS, whereas none are able to be written back up under US GAAP.

Under both IFRS and US GAAP, if inventory subject to write-down has otherwise been contracted to be sold at a price higher than the general market conditions, those units are not written down using the contractual price as the selling price in calculating NRV. This requirement is to prevent moving profit to a later period. Also, both standards describe the relationship between raw materials and WIPs in terms of write-downs. Under each statement, if raw materials or WIPs are used to create finished goods that have not experienced a reduction in value, the carrying value of these needed raw materials are not reduced either, unless the materials on hand are in **excess** of those needed to produce those finished goods. In this case, those materials and WIP are subject to evaluation based on the NRV of the raw materials themselves. Both standards also state that when evaluating categories of inventory that are related, the category of inventory may be the best unit of account to calculate write-downs.

US GAAP also stresses that while specific identification of inventory is needed to evaluate a reduction in carrying value, where materials are common to more than one finished good, the selling price and each good are both evaluated to determine if the material is balanced. In other words, the raw materials can be measured against a kind of composite finished good. While IFRS does not specifically state this, this practice is aligned with the *IFRS Framework* and therefore can be used under IFRS.

The concept of NRV not only prevents an entity from overstating assets, but serves the purpose of reflecting a realistic depiction of the profit a company makes from its merchandising efforts versus the financial effects of the supply chain function and general market conditions. This allows user of financial statements to distinguish the relative strengths and weaknesses of competing firms on key aspects of operations. Gross margin measures how well an entity can profitably sell goods. Write-downs of inventory indicate poor purchasing decisions, which is a distinct function within a business. Under US GAAP, due to the prohibition of reversals of write-downs, gross margin performance can be skewed, being low in one period and high in the next.

Both US GAAP and IFRS require that an accrual (US GAAP) or provision (IFRS) be accrued for firm commitments to purchase inventory on which a loss is expected. Under IFRS, providing for a loss from a contract that has not yet expired is called an *onerous contract*, as required by IAS 37, *Provisions and Contingencies*. IAS 37 is applicable for all contracts, not just for purchases of inventory. Conversely, US GAAP permits accruing for future losses on contracts only in narrow instances, inventory being one.

COST OF GOODS SOLD

Inventory is reflected in cost of goods sold (COGS) when revenue pertaining to the item is recognized, or in the case of a write-down. Recognition of revenue and COGS can be at a different point in time than when the inventory is accepted by the customer (this will be covered later in the chapter on revenue recognition).

Because entities can (and do) produce a large number of goods and varieties of those products, necessarily at different points in time, tracking the cost to recognize against applicable revenue can be difficult considering that prices of inputs change, sometimes rapidly. The onerous nature of tracking the cost of each good separately spurred the development of cost-effective methods. These methods include average costs, first-in first-out (FIFO), last-in first-out (LIFO—not permitted under IFRS), as well as specific identification (used when an entity produces few, expensive, or custom products). IFRS and US GAAP also allow using standard costs if they are materially the same as the other methods. In order to be valid, standard costs must be monitored and updated frequently if costs change materially. A corridor of 2% actual costs under or over standard cost is an acceptable range.

INVENTORIES ABOVE COSTS

US GAAP specifies circumstances under which inventories can be recognized above cost:

ASC 330-10-35

16 *It is generally recognized that income accrues only at the time of sale, and that gains may not be anticipated by reflecting assets at their current sales prices. However, exceptions for reflecting assets at selling prices are permissible for both of the following:*

   a. *Inventories of gold and silver, when there is an effective government-controlled market at a fixed monetary value*
   b. *Inventories representing agricultural, mineral, and other products, with all of the following criteria:*

      1. *Units of which are interchangeable*
      2. *Units of which have an immediate marketability at quoted prices*
      3. *Units for which appropriate costs may be difficult to obtain*

IAS 41, *Agriculture,* requires biological assets to be recorded at fair value at the time of harvest. Thereafter, IAS 2, *Inventories,* applies. Additionally, inventory held primarily for trading purposes are carried at fair value. IAS 2 also does not apply to the same types of products as described in 330-10-35-16:

IAS 2

3 *This standard does not apply to the measurement of inventories held by*

   a. *Producers of agricultural and forest products, agricultural produce after harvest, and minerals and mineral products, to the extent that they are measured at net realizable value in accordance with well-established practices in those industries. When such inventories are measured at net realizable value, changes in that value are recognized in profit or loss in the period of the change.*

DISCLOSURES

Disclosures for IFRS and US GAAP for inventory are similar. Since inventory write-downs cannot be restored in a subsequent annual period under US GAAP, annual statements under US GAAP do not include disclosures for write-ups of inventory. Both standards require disclosures of cost flow and inventories carried at other historical costs.

5 PROVISIONS AND CONTINGENCIES

Under IFRS, a provision is a liability of undermined timing or amount. This contrasts with an accrual or accounts payable obligation that is fixed in terms of the amount and timing needed to satisfy the obligation. The estimated accrual of goods or services received but not invoiced does not qualify for treatment as a provision. Accounts payable accruals are part of the normal estimation processes that are part of routine accounting practices.

Under IFRS, the measurement of a provision at the end of a reporting period must be the most likely amount that would be required to settle the obligation at the date of the financial statements. This is true even if the entity believes that further actions on the part of the entity or obligee(s) could potentially change the settlement amount. To determine the carrying value of the provision, an entity must choose the most likely amount in a range of scenarios, unless a number of other estimates are materially higher or lower than the likely amount, in which case the amount is adjusted to reflect the other values. Under US GAAP, the minimum in a range of estimates is recognized. Additionally, provisions are recorded if the probability of payment is more likely than not, which translates to just over 50%. The US GAAP threshold is generally higher. Following is an example of the estimation of a legal provision.

IAS 37

36 The amount recognized as a provision shall be the best estimate of the expenditure required to settle the present obligation at the end of the reporting period.

37 The best estimate of the expenditure required to settle the present obligation is the amount that an entity would rationally pay to settle the obligation at the end of the reporting period or to transfer it to a third party at that time. It will often be impossible or prohibitively expensive to settle or transfer an obligation at the end of the reporting period. However, the estimate of the amount that an entity would rationally pay to settle or transfer the obligation gives the best estimate of the expenditure required to settle the present obligation at the end of the reporting period.

39 Uncertainties surrounding the amount to be recognized as a provision are dealt with by various means according to the circumstances. Where the provision being measured involves a large population of items, the obligation is estimated by weighting all possible outcomes by their associated probabilities. The name for this statistical method of estimation is "expected value." The provision will therefore be different depending on whether the probability of a loss of a given amount is, for example, 60% or 90%. Where there is a continuous range of possible outcomes, and each point in that range is as likely as any other, the midpoint of the range is used.

Example: Determination of initial recognition of legal provision under IFRS

The chief legal counsel for Company A has just received a notice from a law firm that it is being sued for patent infringement on one of its products, EnviroGone. After discussing the matter with the Chief Executive Officer, the chief counsel confers with external lawyers to gage likelihood of the case resulting in damages. Among other issues discussed, the external lawyer recalls a similar case against Company A brought five years ago. The product line revenues were approximately the same as the EnviroGone and had been sold for about the same number of years. Company A settled by paying $10 million USD. Defense costs were $1 million USD.

Chief counsel noted that the product was part of a different division, so any settlement amount, despite the similar revenues, could be materially different. The external lawyer agreed and explained that the industry of the product was more litigious than EnviroGone, and cited several recent cases about similar products where the plaintiff had been more successful than in the past due to the change in judges for the circuit that the case would be tried in. The external lawyer estimated that the case had a 25% chance of being accepted by the court. If it were tried, the likelihood of a payout was from 50 to 60%, with the estimated damages of about $10 to 20 million USD. External counsel also noted that this industry was very specialized and that billing rates would be higher.

After the conversation, Chief legal counsel considered what he had learned and met with the CFO. The CFO conveyed that Company A had a history of settling suits out of court to limit financial and reputational risk.

The CFO then talked to the controller and directed him to assess the provision, if any, that needed to be booked. It was one week before the end of the quarter, and the controller advised the CFO that she was unlikely to be able to get all the information she needed, but would make an estimate.

After the controller spoke to a manager at the external law firm, she calculated the following possible damages:

Product Z
Range of legal settlement

Aspect	Amount thousand USD	Percent	Notes
Likelihood of settling	N/A	40%	25% chance of having court accept case decreases likelihood company will settle out of court
Likelihood of paying damages	N/A	55%	Mid-range of 50-60% that external counsel gages probability of losing case

Range of payments			
Scenario 1	5,000	15%	750
Scenario 2	8,000	25%	2,000
Scenario 3	12,000	20%	2,400
Scenario 4	17,500	15%	2,625
Scenario 5	20,000	15%	3,000
Scenario 6	25,000	10%	2,500
		100%	13.275

Average of scenarios: 3 to 6   18,625

The controller then drafted the following proposed disclosure and recommendation:

Don,

Here is my draft disclosure:

During the quarter, the Company received notice of a patent infringement action taken by one of its competitors (the plaintiff). The Company is currently assessing the damages, if any, that would be payable. Because the Company does not believe at this time that the plaintiff has sufficient evidence of infringement, there was no provision recognized during the quarter. The company estimates that if the case is accepted in the circuit court of jurisdiction, the charge could be between $12.5 to 20 million USD.

Reasoning:

Because there is only a 25% chance of the case seeing the inside of a courtroom, my judgment is that this probability is not high enough for the company to even consider settlement. If the case does go to court, based on the probability of a plaintiff success, I recommend accruing $12.5 at the start. While external council's highest probability (25%) is for $8 million USD, the other payouts are mostly higher. I settled on $12.5 million because we can usually settle for a smaller amount and we would not incur as much in litigation costs. It's higher than the EnviroGone case since external council advises that the climate in this circuit, product segment, and recent cases point to a higher potential settlement. As the case progresses, we need to regularly check in with counsel on progress. If the prospects of settlement diminish significantly, I recommend accruing $18.5 million USD for the average of settlements above the most likely.

I'm in all week; let me know if you want me to stop by and discuss.

Thanks,

Emma

To examine the differences in approaches between IFRS and US GAAP, it can help to consider that all provisions at some point in the life cycle are contingent, meaning that the ultimate outcome of the settlement depends on the occurrence of one or more future events. These potential obligations comprise a type of potential obligation inventory. These potential liabilities are continuously evaluated for the likelihood that the entity will need to satisfy the obligation, regardless of the amount. The underlying definition of a liability under both standards is effectively identical. It is in the application of the probability of satisfaction that determines if a contingency is recognized as a liability under each standard.

Below is an example from the Codification for litigation involving patent infringement.

Example: Illustrative Disclosure

ASC 450-20-55-36: Entity A is the defendant in litigation involving a major competitor claiming patent infringement (Entity B). The suit claims damages of $200 million. Discovery has been completed, and Entity A is engaged in settlement discussions with the plaintiff. Entity A made an offer of $5 million to settle the case, which was rejected by the plaintiff; the plaintiff made an offer of $35 million to settle the case, which was rejected by Entity A. Based on the expressed willingness of the plaintiff to settle the case along with information revealed during discovery and the likely cost and risk to both sides of litigating, Entity A believes that it is probable the case will not come to trial. Accordingly, Entity A has determined that it is probable that it has some liability. Entity A's reasonable estimate of this liability is a range between $10 million and $35 million, with no amount within that range a better estimate than any other amount; accordingly, $10 million was accrued.

Entity A provides the following disclosure in accordance with Section 450-20-50.

On March 15, 19X1, Entity B filed a suit against the company claiming patent infringement. While the company believes it has meritorious defenses against the suit, the ultimate resolution of the matter, which is expected to occur within one year, could result in a loss of up to $25 million in excess of the amount accrued.

While it is difficult to determine exactly what the company in this example would have done had IFRS been applied, since judgment is involved and we do not know how many estimates there were, the excerpt from IAS 37.39 (…. Where there is a continuous range of possible outcomes, and each point in that range is as likely as any other, the **midpoint of the range is used** …) is indicative that some point in the middle would be accrued. Under IFRS, the minimum would not be the amount accrued in any case in this example.

Both standards require the disclosure of contingent liabilities. The disclosures include the description, nature, and progress in determining the recognition of a liability. IFRS requires a roll forward of provisions displaying the beginning balance, additions, payments or reductions, and unwinding of discounts.

EFFECT OF TIMING OF SETTLEMENT

Under IFRS, all liabilities (not just provisions) that will be settled in more than one year must be discounted to reflect the time value of money. The concept of the time value of money is basically that a unit of currency received later is worth less than it would be if it is received today due to inflation and uncertainty. The impact on measuring provisions, at a high level, is that it is always recorded at an amount different from its nominal value, or rather, the amount of currency units that must be relinquished to settle the obligation. In periods of inflation, this means that the discounted value will always be less than the nominal value. This discount reduces the carrying amount of the nominal provision. As time passes, the discount is unwound into finance expense (interest).

Example: Discounting

In 201X Company A, upon the building of a new plant, recognizes the obligation imposed by a government that it must restore the land to the original state when the plant is closed. Company A estimates that it will cost $30 million dollars to restore the land; additionally, the company estimates that decommissioning will begin in 204X and take five years to complete. Below is a schedule of cash flows for the restoration:

204X: $10m, 204X+1: $8m, 204X+2: $5m, 204X+3: $4m, 204X+4 $3m

Because IFRS requires the discount rate to be the pretax rate specific to the obligation, the company uses 8%. Below is a table used to calculate the discounted value.

Discount Rate: 8%

Year	Nom Spend	Factor	Discounted
1	10.0	1.08	9.3
2	8.0	1.17	6.9
3	5.0	1.26	4.0
4	4.0	1.36	2.9
5	3.0	1.47	2.0
	30.0		25.1

Discount back to date of plant commissioning
25.1 m at 8% at 30 years   10.06   3.0

The entry to establish the provision is

Retirement asset	$3m	
Retirement obligation		$3m

Each period, the entry to unwind the discount is

Interest expense	$x	
Asset retirement obligation		$x

Where x is the interest component computed is based on the balance at the beginning of the period. The interest for the first month is $20,000:

> Balance at inception: $3m
> Multiplied by 8% = $240,000
> Divided by 12 months

The obligation will build up over 30 years to the $25.1m. The discount continues to unwind over the years that the funds are spent.

Under IFRS, at each annual reporting period, the discount rate is assessed. If the discount rate changes, the discount amount is recalculated for the remaining discount period. The change in the obligation is debited or credited to the retirement asset and obligation. It follows that the monthly interest accretion changes upon a change in discount. If the discount rate remains the same, the monthly entry amount will also change (increase) to reflect the large balance. In this example, the interest for the next year would be 8% multiplied by $3,240,000, or $259,200, assuming no change in the estimated costs. Retirement assets are depreciated just as any other assets.

Under US GAAP, the discount rate is the risk-free rate of return adjusted for the entity's credit rating. The risk-free rate is the one paid by the sovereign government of the company's country of incorporation. If the nominal cost of the obligation then increases, the discount rate applied for that layer is the current rate. The prior "layers" are kept at the origination rate. If layers are eroded (i.e., the nominal cost of the obligation is reduced because of, for instance, changes in technology), the unwinding is at the original rate until (and if) the nominal cost is reduced below the current layer.

Below is an example that illustrates differences between IFRS and US GAAP with regard to asset retirement obligations:

IFRS vs. US GAAP
Asset Retirement Discounting Example

Expenditures begin in year 30   **Interest Costs** [Note 1]

Year	Nominal costs*	Discounted liability— IFRS	Rate— IFRS	Discounted liability—US GAAP	Rate—US GAAP**	IFRS	US GAAP	Note
1	25	2.48	8%	4.35	6%	0.20	0.26	
2	25	3.51	7%	4.61	6%	0.25	0.28	
3	30	4.51	7%	5.64	7%	0.32	0.35	2
4	30	6.22	6%	5.99	7%	0.37	0.37	2
5	30	8.44	5%	6.36	7%	0.42	0.39	2
6	27	7.97	5%	6.29	6%	0.40	0.43	
7	27	8.37	5%	6.67	6%	0.42	0.40	
8	23	7.49	5%	6.02	6%	0.37	0.36	

* *Total nominal cost to restore asset. This can change each year for changes in technology regulations, etc.*
** *For US GAAP, increase in costs is considered a new liability. The current rate is applied only to this increase.*

Note 1: IFRS presents accretion as interest expense. US GAAP presents it as operational expense.
Note 2: For US GAAP column, the interest is calculated on two pieces, the original 25 and incremental 5.

APPLICATION OF DISCOUNTING

US GAAP only requires discounting if the cash flows can be reliably predicted. Thus, generally under US GAAP, environmental obligations are generally not discounted. This is not the case under IFRS where all provisions that the time value of money is material requires discounting.

Thus in summary, generally, the IFRS obligations will be smaller at a given point in time and the interest impacts greater and more volatile (due to the higher discount rate and annual recalculation of discount, respectively).

EXIT COSTS

Exit costs are those that an entity incurs for a restructuring or closure of part of a business. Examples include cost of employee termination payments (severance), closure of facilities, cancellation of leases, or other obligations. Under both IFRS and US GAAP, some costs are provided for or accrued at the point in time that the entity is committed to the plan of restructuring or disposal, and other costs are recognized as incurred.

IFRS and US GAAP require that a plan of disposal or restructuring be committed to by a public announcement and be expected to be carried out. The communication must also be specific enough that those affected by it know, in sufficiently specific terms, what the consequences will be for them. The requirements of commitment and specificity are necessary to both create the obligation and to reduce the likelihood that an entity attempts to present operational problems as unusual events. If it were too easy to back out of a plan, an entity could engineer results in a given period, thus reducing the usefulness, reliability, and relevance of the financial statements.

Both standards prohibit the accrual of costs that relate to the ongoing running of the business. These include relocation, retraining, or other costs that are not directly related to the plan. Even incremental costs that would not have been incurred had the plan not been executed are not accrued.

However, there are different obligating events for recognition of a liability or provision for exist costs. US GAAP bifurcates the recognition of employee termination benefits. IFRS does not. Below is an excerpt from IAS 37.

IAS 37

71 *A provision for restructuring costs is recognized only when the general recognition criteria for provisions set out in paragraph 14 are met. Paragraphs 72-83 set out how the general recognition criteria apply to restructurings.*

72 *A constructive obligation to restructure arises only when an entity:*

(a) *Has a detailed formal plan for the restructuring identifying at least*

   (i)   *The business or part of a business concerned*
   (ii) *The principal locations affected*
   (iii) *The location, function, and approximate number of employees who will be compensated for terminating their services*
   (iv) *The expenditures that will be undertaken*
   (v)   *When the plan will be implemented*

(b) *Has raised a valid expectation in those affected that it will carry out the restructuring by starting to implement that plan or announcing its main features to those affected by it*

US GAAP ASC subsections of 420-10 are below.

Determining When to Recognize a Liability

25-1 *A liability for a cost associated with an exit or disposal activity shall be recognized in the period in which the liability is incurred, except as indicated in paragraphs 420-10-25-6 and 420-10-25-9 (for a liability for one-time employee termination benefits that is incurred over time). In the unusual circumstance in which fair value cannot be reasonably estimated, the liability shall be recognized initially in the period in which fair value can be reasonably estimated (see paragraphs 420-10-30-1 through 30-3 for fair value measurement guidance).*

25-2   *A liability for a cost associated with an exit or disposal activity is incurred when the definition of a liability included in FASB Concepts Statement No. 6,* **Elements of Financial Statements**, *is met. Only present obligations to others are liabilities under the definition. An obligation becomes a present obligation when a transaction or event occurs that leaves an entity little or no discretion to avoid the future transfer or use of assets to settle the liability. An exit or disposal plan, by itself, does not create a present obligation to others for costs expected to be incurred under the plan; thus, an entity's commitment to an exit or disposal plan, by itself, is not the requisite past transaction or event for recognition of a liability.*

25-3   *This subtopic requires that future operating losses expected to be incurred in connection with an exit or disposal activity be recognized in the period(s) in which they are incurred. Because future operating losses are the summation of individual items of revenue and expense that result from changes in assets and liabilities, those expected losses, in and of themselves, do not meet the definition of a liability.*

One-time Employee Termination Benefits

25-4   *An arrangement for one-time employee termination benefits exists at the date the plan of termination meets all of the following criteria and has been communicated to employees (referred to as the communication date):*

   a. *Management, having the authority to approve the action, commits to a plan of termination.*
   b. *The plan identifies the number of employees to be terminated, their job classifications or functions and their locations, and the expected completion date.*
   c. *The plan establishes the terms of the benefit arrangement, including the benefits that employees will receive upon termination (including but not limited to cash payments), in sufficient detail to enable employees to determine the type and amount of benefits they will receive if they are involuntarily terminated.*
   d. *Actions required to complete the plan indicate that it is unlikely that significant changes to the plan will be made or that the plan will be withdrawn.*

A comparison of the above guidance for exit costs demonstrates that exit costs for termination benefits will usually occur earlier under IFRS. The point of recognition for other costs is less clear. US GAAP refers (uncharacteristically) to FASB Concept Statement No. 6, *Elements of Financial Statements.* However, ASC 420-10-25-2 (see underlined text) is consistent with guidance in IAS 37 that both a plan of exit and communication of the plan are both needed to recognize a liability for exit costs:

IAS 37

75   *A management or board decision to restructure taken before the end of the reporting period does not give rise to a constructive obligation at the end of the reporting period unless the entity has, before the end of the reporting period*

   (a) Started to implement the restructuring plan

> *(b) Announced the main features of the restructuring plan to those affected by it in a sufficiently specific manner to raise a valid expectation in them that the entity will carry out the restructuring*

Since US GAAP generally requires a higher degree of certainty to accrue costs (e.g. legal or contractual), it is likely that exit cost liabilities will be incurred at a later point in time than under US GAAP.

IFRS, however, does impose some restrictions on recognizing a provision for restructuring plans that include the sale of operations:

IAS 37

78 *No obligation arises for the sale of an operation until the entity is committed to the sale, (i.e., there is a binding sale agreement.)*

79 *Even when an entity has taken a decision to sell an operation and announced that decision publicly, it cannot be committed to the sale until a purchaser has been identified and there is a binding sale agreement. Until there is a binding sale agreement, the entity will be able to change its mind and indeed will have to take another course of action if a purchaser cannot be found on acceptable terms. When the sale of an operation is envisaged as part of a restructuring, the assets of the operation are reviewed for impairment, under IAS 36. When a sale is only part of a restructuring, a constructive obligation can arise for the other parts of the restructuring before a binding sale agreement exists.*

Other provisions that will be covered later in the book include pension, post-retirement, and other employee benefits.

6 INTANGIBLE ASSETS

Under both IFRS and US GAAP, intangible assets lack physical substance, but meet the definition of an asset (i.e., it is expected to benefit the organization for more than a year). Examples include patents, trademarks, copyrights, right-of-ways (easements), and others. Goodwill is also an intangible asset, but can only be recognized upon acquisition of a business. Goodwill is covered extensively in a later chapter.

One significant difference in accounting for intangible assets between the two standards is that under IFRS, **certain** development costs can be capitalized. Under US GAAP, development costs are always expensed, except in certain circumstances in accounting for a business acquisition. More simply said, in the course of ordinary business, development costs are never capitalized under US GAAP, but can be under IFRS. Research costs are expensed under both IFRS and US GAAP. However, IFRS does specify costs that can never be capitalized. These include training of employees, internally-generated goodwill, creation of images, and others. Internal Web sites can be capitalized under IFRS and, under certain conditions, US GAAP (ASC 985). ASC 985 aligns with fixed-asset accounting. The section provides guidance on stages of production that indicate if costs can be capitalized. IFRS covers software development costs in IAS 38, *Intangible Assets*. IAS 38 includes accounting for software in the description of all intangible assets. Therefore there is no specific guidance. The guidance of ASC 985 does fit into the *IFRS Framework*. Consequently, it can be used for software development costs pursuant to IAS 8, *Accounting Policies and Errors*.

Because IFRS requires development costs to be capitalized if they meet certain criteria, and these costs are always expensed for US GAAP (except for own-use internally developed software), the following sections will focus on IFRS.

For development costs to be capitalized under IAS 38, they must first meet the criteria for recognition. The criteria are the ability to separately identify the assets from other expenditures, control of the benefits, and the reasonable expectation that future benefits will flow to the entity. IAS 38 specifies that only rarely will subsequent expenditures (i.e., after the costs of development are complete) qualify for recognition because it is difficult to determine future benefits of additional expenditure from the original asset.

IAS 38

Identifiability

11 The definition of an intangible asset requires an intangible asset to be identifiable to distinguish it from goodwill. Goodwill recognized in a business combination is an asset representing the future economic benefits arising from other assets acquired in a business combination that are not individually identified and separately recognized. The future economic benefits may result from synergy between the identifiable assets acquired or from assets that, individually, do not qualify for recognition in the financial statements.

12 An asset is identifiable if it either

1. *Is separable, that is, capable of being separated or divided from the entity and sold, transferred, licensed, rented or exchanged, either individually or together with a related contract, identifiable asset, or liability, regardless of whether the entity intends to do so; or*
2. *Arises from contractual or other legal rights, regardless of whether those rights are transferable or separable from the entity or from other rights and obligations.*

Control

13 An entity controls an asset if the entity has the power to obtain the future economic benefits flowing from the underlying resource and to restrict the access of others to those benefits. The capacity of an entity to control the future economic benefits from an intangible asset would normally stem from legal rights that are enforceable in a court of law. In the absence of legal rights, it is more difficult to demonstrate control. However, legal enforceability of a right is not a necessary condition for control because an entity may be able to control the future economic benefits in some other way.

For both IFRS and US GAAP, nongoodwill intangible assets (other intangibles) can also be recognized as part of a business acquisition. Other intangibles acquired in an acquisition usually have much higher values than ones created in the ordinary course of business. This is because often a business is a target for acquisition due to its position in the marketplace, that is, its profitability as compared to its peers, which is often attributable to market positioning, geographic situation, or brand recognition.

The different treatment of intangibles between routine accounting and acquisition accounting, at first, appears to be inconsistent. However, in an acquisition, what the acquiring entity paid for the intangible asset can be measured, and the recognition of it complies with the historical cost principle. While it is true that two comparable companies, one never acquired, the other recently acquired, will have different balance sheets, all things being equal, the profit of the nonacquired entity will be lower than it would have been if not for the expenditures it incurred to generate the value of the intangible. The acquired company will not incur these expenses, thus its return on assets should approximate the return of assets from the nonacquired company.

Since IFRS 3 was issued jointly by the IASB and FASB and effective in 2009, there are currently very few differences in accounting for business combinations.

DERECOGNITION

Other intangible assets are either amortized or assessed for impairment on the same basis as property, plant, and equipment, or not amortized and subject to annual impairment testing.

Upon recognition, if an intangible asset's economic life can be estimated, it is amortized during that life. If the useful life cannot be estimated, and it otherwise qualifies as an asset (i.e., has future value), it is not amortized.

When it is determined that an intangible asset's life is estimable, the asset is prospectively amortized and then treated as other amortized intangible assets.

Impairment of other intangibles is similar to that of PP&E (impairment is covered later in the text). Fair value of intangibles is often based on a margin analysis comparison between branded and unbranded products. For companies with both types of lines of goods and services, margin comparison of each line is relatively simple. For companies that do not have an unbranded version of its products, comparison to competitors is often used.

7 SHARE-BASED COMPENSATION

IDENTIFICATION OF A SHARE-BASED COMPENSATION PLAN

The accounting and reporting for share-based compensation (SBC) plans is one of the most difficult and subjective areas. Every transaction in the life cycle of the plan—measurement date, measurement amount, recognition, amortization, de-recognition, balance sheet classification, exercise, and tax effects—requires multiple inputs, assumptions, and judgment.

Below is a table that lists the major events in the life cycle of SBC plans with the operational variables that affect them.

Accounting Events Table

Measurement date	Measurement amount	Remeasurement	Recognition	Amortization	Derecognition	Classification	Exercise	Tax effects
Grant date	Montecarlo	Performance condition	Compensatory	Vesting time	Cancellations	Liability	Vs. FV at exercise	Tax rate
Agreement date	Black-Scholes Intrinsic value	Market condition	Grant date reload feature		Acqu/Divestee retirement	Equity operating gain/loss disposal Goodwill	Excess/ surplus	
			Replacement forfeiture rate					

The first issue in accounting for SBC plans is to assess whether an entity has a share-based compensation plan. Under IFRS, if employees or others (vendors, directors) receive shares, options, or other instruments based on an entity's shares, except in rare circumstances, a company is considered to have an SBC plan. Under US GAAP, certain criteria must be met. For large-scale programs, criteria include an assessment of the relative amount of price reduction a recipient can receive from the general market participants. Generally, IFRS and US GAAP are similar in terms of whether the entity has an SBC plan (the accounting is different in several respects, which will be covered later).

Under both standards, share-based compensation can be awarded to employees and nonemployees. IFRS also extends the accounting for employees to parties performing similar type work (e.g., contractors). US GAAP defines employees specifically as those that are recognized as such under the US Internal Revenue Service code. This excludes virtually all individuals who are not legal employees. This distinction is different because, as will be covered in this chapter, the recognition patterns of SBC costs are different between employees and other grantees.

MEASUREMENT DATE AND VALUE

Under IFRS, the value of an SBC is the fair value at the measurement date. The measurement date is the earlier of the grant date or the date that the agreement is effective. The agreement can be verbal. The determination of the measurement date is similar under US GAAP. Under each, the date at which mutual understanding of the key terms and conditions is reached is the measurement date. However, US GAAP includes conveniences such as assumptions of an SBC plan the date at which an award is granted in a process performed under company policy, such as approval of awards by the board of directors.

For nonemployees, US GAAP also includes a commitment date, which is the date that the nonemployee commits to the work. From the commitment date through to the date of delivery, (e.g., completion of the project), the SBC award is measured at fair value using general IFRS principles. Consequently, the value per share is not fixed until the date of performance.

For employees and, under US GAAP, for nonemployees who do not commit before the delivery date, once the measurement date is determined, the value per instrument must be established. While fair value can be calculated a number of ways, for options, companies usually use statistical methods such as the Black-Sholes or Montecarlo method. IFRS discourages the use of Black-Sholes if there is a significant delay between the vesting date (the date the recipient can first exercise) and the expiration date since this model assumes exercise at expiration. US GAAP, conversely, encourages use of Black-Sholes (and others), but if there is a significant period between the vesting and expiration dates, the result of the model must be adjusted to factor in the possibilities of exercise before the expiration date. So, effectively, a modified Black-Sholes model can be used for both standards. IFRS and US GAAP permit a strict Black-Sholes result if the vesting and expiration are relatively close.

For shares, the fair value is usually the market price at the grant date. This works well if the securities are traded on an active market. However, if they are not, other methods can be used, being careful to include the impact restrictions (i.e., holding period, after vesting, no right to dividends).

IFRS and US GAAP differ significantly on the use of *intrinsic value*. Intrinsic value is the value of the instrument to the grantee on date of grant less the cost to the grantee on that date, in essence, the discounted value on that date. Intrinsic value is usually zero, since the grant date value is typically used, and no payment is due. US GAAP allows intrinsic value only if an entity is *non*public and it cannot reasonably estimate the fair value. IFRS allows public entities to use intrinsic value. However, both standards require an entity using intrinsic value to update the value at each reporting date, and thus change the expense associated with those instruments that would have been reflected had the remeasurement not occurred.

The total value at the measurement date is not simply the value per instrument times the share allotment. Under both IFRS and US GAAP, estimates of the number of shares that will vest (not exercised) must be estimated throughout the vesting period. One typical factor is forfeiture, which is the result of employee terminations or demotions. The difference between the shares granted and the number expected to vest recipients compounded each year is factored into the aggregate value.

Example: Forfeiture

Company A has experienced over the past several years that employees eligible for their SBC leave at a rate of 5%. If 100 people are granted awards, the number of forfeitures can be calculated as follows:

End of Year 1: 95 = 100 x 95%
End of Year 2: 90 = 95 x 95%
End of Year 3: 87 = 90 x 95%

The total value at recognition would be calculated as 87 times the fair value per instrument. This result is the amount that is amortized over the vesting period. This is because 87 is the number of recipients that are expected to vest and thus be entitled to exercise the instruments.

SUBSEQUENT ACCOUNTING

The amount of expense recognized in any one subsequent period depends not only on the vesting period, but also the conditions that determine what the payout will be at exercise date. There are three classes of conditions:

1. Performance
2. Vesting
3. Market

Performance conditions, which are usually present in all SBC plans, are achievements that must be made to qualify for payout. In executive plans, this usually involves some profitability metric such as return of assets, return on equity, compound average growth rate, and others. Each period, the likelihood of achieving those measures is evaluated. If in a particular period subsequent to recognition, it is probable at the financial statement date that the performance metric will not be achieved, the amortization is reversed. In the case of an instrument with multiple payout levels, the expense in the period is the amount necessary to record the inception-to-date amortization at that date. This type of catch-up is often referred to as a "true-up." Awards consisting of multiple levels, or legs are adjusted each reporting period for the tranches that are expected to be achieved. Evaluating the probability of the legs is another aspect.

A vesting condition is a date or event at which the grantee obtains an irrevocable right to the award. This is the date, theoretically, that the recipient is no longer motivated to provide any other service or deliver any goods to obtain the shares. Thus, it marks the end of the attribution period, so no expense or reversals of expense are permitted on or after vesting. Forfeitures and cancellations have no effect on the expense already recorded. Except for market vesting conditions (covered later), vesting conditions have no impact on the value per share. Instead, the effect on total compensation is calculated by adjusting the number of shares that are expected to vest.

A market condition is one that is dependent on the price of the instrument achieving a set price per share over some period of time. Market conditions are factored into the calculation of the measurement date fair value.

Example: True-up of expense in year 2 of a four-year vesting period		
Grant date	7/1/2010	
Grant	100,000	options
FV at grant date	$10.72	each option
Vesting date	6/30/2014	
Expiration date	6/30/2019	
Yrs to vest	4.00	
# Recipients	100	each, assuming ma performance
Est. attrition rate	3%	per year
# Recipients expected to vest	83	
Grant date aggregate value	$88,976.00	
Amortization at 12/31/2010	11,129.62	(88,976/4 years/12 months × 6 months)
At end of year 2		
Inception-to-date amort.	$44,518.47	
Reversal of 25 shares each	$(11,129.62)	
Accumulated amort. at end yr 2	$33,366.00	
Expense in year 2	$11,122.00	
Expense in year 1	$22,244.00	

The above example assumes that attrition rate remains at 3 %. For each grant, the same calculation is performed. Thus, in practice, there are often layers of calculations.

BALANCE SHEET CLASSIFICATION

The offset of the SBC expense can be either stockholders' equity or a liability. The characteristics of the instrument, as well as the method of redemption available to the holder, determine what classification and award is present.

Generally speaking, when the holder of the instrument has the ability to demand cash upon vesting, the instrument is reflected as a liability. Otherwise, it is presented as equity. There are gray areas that are addressed with different degrees of detail in the respective guidance. The complexity of the instrument terms can also cause the classification of the instrument to change over time depending on the outcome of contingencies.

US GAAP is much more detailed regarding the classification of instruments with complex terms. A puttable instrument, that is, one that allows the holder to return the instrument, to require the issuer to sell the shares and remit the proceeds that is outside the control of the issuer is classified as a liability. Contingent events that would give the holder this right are not classified as liabilities until such an event occurs. Even if the issuer has the choice of settlement between cash and instruments and normally settles in cash, the award must be classified as a liability. Obviously, judgment is involved in this decision. Under IFRS, conversely, if a holder has an option to settle in cash or shares, and that award is calculated directly from the fair value of the goods or services, the difference between the fair value of the instruments and the directly measured value is recorded in equity. This is because under IFRS, the issuance of an instrument that gives the holder the choice of settlement has issued a compound instrument, with both a debt and equity component. However, most of the award is still presented as a liability under US GAAP. Moreover, if the values are the same, there will be no equity component.

When an award is classified as a liability, the change in fair value of the instrument is adjusted each period to true-up the balance to what amount of cash will be required to settle. This contrasts with an equity award where each unit is not re-measured (only the number of instruments expected to vest are changed, which thus changes the total costs and equity).

SETTLEMENT

Settlement occurs when the issuer delivers the compensation to the holder of the instrument. For awards classified as equity, this requires the delivery of shares. For those that are classified as liabilities, settlement can be either in instruments or, if either the company or the holder have a choice of settlement, in cash. If cash is used, the difference between the actual cash disbursed and the liability on the date of settlement is handled in two different ways. If the liability is greater than the amount of cash required, the excess credit is reflected in equity. If the liability is less than the cash required, the excess debit is booked to compensation expense.

The withholding of shares equal to the payroll taxes due on the exercised shares does not require classification as liabilities. However, under US GAAP, any amount in excess of this amount requires the entire award to be classified as a liability. Under IFRS, the incremental amount over the equity value only would be classified as a liability.

Payroll taxes are classified on the profit and loss statement the same way as they are for cash compensation. Therefore, stock compensation expense will never be different for payroll tax effects. Under US GAAP, payroll taxes are recognized upon exercise. Under IFRS, they are usually recognized through the attribution period. Consequently, all other things being equal, the total expense will be slightly greater under IFRS than US GAAP until settlement, at which point they would be equal.

8 FINANCIAL INSTRUMENTS

BACKGROUND

Financial instruments have been the subject of numerous issuances of technical guidance interpretation, revisions in standards, and harsh criticism from the investor community. While some instruments are recorded at historical cost, similar to property plant, and equipment, many are regularly revalued to fair value. At the date that this text is being written, fair value is handled differently under US GAAP and IFRS, although a pending standard by the IASB is nearly identical to the present US GAAP.

The consternation and division in the user community about the accounting for financial instruments is rooted in the balance between relevance and reliability. Because financial instruments are liquid, meaning they can be turned into cash quickly, the standard setters favor reporting at fair value since it is useful and relevant to users of the financial statements in assessing the amount, timing, and risk of cash flows. This near-cash quality is what makes financial instruments so different from other noncash assets.

As a compromise to counter the volatility that fair value reporting can impart on an entity's results, current rules required the classification of financial instruments into three classes:

1. Held-to-maturity (HTM)
2. Available-for-sale
3. Trading

HTM securities are *deemed* to be most illiquid, insofar as the entities' intent and ability to not sell the investment in the foreseeable future. This is the case for a company that has more than adequate funding and a stable capital structure with ample access to other sources of liquidity. The point is that it is unlikely the entity would need to cash in the instruments in the near future. Consequently, the entity does not need to reflect the changes in fair value anywhere in its statements (although there are disclosures required). The accounting reflects that the entity will recover its cash when the instrument matures. Because equity has no maturity, it cannot be HTM.

Conversely, if an entity classifies instruments as trading, that is a signal to the users that these investments can be sold and turned over continuously. Due to this uncertainty of the amount of cash that will be realized, these investments are revalued at fair value in each period, with the difference reflected in income.

Instruments that meet neither of these definitions are classified as available for sale (AFS). While these investments are carried at fair value, normal changes in value are reflected in other comprehensive income (OCI). Under US GAAP, reductions in value or impairments of AFS that are determined to be other than temporary (OTT) are reflected in income. IFRS has no such rule of AFS securities since write-ups of impairments are permitted (write-backs of impairments are also required for PP&E as well as inventory). As will be covered later, both standards require impairment of HTM securities to be reflected in income.

IFRS also provides an option for entities to designate changes in fair value for any AFS or HTM instrument to be recognized in income if it reduces an *accounting mismatch*. A mismatch occurs usually in the context of hedging. Hedging occurs when an entity purchases instruments that respond inversely to each other in response to the same economic event; or obtaining a fixed price for a commodity when the selling or purchase price is fixed. For instance, a company that manufactures and sells ethanol at a fixed cost or an index can purchase an instrument to purchase corn at the current price or the same index at a certain point in the future to lock in the profit. The technique of hedging may or may not qualify for *hedge accounting* (covered later).

As another support to the risk inherent in accounting for financial instruments, both standards require extensive disclosure, including a narrative of how the entity determines fair value and details about reclassifications in and out of the categories, which are indicated by the respective standards to be a rare event. In other words, entities are not permitted to randomly change accounting for instruments to prevent them from using accounting to achieve a desired financial result (rather than reporting on the actual economics of the business).

According to the standards, fair value is computed using factors that fall into categories of inputs, which are intended to reflect their accuracy with regard to the instruments' actual market value at the balance sheet date.

There are three tiers of inputs:

1. Observable values (OV)
2. Observable inputs (OI)
3. Unobservable inputs (UI)

The above list is in order of riskiness with regard to accuracy, from least to most. In other words, OVs are the most accurate while UIs are the least. One must keep in mind that since these are values at a moment in time, twelve midnight on the last day of the reporting period, that accuracy should be construed in a relative sense. Explained another way, over time and across multitudes of financial instruments, OVs are thought to be more accurate, and thus, relative to UIs, over time, more indicative of the market value. However, in a microeconomic sense, a company that has, say, an investment in a private equity firm and has direct access to management, may very well be in a position to have a UI be more accurate than an OI. In this case, the proximity to the operations of the company may offset the lack of observers (bidders) in a market.

The above dissonance is another reason why disclosure of financial instruments are so relevant and thus useful to the user of the financial statement. However careful the standard setters have been in crafting these standards to balance the relevance and reliability of reporting on financial instruments, their volatile nature lends itself to ample, and sometimes vehement opposition.

The financial crisis of 2008 was one such event. In 2008, the credit markets in the United States froze because of the uncertainty of the value of investments held by numerous banks, specifically subprime mortgage-backed securities. The tipping point in the crisis was when it was learned publicly that Lehman Brothers, a storied and long-lived investment bank, could no longer re-fund its massive short-term obligations. Banks were wary of lending to Lehman, which meant it did not have the funding to pay off its creditors, who in turn were short on cash for their creditors. This cascading effect bred astonishingly rapid mistrust among traders at other financial firms, leading to a severe reticence for the firms to lend to anyone, particularly those firms with large exposures to mortgage-backed securities. Additionally, because of the lack of transparency about the owners of the instruments, who bore the eventual risk due to layers of derivatives based on the securities, the impact was multiplied, which caused the crash of even ultrasafe money markets (which are deemed to be so liquid that they are near cash).

The crisis led to a truly epic bailout via government stimulus in the United States and Europe, totaling close to $2 trillion USD. The central banks of the United States and some in Europe also tendered unlimited guarantees of securities, thereby providing liquidity to the seized gears of the international funding system.

Companies complained loudly that fair value accounting was the *cause* of the crisis because it "forced" them to write down their investments which, in their estimation, caused a downward spiral. To many, especially in the accounting profession, this argument was at best disingenuous and at most, dangerously misleading. Some in the investor community had for years eschewed financial statements as backward-looking due to their reliance on historical information. Moreover, it is widely known, and stated throughout accounting literature, that financial statements are one tool in a tool chest of implements that investors must use to gage the performance, and future performance, of investments. To believe that suddenly, and conveniently for them, companies regarded financial statements as the seed of the crisis was incredulous.

Another response to the crisis was the formation of the Financial Crisis Advisory Group (FCAG). This multinational board of accounting standard setters, central bankers, and market regulators met for several months to uncover the root causes of the crisis and propose steps forward to avert another. While the conclusion was multifaceted, two in particular held profound meaning for the accounting profession.

The FCAG held that more rapid, not slower, global convergence of accounting standards should be continued. It is in harmonizing the present differences in accounting for financial instruments between IFRS and US GAAP that the findings held as being pivotal to averting another crisis. The other pertinent conclusion was that financial statements were just one of many tools that investors should use. This appeared to vindicate the stance of the accounting community that fair value accounting was not the cause of the crisis.

However intricate the accounting for investments held by companies at the balance sheet date is, the more difficult facet is when to derecognize financial instruments. The simple answer is that financial instruments should be removed from the books when they are sold. However, financial instruments are often the subject of very complex arrangements. Among these are transfers of securities as collateral, transfers with the right or obligation to repurchase them, as well as contingent rights and obligations to perform these actions. Securitizations also enter into the decision model on derecognition. Intent and capability of the transferee to sell the securities also bears on the decision to derecognize.

WHAT IS A FINANCIAL INSTRUMENT?

What qualifies as a financial instrument is the first question that must be answered before embarking on accounting or reporting for an investment. Let's start with the definitions under respective standards:

Under US GAAP, a financial instrument is defined as follows:

Cash, evidence of an ownership interest in an entity, or a contract that both

1. Imposes on one entity a contractual obligation either

   a. To deliver cash or another financial instrument to a second entity
   b. To exchange other financial instruments on potentially unfavorable terms with the second entity

2. Conveys to that second entity a contractual right either

   a. To receive cash or another financial instrument from the first entity
   b. To exchange other financial instruments on potentially favorable terms with the first entity.

Under IFRS, the definition (partial) is as follows:

A financial asset is any asset that is

1. Cash
2. An equity instrument of another entity
3. A contractual right

   a. To receive cash or another financial asset from another entity
   b. To exchange financial assets or financial liabilities with another entity under conditions that are potentially favorable to the entity

A financial liability is any liability that is

1. A contractual obligation

   a. To deliver cash or another financial asset to another entity; or
   b. To exchange financial assets or financial liabilities with another entity under conditions that are potentially unfavorable to the entity

The definitions are nearly identical. While the second part of the US GAAP definition alludes to the fact that it is defining a financial liability, the IFRS is explicit. In theory both standards are referring to the same thing, although the accounting can be different.

It is also important to note that certain assets that do not meet the above definitions are also accounted for as financial instruments. This will be covered in later chapters.

A unique aspect of some financial instruments is that they can transform from an asset to a liability and back again an unlimited number of times. In this sense, the definition is two-sided; the same contract can be either a right or an obligation at a particular point in time depending on the contract and the prevailing circumstances. There is no other element in the accounting realm where this is the case. These types of contracts are employed to lock in profit. In other words, its only function is to preserve the impact of profitability on an entity, not to be lucrative in and of itself. The company is essentially de-risking part of its business.

While the universe of financial instruments appears to be boundless, some of the classes of financial instruments are derivatives, call options, put options, swaps (usually for interest rates) or a combination of these. Securitizations are groups of financial instruments that are packaged together and sold in units to investors.

MEASUREMENT OF FINANCIAL INSTRUMENTS

Held-to-Maturity/Measured at Amortized Cost

HTM instruments are ones that an entity has both the intent *and* ability to hold until maturity. IFRS uses the term *measured at amortized cost* rather than HTM. Because equity has no maturity date, an equity instruments cannot be HTM. The value moves steadily up so that the return on the instrument produces a steady rate of return. This is called the effective rate. It is the interest rate that equates the purchase cost of the asset with the amount that the entity will receive at maturity. If an instrument is purchased at either a discount or premium (i.e., above or below the face value), the effective rate will be different than the face or coupon rate to compensate for the higher or lower purchase price. While IFRS and US GAAP have slightly different definitions, the meaning is the same.

It is not enough for an entity to say that it will hold the instrument to maturity—it must also have the ability. The ability to do so is directly dependent on the adequacy of financing. If the entity would foresee any need to sell all or part of the instrument, it cannot be classified as HTM. Naturally, even if it has the ability, if the entity does not intend to hold it, the security also cannot be classified as HTM.

Trading Instruments

Trading instruments are ones that the entity intends to buy and sell actively. The bar for this definition is low. The standards give only narrow leeway for an entity to classify investments as HTM. Trading classification, conversely, in some ways, is the default classification. While the last classification, termed available-for-sale, are instruments that are neither HTM nor trading, and have the appearance of a default, the fact that the gains and losses are reflected in OCI gives auditors more caution than the trading classification since all gains and losses for nonhedged trading instruments are reflected in income.

Available-for-Sale

AFS instruments are ones that are neither HTM nor trading. Typically these would be instruments of a nonfinancial company that uses them to make returns for cash that is not currently employed for working capital, capital expenditure, or dividends. Companies may maintain seasonal funds, that is, money waiting for seasonal ramp-up of production.

Like securities in the trading class, AFS are remeasured each reporting period to fair value. The difference is that changes in value are reflected in OCI. When the instrument is sold, the balance in OCI is reclassified to profit and loss. Thus, at that point, the ultimate gain or loss on the holding is recognized in income.

Designated Through Profit and Loss

IFRS also allows an entity to designate a financial instrument as recognized through profit and loss, regardless of the required classification, if it would reduce an accounting "mismatch." A mismatch is generally a factor in hedging, whether or not the hedge qualified for hedge accounting. This option means that for a given financial instrument, the change in fair value can be reflected in OCI under US GAAP while in income for IFRS.

IMPAIRMENT

Since trading securities are marked to market, impairment, or nontemporary decreases in value, they are not a separate accounting issue since all movements are reflected in income. However, for HTM and AFS, impairments are reclassified to income from the balance sheet and OCI, respectively.

The decision to reflect a decrease in value in a financial instrument is predicated on whether the value will return before it is realized into cash or another financial instrument. For HTM instruments, this is based on the expected cash flows to maturity, or, in extraordinary circumstances, before it is sold, since only in rare cases should HTM investments be realized before redemption from the issuer.

Cash flows are discounted using the effective interest method as a gage of whether future cash flows are sufficient to recover the carrying value. During a period that the entity decides to sell an instrument is when the determination of any impairment is recognized, even if it is not sold until a subsequent period.

Under US GAAP, if an entity determines that an AFS instrument is impaired, but it is not deemed OTT, it must test for impairment each period until either it is sold or the value increases above the carrying value. If at any point an impairment of an AFS investment is determined to be OTT, the balance in OCI, if greater than the carrying value, is reclassified to income. IFRS does not specify that impairments of AFS securities be reclassified to income.

Impairment reversals under US GAAP are prohibited. However, under IFRS, reversals are required if the impairment indicators that bore on the calculation improve.

The unit of account (UOA) for impairment is at the individual security level for US GAAP, or it can be a collection of instruments that represent the same security (e.g., CUSIP). IFRS can be for a particular instrument or a group of instruments with similar risk characteristics. Individually significant securities are first assessed for impairment by themselves. If not impaired individually, that instrument is included in the related group so, in effect, it can be measured twice. However, the impairment of a group of instruments is an intermediate step, pending the outcome of impairment performed in individual instruments within that group, which is removed from the group valuation prior to calculating the impairment. Consequently, IFRS allows potentially for gains on some instruments to offset losses on another. It should be noted, however, that IFRS (and US GAAP) generally allows offsetting only under very specific circumstances. Moreover, the *IFRS Framework* includes a strong concept of substance over form. Thus, if a particular security, though sharing characteristics with a group, is obviously impaired, the IFRS prudence concept would dictate that impairment be done on that instrument alone, or with other instruments based on the same issuer, similar to US GAAP.

INDICATORS OF IMPAIRMENT

Both IFRS and US GAAP use objective indicators of impairment which must be assessed each reporting period. As mentioned above, the key is to make a professional judgment if the future cash flows will be sufficient to recover the value. Among these indicators are the financial health of the issuer, taking into account bankruptcy filings and other evidence of financial distress, such as failure to make scheduled debt payments. The disappearance of a market for the issuer's securities is, not in and of itself, a reason to recognize an impairment. However, a disappearance of a market due to the issuer's financial distress should be considered. General impairment indicators similar to the ones used for PP&E (e.g., internal and external factors such as deep drops in sales prices, changes in regulation or market demand) must be considered for assessing impairment. US GAAP includes more specific guidance including considering analyst reports and general industry difficulties.

SPECIFIC US GAAP GUIDANCE

While IFRS explicitly includes some of the more specific guidance of US GAAP, the general guidance can fit within the applicable US GAAP guidance. IFRS, in IAS 8, *Accounting Policies*, allows the reference to the current guidance of another standard setter with a common framework to IFRS when no direct or analogous guidance exists.

US GAAP includes guidance about the impact that the pending sale of a security, or even a bona fide offer to sell, whether or not solicited, is below the original amortized costs and has on the incidence and measurement of impairment. For debt securities, if an entity intends to sell, or more likely than not will be required to sell an AFS or HTM security, if the fair value is less than the original cost of the investment, an OTT impairment is deemed to have occurred. If the entity will sell or will more likely than not be required to sell the investment, the entire difference between the amortized costs and the fair value is recognized in earnings. Otherwise, only credit losses are recognized in income, with the remainder recognized in OCI.

After an OTT impairment, the impaired value is the new cost basis, and subsequent recoveries are prohibited. (IFRS requires recoveries if impairment indicators have improved). HTM debt securities are subsequently accounted for using the effective interest rate method, using the rate that equates the expected future cash flows with the new cost basis. Subsequent increase in cash flows received or expected to be received are recognized over the life of the instrument as an adjustment to the acceptable yield. Effectively this means that any recovery would be amortized over the remaining holding period at an even rate, not as a significant, one-time reversal, which would be the case under IFRS.

TRANSFERS

Transfers of securities can either qualify as a sale or not qualify. If the transfer does qualify, the financial instrument is removed from the balance sheet and any difference between the proceeds and carrying value is recognized in income. Additionally, for any AFS financial instruments, the balance in OCI is also reclassified to income, thereby recognizing the gain or loss experience on the instrument from inception. If a transfer does not qualify as a sale, the proceeds received are offset by a liability. Consequently, the balance sheet is grossed up, signifying that the entity will likely need to return the proceeds under certain circumstances, and thus it cannot be recognized as income.

Generally speaking, a transfer qualifies as a sale if the risks and rewards of ownership have passed to the transferee. This is a common concept in IFRS and US GAAP with regard to revenue recognition. The key is that *both* the risks and rewards must be relinquished. This is important since entities can gain income from securities they transfer without off-loading the risk of loss.

Transfers that generally do not qualify as sales are arrangements in which the transferor must repurchase the securities, either unconditionally or under certain conditions that are probable. An example would be executing deals known as *repos*. This transaction has two legs in which the transferor exchanges securities for use of cash for a short time and is then obligated to purchase those securities back. In essence, this is a loan backed by collateral.

US GAAP has much more detailed guidance on transfers that do not qualify as a sale. One such situation is where a transferee does not have the capability, say access, to a market for the instrument exchanged, and business expectations, either contractually or by custom, are that the transferor will buy back the securities if the transferee cannot sell them. In this case, when the transferee makes a transfer that qualifies as a sale, the transferor could recognize a sale. The transferor would offset the transferred assets with the liability booked as a transfer and recognize any difference in income. Effectively, the transferor needs to look down the supply chain as to when to recognize income.

One arrangement whereby the transferor can recognize a sale but still has involvement in the cash flows for the instrument is when it agrees to *service* the assets. Servicing the assets in this context means that the entity collects the income but only as a custodian, retaining a fee for the service, and remitting that cash to the transferee. This occurs frequently in the mortgage security market where the originator-seller has a robust capability to provide a collection of income more efficiently than the buyer, who profits from asset appreciation or trading.

HEDGING AND HEDGE ACCOUNTING

Hedging is a grouping of transactions designed to mitigate the variability of the ultimate profitability of those transactions. In a hedging relationship, a hedging instrument or agreement is entered into contemporaneously with the hedged item in a way that offsets the variability in value of the hedged item. Hedges have varying degrees of *effectiveness*. Effectiveness is the degree to which the hedge cancels out the variability of the hedged item. If a hedge is designed to be 80% effective, this means that the entity will still experience 20% of the up or down movement on the value.

In practice, there are rarely perfect hedges. One of the reasons for this is that except in commodity firms, an entity often purchases a contract that is similar to the hedged item because an exact hedge, that is, an instrument that references the same exact hedged item, is not available, or would only be available at a cost that exceeds the benefit. For example, an oil refinery may sell forward jet fuel and purchase a hedge based on kerosene, which is derived from some of the same feed stocks, but has different market demand. When the jet fuel is sold, if the hedge and the hedged item are of the value as planned, the gain or loss on the contracts should cancel each other out, leaving a normal, predictable profit (less the cost of the hedge). This is attractive to entities because it locks in the profitability, or to a degree at least, at the date the deal is struck, which is based on the economics at that time. It is a way to neutralize the variability in the entity's supply chain.

Hedge *accounting* can only be applied under certain circumstances. While a company can hedge however and whenever it wishes, to gain the advantage of hedge accounting, which is the deferral or avoidance of recognizing volatility in profitability, it must design, document, and commit to a practice that has a reasonable probability of achieving effectiveness.

Just as the classification of financial instruments among HTM, AFS, and trading, together with ample disclosure, is a compromise balancing the relevance of changes in the investment values of an entity against the assessing management's effectiveness so reliably, so too is hedge accounting. By deferring the gain or loss on the hedge of a financial transaction, management can demonstrate the effectiveness of its operations in a concise manner, that is, within a single period. However, if the hedge is not operating as designed inside of a corridor, the gain or loss is recognized immediately, thereby giving way to relevance.

Types of Hedges

Hedge accounting applies to three different types of items.

Fair value hedge. A hedge of the exposure to changes in fair value of a recognized asset or liability, or an unrecognized firm commitment, or an identified portion of such an asset, liability or firm commitment, that is attributable to a particular risk and could affect profit or loss. An unrecognized firm commitment is an agreement to supply or purchase goods or services over a period of time.

Cash flow hedge. A hedge of the exposure to variability in cash flows that (1) is attributable to a particular risk associated with a recognized asset or liability (such as all or some future interest payments on variable-rate debt) or a highly probable forecast transaction, and (2) could affect profit or loss.

Hedge of a net investment in a foreign operation as defined in IAS 21.

IFRS does not limit the type of item that can be hedged; however, nonfinancial instrument items can only be used as a hedge of a net investment in a foreign operation.

Implicit in the definitions above is that what is actually hedged is not the item itself, but rather a risk associated with it. While this distinction is often irrelevant in some hedges, perhaps in the example above in hedging future oil purchases, hedging of financial instruments with an interest component can be extremely complex.

US GAAP is much more detailed about how interest rate hedges qualify for hedge accounting. US GAAP requires that when hedging against a benchmark rate, that the same rate be used for similar instruments. Departures from the benchmark rate should be rare and justified. While IFRS does not have such a specification, using a consistent benchmark would certainly fall within the allowable boundaries of IFRS. IFRS standards reference benchmark rates and propose that these rates can be used to base hedges on. From a practical perspective, under both IFRS and US GAAP, the use of benchmark rates adds an element of reliability to measuring hedge effectiveness. The measurement of effectiveness, which will be covered later in the chapter, is a critical aspect of being able to use hedge accounting.

Both IFRS and US GAAP allow for hedging a portfolio of instruments, although hedging a net position of assets and liabilities is not permitted. Consequently, only a portfolio of asset **or** liabilities can be hedged items. US GAAP further specifies that to qualify for hedge accounting, the individual instruments in a portfolio must be expected to respond proportionately to changes in the risk being hedged, in this case, interest rates. This implies that the instruments must have similar characteristics, such as simple interest rate terms, not varying degrees of complex rate features. However, even if a portfolio of instruments is complex, if they are expected to respond proportionately to changes in rates, and have been shown to actually exhibit this behavior, the portfolio can qualify (measuring effectiveness is covered later in the chapter).

Hedges can be groups or sequences of financial instruments, which can offset groups of hedged items. In other words, if the hedges are all mitigating the same type of risk (e.g., change in interest rates), an entity can combine instruments so long as the instruments are not specifically prohibited by the applicable standards, the strategy is defined in the hedging documentation, and effectiveness can be demonstrated using a reliable measure.

Portions of items can also be hedged, as well as (as described above) up to certain effectiveness (e.g., the hedge is designed to be 60% effective). Partial-term hedges (that is, hedging for only part of the "life" of a hedged item) are viewed differently in IFRS and in US GAAP. While both standards allow partial-term hedging, the verbiage in US GAAP guides the user to only apply this where instruments are very closely matched in key terms. US GAAP uses the example that hedging interest rate risk of a ten-year bond with a three-year swap would be difficult since it would be rare to find a three-year derivative that can be shown to effectively offset the changes on a ten-year note. IFRS has the same underlying principles, but the guidance gives a range of 85 to 120% effectiveness as being deemed effective.

Designation of a Hedge

At the inception of a hedge, the entity must have in place a properly authorized, articulated, and documented hedging strategy applicable to the hedge being entered into. The document must describe why and how to measure effectiveness. This document is important since it will be referenced throughout the life of the hedge to determine, based on the performance of the instruments, if hedge accounting can still continue.

Effectiveness is the degree to which a hedge **negates** the *change* in the value of the hedged item. An entity can choose to hedge less than 100% of the hedged item.

Under IFRS, a hedge is deemed to be ineffective if it does not offset the variability in a range between 85 and 120%. For example, in a 100% hedge, if the change in the forecast purchase of Columbian coffee compared with a hedge of a Peruvian coffee derivative is 80/100, meaning that if the price of Columbian coffee increases 20 CUs for unit in a period, but the hedge only decreases by 15 CUs, the hedge is ineffective since 15/20 = 75%.

If the hedge is deemed to be ineffective at any point before maturity, hedge accounting for that instrument is discontinued prospectively. If the hedged transaction is no longer expected to occur, then all future gains and losses are recognized in income in that period and subsequent periods. For cash flow hedges that are reflected in OCI (as will be covered later), the cumulative amount is also reclassified income. If the hedged transaction is still expected to occur, the accounting for the hedge is frozen. For hedges accumulated in OCI, the amount that is expected not to be recovered is reclassified into profit and loss in that period. Any remaining amount in OCI is taken to income upon the realization of the hedged item. It follows that until a cash flow hedge is realized, the cumulative amount in OCI is revaluated each period with the part not expected to be realized reclassified to income.

Hedge effectiveness measurement is the single most important factor in beginning, ending, and planning a hedge. If the effectiveness cannot be reliably measured, it cannot be designated to begin with, or, in the case of changes in the financial markets or economy, it can lead to the suspension of hedge accounting. The expectation of effectiveness must also take into account the counterparties' capability and intent to perform. This condition is to prevent hedge accounting from being applied even in a well-matched hedge where the hedging entity has reason to believe that ultimately the hedge will not be fulfilled.

IFRS and US GAAP differ somewhat in documenting what determines an effective hedge. IFRS in application guidance does require that an entity look at both historical and projected movements of hedges and the hedging instruments. Common methods include various statistical models such as regression analysis. US GAAP specifies that both past and future assessments of effectiveness are required to maintain hedge accounting. US GAAP gives users a choice of a cumulative or period-by-period approach. The cumulative approach requires that the test for effectiveness examine the inception-to-date net changes in the hedge and the hedging instrument. The period-by-period approach looks at each period in isolation, that is, it compares the respective changes in the item and the hedging instrument for a particular period. US GAAP specifies further that the length of the period in period-by-period cannot be longer than three months.

US GAAP allows what is known as the "short-cut method" (SCM) for testing effectiveness. The SCM, in summary, allows a company to assume effectiveness of a hedging relationship throughout the hedge period in the absence of obvious evidence to the contrary. It is a negative assurance—the company does not know that the hedge is definitely not working.

To qualify for SCM, first it must be an interest rate hedge. Other hedges are prohibited. The hedge must be expected to be highly effective. All the following conditions must be met in order to use the SCM. The terms of the item and hedge must be nearly identical. To define the degree of similarity of the terms, US GAAP further requires that notional amounts of the pair be the same. In a simple interest rate swap, either the fair value of the instrument must be zero at hedge inception or differ only due to the bid-ask spread between an entry and exit price as covered earlier (US GAAP fair value must be an exit price, not an entry price).   If the hedging instrument is a compound derivative composed of an interest rate swap, a mirror call, or put option, the premium paid for the put option or mirror call must be paid in the same manner as the hedged item. The formula for computing the net settlement for the interest rate swap is the same for each net settlement. This means that the fixed rate is the same throughout the term and that the variable rate is the same index and the spread (or no spread) is constant. The interest-bearing asset or liability must **not** be prepayable, that is, able to be redeemed before maturity, unless it is due solely to an embedded call option in a compound derivative composed of an interest rate swap and a mirror-call option. Any other terms of the hedged item must be typical and not invalidate the effectiveness.

For fair value hedges only, the maturity date of the hedged item and the expiration date of the swap must be identical. There must be no floor or cap on the variable portion.

MEASUREMENT AND ACCOUNTING

Fair Value Hedges

In a fair value hedge (FVH), the deferral or elimination of the volatility of the fair value of a hedged item is effected by recording the changes in a hedged item that would not yet qualify for recognition. For instance, a firm commitment is not recognized as an asset. Only after the sale or purchase is completed can the asset or liability be recognized. FVH accounting requires the entity to record the change in the fair value of the hedged item in income, with the offset as an asset or liability in the case, respectively, of a gain or loss. If the hedge is effective, at least some of the gain or loss is offset in income from the loss or gain of the hedging instrument.

When the commitment (or part of it) is realized, say the purchase of inventory, the hedged item asset or liability become part of the cost of the item. So in the case of a purchase of inventory, a hedge asset would be added to the cost of the inventory, or a liability subtracted.

Example: Hedge of a firm commitment to purchase inventory

Home Stop retail stores have agreed with Mower, Inc. to purchase 1,000 mowers over the next six months. The gross margin on mowers has been near a historical high in the current month and Home Stop wants to lock in these margins. However, the pricing in the contract is fixed only 10 days prior to the delivery of the mowers at the spot price of steel on that day. The same day that the contract is executed, the CFO of Home Stop purchases a derivative on the type of steel used to make a majority of the mower's housing. The hedge is designed to offset the rise or fall in the price of steel by receiving cash or paying cash to the counterparty based on the increase or decrease, respectively of steel relative to the spot price on the date of purchase. The derivative expires 10 days prior to the delivery of the first batch of 400 mowers. The CFO documents this strategy, including the fact that the hedge is designed to offset 75% of the variability in the price of the mowers. The CFO structured the hedge to purchase nominal tons of steel to correspond with the steel content of the mowers.

At the end of the current month, the spot price of the grade of steel used to make the mowers has increased by 5%. Because of the mix of steel used to make the mowers, the Mower Inc. purchasing manager tells the Home Stop CFO that the mower price has increased 35% since the date the agreement was signed. The controller is preparing the month-end financial statements and calculates the following entries:

FV of derivatives—hedges (B/S)   200
    Gain on FV of derivatives—hedges   200
To record the gain on steel price derivatives contract # 2010-23

Loss on FV of hedged item   190
    FV of hedge (B/S)   190
To record the loss on the hedge of a firm commitment contract# 2010-23

The two journal entries above net to a $10 gain that is reflected in income in the current period. Because the ratio of the change is 95% (190/200), the hedge is deemed effective since the ratio is between 80 to 125%, which is established by IFRS standards.

In the subsequent two months leading up to the purchase, the cumulative changes in the fair value, and thus the balances of the hedge and hedging instruments are 90 CU and 100 CU. The hedges were tested and deemed effective in each period.

The controller directs that the collection of cash from the counterpart of the hedging instrument is booked as follows:

Cash   100
    Fair Value Hedge—Asset   100
To record the settlement of contract # 2010-23

The purchase of the inventory of the 400 units triggers the following entry:

FV of Hedge (B/S)   90
    Inventory   90

When the inventory is sold, the cost of sales will be 90 CU lower than the current purchase price. Thus, this locked in 95% of the gross margin that existed on the date of the commitment.

If the hedge had been deemed ineffective at any point in this example, the company would stop recording the change in the hedge item fair value (the firm commitment). Since the derivative (hedging instrument) needs to be accounted for under fair value no matter what the effectiveness of the hedge is, Home Stop's income would have increased or decreased each period by the change in fair value of the derivative. While the ultimate profitability is the same (cash is cash), under effective hedge accounting the volatility in income over the preceding months leading up to the purchase of the inventory was all but eliminated.

Cash Flow Hedges

A cash flow hedge is designed to mitigate or eliminate the variability in an expected cash flow. Like FVHs, to qualify for hedge accounting, cash flow hedges must have a documented strategy, tested each period for effectiveness, discontinued if ineffective, and reflected in income when it is known that the hedge will be ineffective. The two main differences in hedge account as compared to FVH, are that the effect of the variability in the hedged item is **not** recorded in the period, and the change in the fair value of the hedging instrument is reflected in OCI to the extent effective.

As covered earlier in the chapter, cash flow hedges are hedges of particular risk of a recognized asset or liability (e.g., a bond payable or bond investment) or a highly probable forecast transaction. For instance, if an entity has issued variable rate bonds to finance a project but wants to fix the rate it pays in interest to ensure that the project is profitable in accordance with its projected returns, it can enter into an interest-rate swap in which it pays a fixed rate and receives the variable rate in return. Thus it is always reimbursed for the interest payments it will make (or up to the number of bond hedges) and always pays a fixed rate.

9 LEASES

PREFACE

In 2011, the Financial Accounting Standards Board and International Accounting Standards Board issued an Exposure Draft of a converged leasing standard. The standard is still being finalized; however, with few exceptions, under both IFRS and US GAAP, entities would be required to record a leased asset on its balance sheet regardless of the terms. Operating leases would cease to exist as an accounting concept. In broad terms, lessees would recognize a right-to-use asset offset by a lease obligation. The asset would be depreciated in a similar way to fixed assets but would be separated from general classifications. Lessors would be required to also recognize an asset to represent the right to receive cash flows (essentially a discounted receivable) and an obligation. The remainder of the cost of the asset leases would be carried on the balance sheet in property, plant, and equipment.

CURRENTLY EFFECTIVE STANDARDS

A lease, in business terms, is a right to use an asset for a specific period of time in exchange for cash or other consideration. At the end of the lease, the lessee (the party that pays and uses the asset) has the right and obligation to return the asset control back for the lessor (the party that owns the asset). In a more general sense, most people consider this rent.

The objective of financial reporting under both IFRS and US GAAP includes enabling the user of the financial statements to assess the amount, timing, and risk of cash flows. In a basic sense, assets enable an entity to receive cash. Liabilities require an entity to hand over cash. Although sometimes the cash is not immediately received or paid, ultimately, it is. So lease accounting must consider this. Another critical aspect of financial reporting is to reflect on the financial impact of management decisions. This way, if an entity enters into a commitment, it needs to be considered for recognition as a liability.

Current accounting under both standards provides two types of lease accounting

1. Capital or finance (under IFRS)
2. Operating

In summary, a capital or finance lease requires the entity to record an asset and liability for the present value of the obligation. This is not the case in operating leases as they require more disclosure.

The decision on the classification of a lease turns on an evaluation of whether the agreement transfers substantially the risks and rewards of ownership to the lessee. If it does, then the lease is effectively a purchase, even though the legal form of the contract may indicate otherwise. The reason for this standard is to promote comparability among companies and across reporting periods of the financial position and performance of an entity regardless of the means used to finance it. If two companies are otherwise identical, and one leases while the other purchases, the lease standards require similar accounting to the purchase if the economic substance is a purchase. The fact that the entity has the right to return the asset at the end of the lease does not in and of itself mean that it does not have obligations similar to one that owns the asset.

While both IFRS and US GAAP require an entity to base the decision of operating or capital (finance lease in IFRS) classification, US GAAP provides bright-line criteria. IFRS does not. The IFRS assessment is based on whether the risks and rewards of ownership have been transferred to the lessee.

ASC 840-10-25

29 *If at its inception a lease meets any of the four lease classification criteria in paragraph 840-10-25, the lease shall be classified by the lessee as a capital lease.*

1 *A lessee and a lessor shall consider whether a lease meets any of the following four criteria as part of classifying the lease at its inception under the guidance in the Lessees Subsection of this Section (for the lessee) and the Lessors Subsection of this Section (for the lessor)*

   1. *Transfer of ownership. The lease transfers ownership of the property to the lessee by the end of the lease term. This criterion is met in situations in which the lease agreement provides for the transfer of title at or shortly after the end of the lease term in exchange for the payment of a nominal fee, for example, the minimum required by statutory regulation to transfer title.*
   2. *Bargain purchase option. The lease contains a bargain purchase option.*
   3. *Lease term. The lease term is equal to 75 percent or more of the estimated economic life of the leased property. However, if the beginning of the lease term falls within the last 25 percent of the total estimated economic life of the leased property, including earlier years of use, this criterion shall not be used for purposes of classifying the lease.*
   4. *Minimum lease payments. The present value at the beginning of the lease term of the minimum lease payments, excluding that portion of the payments representing executory costs such as insurance, maintenance, and taxes to be paid by the lessor, including any profit thereon, equals or exceeds 90 percent of the excess of the fair value of the leased property to the lessor at lease inception over any related investment tax credit retained by the lessor and expected to be realized by the lessor. If the beginning of the lease term falls within the last 25 percent of the total estimated economic life of the leased property, including earlier years of use, this criterion shall not be used for purposes of classifying the lease.*

While IAS 17, *Leases,* requires preparers to consider the proportion of fair value that the minimum lease payments are of fair value and the term of the lease in comparison to the useful life and a bargain purchase option, it does not contain the bright lines of ASC 840-10. IAS 17 also includes language of other factors that could, either individually or in conjunction with other factors, require a lease to be in the balance sheet:

IAS 17

10 *Whether a lease is a finance lease or an operating lease depends on the substance of the transaction rather than the form of the contract.* Examples of situations that individually or in combination would normally lead to a lease being classified as a finance lease are*

1. *The lease transfers ownership of the asset to the lessee by the end of the lease term*
2. *The lessee has the option to purchase the asset at a price that is expected to be sufficiently lower than the fair value at the date the option becomes exercisable for it to be reasonably certain, at the inception of the lease, that the option will be exercised*
3. *The lease term is for the major part of the economic life of the asset even if title is not transferred*
4. *At the inception of the lease the present value of the minimum lease payments amounts to at least substantially all of the fair value of the leased asset*
5. *The leased assets are of such a specialized nature that only the lessee can use them without major modifications*

* *See also SIC-27, **Evaluating the Substance of Transactions Involving the Legal Form of a Lease.***

11 *Indicators of situations that individually or in combination could also lead to a lease being classified as a finance lease are*

1. *If the lessee can cancel the lease, the lessors losses associated with the cancellation are borne by the lessee*
2. *Gains or losses from the fluctuation in the fair value of the residual accrue to the lessee (for example, in the form of a rent rebate equaling most of the sales proceeds at the end of the lease)*
3. *The lessee has the ability to continue the lease for a secondary period at a rent that is substantially lower than market rent*

12 *The examples and indicators in paragraphs 10 and 11 are not always conclusive. If it is clear from other features that the lease does not transfer substantially all risks and rewards incidental to ownership, the lease is classified as an operating lease. For example, this may be the case if ownership of the asset transfers at the end of the lease for a variable payment equal to its then fair value, or if there are contingent rents, as a result of which the lessee does not have substantially all such risks and rewards.*

The differing criteria can and often do result in identical leases being recorded as operating leases under US GAAP, and finance leases for IFRS. One such example is an open-ended auto lease for a fleet of cars. If the lessee assumes the risk of reimbursing the leasing company for a market price below the residual value, or receives the proceeds for the opposite circumstance, there is a strong indication that the risks and rewards of ownership have passed to the lessee even though the lease term may be short.

Another difference between the two standards relates to guarantees of residual value. Under IAS 17, a guarantee of residual value by a third party is included in the minimum lease payments of the lessee. Under US GAAP, third-party guarantees are specifically excluded.

CLASSIFICATION OF LEASES

Because the classification of leases is greatly influenced by the proportion of the fair value and useful life of the asset(s) being leased, it is necessary to examine the differences between IFRS and US GAAP for areas that US GAAP contains specific guidance.

ASC 840-10-25 contains specific guidance for classification of leases involving land and other assets:

ASC 840-10-25

Classification of a Lease Involving Real Estate

18 *This guidance on applying the four lease classification criteria in paragraph 840-10-25-1 to leases involving real estate is organized as follows:*

1. *Lease involving equipment and real estate*
2. *Lease involving both land and buildings*
3. *Lease involving only part of a building*
4. *Lease involving facilities owned by a government unit or authority*

ASC 840-10-25-19 to 20 directs that where land and equipment are part of the same lease, any reasonable means to separate the minimum lease payments to the equipment are used, with the remainder attributable to the land. This approach is consistent with IFRS.

ASC 840-10-25-21 to 22 requires that where a lease incorporates both buildings and land, and there is a residual value guarantee, how is the 90% test (based on fair value of asset leased) apportioned? The guidance directs that where land is 25% or more of the total leased value, the minimum lease payments attributable to the land are

ASC 840-10-25

22 *Paragraphs 840-10-25-38(b) (2) and 840-10-25-67 state that the annual minimum lease payments applicable to the land are determined for both the lessee and lessor by multiplying the fair value of the land by the lessee's incremental borrowing rate. As a result, the remaining minimum lease payments, including the full amount of the residual value guarantee, are attributed to the building.*

This is not permissible under IFRS. IAS 17 requires that preparers allocate the minimum lease payments based on the fair values of the leasehold interests in the land and building elements.

IAS 17

> *15 When a lease includes both land and building elements, an entity assesses the classification of each element as a finance or an operating lease separately in accordance with paragraphs 7-13. In determining whether the land element is an operating or a finance lease, an important consideration is that land normally has an indefinite economic life.*
>
> *16 Whenever necessary in order to classify and account for a lease of land and buildings, the minimum lease payments (including any lump-sum up-front payments) are* allocated between the land and the buildings elements in proportion to the relative fair values of the leasehold interests in the land element and buildings element of the lease at the inception of the lease. *If the lease payments cannot be allocated reliably between these two elements, the entire lease is classified as a finance lease, unless it is clear that both elements are operating leases, in which case the entire lease is classified as an operating lease.*

The fair value of the land element could be the rental cost of a similar lot without a building. This should be obtainable from a real estate agent or firm at minimal cost.

IAS 17 also states that where the land element is immaterial, it is rolled up into the building value. From that point, the classification of the lease is determined based on the economics of the entire lease agreement:

IAS 17

> *17 For a* lease *of land and buildings in which the amount that would initially be recognized for the land element, in accordance with paragraph 20, is immaterial, the land and buildings may be treated as a single unit for the purpose of lease classification and classified as a finance or operating lease in accordance with paragraphs 7-13. In such a case, the economic life of the buildings is regarded as the economic life of the entire leased asset.*

ASC 840-10-25-3 to 4 states that if a lease is for part of a building, like the ASC 840-10-25-19 to 20 on the subject of land and equipment, reasonable attempts have to be made to estimate the fair value of the portion leased. This is consistent with IAS 17.

ASC 840-10-25-20 covers leases from government authorities. In summary, the guidance explains that because leases with governmental entities rarely (if ever) transfer ownership and the life of the property is in many senses unlimited, that virtually all leased government properties are classified as operating leases.

IFRS includes separate guidance for these types of agreements. IFRIC 12, *Service Concession Arrangements,* covers instances where a private operator is granted rights to use public property. IFRIC 12 is a comprehensive piece of guidance (though not voluminous) that establishes a decision tree, based on the outcomes of judgments made by the entity as to whether an arrangement is recognized as a lease. This decision turns on whether the operator controls the asset. This reliance on control illustrates the emphasis IFRS puts on adhering to the *IFRS Framework.*

IFRIC 12 refers to IFRIC 4, *Determining Whether an Arrangement Contains a Lease*. IFRIC 4.9 specifies that an arrangement contains a lease if the user of the asset has the ability to control the use of the specific asset for its own economic purposes, which conveys the rights of ownership. Even though IFRIC 4 excludes arrangements covered in IFRIC 12, IFRIC 4 uses the Basis of Conclusions to underpin the treatment specified in IFRIC 12:

IFRIC 12

Treatment of the operator's rights over the infrastructure (paragraph 11)

BC20 The IFRIC considered the nature of the rights conveyed to the operator in a service concession arrangement. It first examined whether the infrastructure used to provide public services could be classified as property, plant, and equipment of the operator under IAS 16. It started from the principle that infrastructure used to provide public services should be recognized as property, plant, and equipment of the party that controls its use. This principle determines which party should recognize the property, plant, and equipment as its own. The reference to control stems from **The Framework:**

1. An asset is defined by **The Framework** as "a resource controlled by the entity as a result of past events and from which future economic benefits are expected to flow to the entity."
2. **The Framework** notes that many assets are associated with legal rights, including the right of ownership. It goes on to clarify that the right of ownership is not essential.
3. Rights are often unbundled. For example, they may be divided proportionately (undivided interests in land) or by specified cash flows (principal and interest on a bond) or over time (a lease).

BC21 The IFRIC concluded that treatment of infrastructure that the operator constructs or acquires or to which the grantor gives the operator access for the purpose of the service arrangement should be determined by whether it is controlled by the grantor in the manner described in paragraph 5. If it is so controlled (as will be the case for all arrangements within the scope of the interpretation), then, regardless of which party has legal title to it during the arrangement, the infrastructure should not be recognized as property, plant, and equipment of the operator because the operator does not control the use of the public service infrastructure.

BC22 In reaching this conclusion the IFRIC observed that it is in control of the right to use an asset that determines recognition under IAS 16 and the creation of a lease under IAS 17, **Leases**. IAS 16 defines property, plant, and equipment as tangible items that "are held for use in the production or supply of goods or services, for rental to others or for administrative purposes . . ." It requires items within this definition to be recognized as property, plant, and equipment unless another standard requires or permits a different approach. As an example of a different approach, it highlights the requirement in IAS 17 for recognition of leased property, plant, and equipment to be evaluated on the basis of the transfer of risks and rewards. That standard defines a lease as "an agreement whereby the lessor conveys to the lessee in return for a series of payments the right to use an asset" and it sets

> out the requirements for classification of leases. *IFRIC 4, **Determining Whether an Arrangement Contains a Lease*** interprets the meaning of right to use an asset as "the arrangement conveys the right to control the use of the underlying asset."

In other words, if the grantor (the public body) controls who the customer base is (e.g., in the case of a tollway, for instance, that all drivers must be permitted on the road) and regulates what it can charge, the grantor effectively controls the asset, and thus the operator is prohibited from applying lease accounting at all (that is not even an operating lease). These arrangements, however, can result in the recognition by the operator of a financial asset for the right to receive cash flows from the grantor (or at the grantor's direction) or an intangible asset for the right to collect user fees. The recognition of other assets is consistent with the parts of the *IFRS Framework* that relate to these rights and obligations.

Financial assets derive their value primarily from market supply and demand. That is, there is a great deal of the value of the asset that is out of the control of the owner of the instrument. So it follows that when an entity retains the right to receive variable cash flows from the grantor, whom it does not control, it has a financial instrument.

Likewise, the right to receive user fees from an asset it does not own or control is an asset in its own right that has the characteristics of other intangible assets. IAS 38, *Intangibles,* indicates that intangible assets lack physical substance and that their recognition and value depend on the ability of the entity to separately identify the asset and to control its use. Since the type of arrangement described in IFRIC 12 describes a contractual right to receive cash flows, and there is only one asset from which this derives, the characteristics of an intangible asset exist.

The fact that US GAAP affords lease treatment to these types of arrangements and IFRS does not highlights a major difference between the *IFRS Framework* and US GAAP, including the Concepts Statements. IFRS is clear that an asset is recognized by an entity based on control, not ownership. While ownership often conveys the right to control, an entity can control an asset that it does not have title to. Since US GAAP is firmly rooted in legal concepts, this is not permitted under US GAAP.

To summarize, in the cases of arrangements using public assets, the use of US GAAP will usually result in an operating lease. Depending on the control of the resources an operator has over public assets in an arrangement, the result for an entity using IFRS can be a lease, an intangible asset, or financial instrument.

IDENTIFYING A LEASE

IFRIC 4, *Determining Whether an Arrangement Contains a Lease,* clarifies application of IAS 17 which requires an assessment of whether a user of an asset has control of it. It also specifies that the substance of an agreement, not the legal form, determines lease accounting. ASC 840-10-15 contains similar guidance for determining whether the substance of an agreement contains a lease.

In summary, both standards specify that agreements such as supply contracts can contain a lease. The lease and other elements need to be separated for purposes of applying the respective lease guidance. Both indicate that the use of a specified asset, or the capability of the supplier to provide an identical asset, are a requisite for lease accounting since this indicates the use of an asset for a specified period of time in exchange for payments. If nonsubstantive provisions make alternative uses by the provider of the asset unlikely, this would not preclude lease accounting. An example would be if the asset is specialized for its geographic location and would effectively prohibit the economic use of the asset for another party's benefit.

In practice, there would be little practical difference in accounting for these types of arrangements.

SALE-LEASEBACKS

Sale-leaseback arrangements involve the sale of an asset by an entity that is immediately leased back from the purchaser. The key issue is how and when to recognize any gain or loss on the transaction. This is because the substance of the transaction often results in the same party controlling the asset before and after the transaction.

Under US GAAP, if substantially all of the rights and use of the property are transferred to the purchaser-lessor, gain or loss is recognized immediately. This set of circumstances would result in an operating lease. IAS 17.61 specifies that if the resulting lease is classified as operating, gain or loss is recognized immediately, unless the sale is at other than fair value. If the sale amount is greater than fair value, the gain or loss is recognized over the lease term. If the sale price is less than fair value, loss is recognized immediately, unless a loss is compensated by below-market rentals, in which case the profit is deferred. Thus where an operating lease is the outcome of a sale-leaseback, US GAAP and IFRS can result in deferral or nondeferral of the profit or loss.

IAS 17.59 states that if a sale-leaseback transaction results in a finance lease, the gain or loss is deferred and amortized over the lease term. Conversely, ASC 840-40-25-3(b) specifies that if the entity retains more than a minor but less than a substantial interest, if the result is an operating lease or a capital lease, profit or loss is recognized immediately. This deferral is based on a threshold of control and use. IFRS, however, uses the definition of a finance lease to make the determination. This is presumably because the IAS 17 classification is based on the substance of an agreement, not a bright line. Thus it is necessary to assume that the entity owns the asset and this profit or loss should be deferred. The US GAAP guidance in a sense suspends the bright-line test of lease classification to assess the substance of the transaction. Because of this disparity, for finance leases, gain or loss will always be deferred for IFRS. However, under US GAAP, deferral depends on proportion of rights retained by the seller-lessee, although the default treatment under US GAAP is to defer a gain.

ASC 840-40-25-3(c) requires where the fair value of the property at the time of the transaction is less than its undepreciated cost, the loss shall be recognized immediately. In terms of losses, then, for assets sold at less than fair value, losses are recognized immediately for both IFRS and US GAAP.

CHAPTER SUMMARY

The classification criteria for leases are conceptually the same; however, US GAAP contains bright lines that determine whether an agreement is a capital or operating lease. IAS 17 bases the classification strictly on the evaluation of the transfer of risks and rewards. This can result in different classification for identical contracts. Both standards, however, require entities to apply the respective lease accounting guidance when agreements include plans to use an asset for a period of time in exchange for payments. Lastly, sale-leaseback accounting differs, but this is due primarily to consequential differences in lease classification. The accounting for operating and finance leases, after classification is considered, is nearly identical. Capital or finance leases result in recognition of an asset and obligation in the financial statements of a lessee that are measured by the minimum lease payments. Operating leases result in rent expense and not balance sheet recognition, although disclosures are more extensive.

10 REVENUE

Revenue, arguably, is the most prominent figure in financial statements. Public company securities are influenced heavily by the revenue trends. Revenue is the lifeblood of a business. Cash flow begins with it. Consequently, the recognition of revenue is one of the most important facets of accounting information. Consistency of application is of utmost importance.

Despite the conventional wisdom that says that IFRS and US GAAP are far apart on revenue recognition, the core principles are the same. These are

1. An enforceable agreement
2. Reliability of measurement of revenue
3. Assurance of collectability
4. It is earned

The language, complexity and placement of the guidance contribute greatly to the difficulty in bridging the two standards. IFRS has six standards that touch revenue recognition. US GAAP contains 20-plus Accounting Standards Codification sections. Prior to the Codification, there were in excess of 100 documents from which US GAAP revenue recognition was garnered.

In broad strokes, US GAAP focuses more on what an entity cannot do, whereas IFRS focuses more on what an entity can do. In helps to understand that the multitude of US GAAP guidance on this subject has its roots in the curtailment of abuses of application. The groundbreaking SOP 97-2, the seminal document for revenue recognition for software companies, and the equally statuesque SAB 101 defined clearly units of account and thresholds over which revenue could be recognized. SOP 97-2 is full of bright lines. While these boundaries are anchored to the principles, they do hold back remuneration that is otherwise probable.

However, despite these artificial lines, many software companies who report under IFRS use the US GAAP guidance for multiple deliverable arrangements. As permitted by IAS 8, *Accounting Policies,* companies such as SAP and Sage apply ASC 985-605. IAS 8 allows companies, after exhausting evaluation of analogous IFRS standards and *The Framework*, to use the recent pronouncement of other standard setters that use a similar framework. US GAAP is often the source.

The use of this US GAAP section underscores an important point of IFRS. Due to the greater amount of judgment used in IFRS as compared to US GAAP, IFRS preparers often seek alignment in accounting policies with their competitors. For instance, European Union preparers use Committee for European Securities Regulators (CESR) releases to supplement accounting techniques. The International Federation of Accountants surveys include a report on the discussions between accounting firms on the application of IFRS. Transparency is a key factor in securities prices. Generally speaking, less transparency means a lower stock price.

However, because IFRS is principles-based, it requires the entity to report transactions that are representationally faithful. There are few bright lines. The objective of IFRS is to allow companies to demonstrate the financial results of the numerous contracts of which a company is comprised. No company is identical to another. Therefore, the financial statements will differ. However, to the extent transactions in two companies are the same, the reported results should be the same.

Obviously there are trade-offs to these qualities—consistency and representational faithfulness. US GAAP tends to define consistency clearly. IFRS gives companies guiderails to be able to apply like accounting for similar transactions. Nonetheless, if a company (and its auditors) determines that adhering to a section of the US GAAP Codification materially represents the transactions, it is free to do so but must do this consistently. If another set of similar transactions is different enough to warrant another application, those transactions must be reported differently. Like US GAAP, IFRS requires retroactive application of a change in accounting. Entities cannot switch whenever they like without transparency. Moreover, market regulators will step in to curb abuses.

Following is a table of the language and position in the literature of guidance in IFRS and US GAAP for revenue recognition for the core principles as defined above.

IFRS	*Para.*	*US GAAP*	*Para.*
Goods:	IAS18.14	Persuasive evidence of an arrangement	605-10-S99-1
(d) It is probable that the economic benefits associated with the transaction will flow to the entity; and			
Services:	IAS18.23.a		
(a) Each party's enforceable rights regarding the service to be provided and received by the parties (after it has agreed… with the other parties to the transaction)			
Goods:	IAS18.14	Delivery has occurred	605-10-S99-1
(a) The entity has transferred to the buyer the significant risks and rewards of ownership of the goods;			
(b) The entity retains neither continuing managerial involvement to the degree usually associated with ownership nor effective control over the goods sold;			
Services:	IAS18.20		
(b) It is probable that the economic benefits associated with the transaction will flow to the entity;			
(c) the stage of completion of the transaction at the end of the reporting period can be measured reliably			

IFRS	*Para.*	*US GAAP*	*Para.*
Goods:	IAS18.14	Fixed or determin-	605-10-S99-1
(c) The amount of revenue can be measured reliably;		able sales price	
Services:	IAS18.23		
An entity is generally able to make reliable estimates after it has agreed to the following with the other parties to the transaction:			
(a) Each party's enforceable rights regarding the service to be provided and received by the parties;			
(b) The consideration to be exchanged; and			
(c) The manner and terms of settlement.			
(d) It is probable that the economic benefits associated with the transaction will flow to the entity	IAS18.14, IAS18.20.d	Realized or realizable	605-10-25

The following is a comparison of the specific US GAAP revenue recognition guidance through the lens of IFRS.

The recognition of revenue of the sale of goods (and only goods) is very similar and there would likely be only minimal differences in practice.

IAS 18

Sale of Goods

14 *Revenue from the sale of goods shall be recognized when all the following conditions have been satisfied:*

(a) *The entity has transferred to the buyer the significant risks and rewards of ownership of the goods.*

(b) *The entity returns neither continuing managerial involvement to the degree usually associated nor effective control over the goods sold.*

(c) *The amount of revenue can be measured reliably.*

(d) *It is probable that the economic benefits associated with the transaction will flow to the entity.*

(e) *The costs incurred or to be incurred in respect of the transaction can be measured reliably.*

16 *If the entity retains significant risks of ownership, the transaction is not a sale and revenue is not recognized. An entity may retain a significant risk of ownership in a number of ways. Examples of situations in which the entity may retain the significant risks and rewards of ownership are*

(a) *When the entity retains an obligation for unsatisfactory performance not covered by normal warranty provisions*

(b) *When the receipt of the revenue from a particular sale is contingent on the derivation of revenue by the buyer from its sale of the goods*

(c) *When the goods are shipped subject to installation and the installation is a significant part of the contract which has not yet been completed by the entity*

(d) When the buyer has the right to rescind the purchase for a reason specified in the sales contract and the entity is uncertain about the probability of return

17 If an entity retains only an insignificant risk of ownership, the transaction is a sale and revenue is recognized. For example, a seller may retain the legal title to the goods solely to protect the collectability of the amount due. In such a case, if the entity has transferred the significant risks and rewards of ownership, the transaction is a sale and revenue is recognized. Another example of an entity retaining only an insignificant risk of ownership may be a retail sale when a refund is offered if the customer is not satisfied. Revenue in such cases is recognized at the time of sale provided the seller can reliably estimate future returns and recognizes a liability for returns based on previous experience and other relevant factors.

ASC 605-15-25

Sales of Product When Right of Return Exists

1 If an entity sells its product but gives the buyer the right to return the product, revenue from the sales transaction shall be recognized at the time of sale only if all of the following conditions are met:

a. The seller's price to the buyer is substantially fixed or determinable at the date of sale.

b. The buyer has paid the seller, or the buyer is obligated to pay the seller and the obligation is not contingent on resale of the product. If the buyer does not pay at the time of sale and the buyer's obligation to pay is contractually or implicitly excused until the buyer resells the product, then this condition is not met.

c. The buyer's obligation to the seller would not be changed in the event of theft or physical destruction or damage of the product.

d. The buyer acquiring the product for resale has economic substance apart from that provided by the seller. This condition relates primarily to buyers that exist on paper, that is, buyers that have little or no physical facilities or employees. It prevents entities from recognizing sales revenue on transactions with parties that the sellers have established primarily for the purpose of recognizing such sales revenue.

e. The seller does not have significant obligations for future performance to directly bring about resale of the product by the buyer.

f. The amount of future returns can be reasonably estimated (see paragraphs 605-15-25-3 through 25-4). Because detailed recordkeeping for returns for each product line might be costly in some cases, this Subtopic permits reasonable aggregations and approximations of product returns. As explained in paragraph 605-15-15-2, exchanges by ultimate customers of one item for another of the same kind, quality, and price (for example, one color or size for another) are not considered returns for purposes of this Subtopic.

• The first paragraph of IAS18.16 alludes to 605-15-25-1.c, that is, risks and rewards of ownership must be passed.

- Paragraph section "b" in both (coincidentally) refer to consignment sales. More specifically, that sell-through requirements are counter to revenue recognition.
- Paragraph IAS18.16.c and 605-15-25-1.e each refer to the completion of the earnings process, specifically that delivery has not occurred if the good(s) is/are not in a condition for the recipient to receive the full benefit.
- IAS18.17 compares nearly identically to 605-15-25-1.f in the requirements for allowances for returns, although the US GAAP section is more prescriptive. The last sentence of paragraph IAS18.17 is the principle in which the factors listed in 605-15-25-3 could "fit into." While the language in this paragraph is couched in terms of guidance and not prescription (the paragraph is full of "may" or "may not"), the mere presence of these factors would likely cause entities to be more conservative in revenue recognition when these circumstances apply. The lack of any similar prescriptive guidance for these factors in IFRS would not encourage a bias. Moreover, the *IFRS Framework* uses the term "prudence" in place of the "conservative" concept that is prevalent throughout US GAAP.
- Paragraph 605-15-25.d is not specifically addressed in IAS 18. This is because of the complex and legalistic consolidation standard in US GAAP as compared to that of IFRS. The IFRS consolidation model uses a "relative influence continuum" model where control is defined by what entity or entities direct the substantive activities of an entity, regardless of legal structure. If an entity is consolidated (under both standards) the revenue would be eliminated and thus not recognized. This is not always the case under the more deterministic US GAAP approach.

FIXED AND DETERMINABLE FEE

US GAAP contains a number of references to when revenue is fixed and determinable. The following US GAAP guidance is part of the ASC section on sales of software. However, other portions of US GAAP refer to this guidance regardless of the product or service being delivered:

ASC 985-605-25

Factors that Affect the Determination of Whether a Fee Is Fixed or Determinable and Collectible

32 The following guidance addresses various considerations related to whether a fee is fixed or determinable and collectible, specifically:

 a. Extended payment terms (see paragraphs 985-605-25-33 through 25-35)
 b. Reseller arrangements (see paragraph 985-605-25-36)
 c. Customer cancellation privileges (see paragraph 985-605-25-37)
 d. Fiscal funding clauses (see paragraphs 985-605-25-38 through 25-40)

The focus of the guidance referred to in subparagraph "a" is that the longer an entity has to wait for payment, the more uncertainty that the fee is likely to be collected. Further, in reference to software, a licensing fee that is not due until after the expiration of the license is not fixed and determinable unless a company has a history of successful collection of these amounts.

IFRS addresses this uncertainty indirectly in IAS 18.18:

> *Revenue is recognized only when it is probable that the economic benefits associated with the transaction will flow to the entity. In some cases, this may not be probable until the consideration is received or until an uncertainty is removed. For example, it may be uncertain that a foreign governmental authority will grant permission to remit the consideration from a sale in a foreign country. When the permission is granted, the uncertainty is removed and revenue is recognized. However, when an uncertainty arises about the collectability of an amount already included in revenue, the uncollectible amount or the amount in respect of which recovery has ceased to be probable is recognized as an expense, rather than as an adjustment of the amount of revenue originally recognized.*

Sentence 2 in IAS18.18 together with IAS18.14.c and d requires that an entity consider the effect of extended payments, although not explicitly. However, the explicit requirement in IFRS that the amount or revenue must be reliably measured would naturally include an assessment as specified in 985-605-25-32.a.

General reseller arrangements are covered in the earlier part of this chapter. Specifically, under both IFRS and US GAAP, revenue is not recognized until sale to the final user if the payment is contingent on that sale. However, ASC 985-605-25-36 lists certain circumstances that, if they exist, require the entity to include them in the evaluation of whether a fee is fixed and determinable. The factors center on the financial viability of the reseller, the difficulty in estimating returns from the reseller, or the existence of repricing rights in light of competitive conditions. IAS 18 does not address these factors specifically, but one would expect them to be included in an evaluation of probability of collectability as well as reliability of estimates. However, the inclusion of these factors in US GAAP would tend to make preparers more conservative in their applicability to determine if revenue is fixed and determinable. IFRS uses the prudence concept in favor of the conservative principle in US GAAP.

IFRS does not specifically address the recognition of revenue in light of customer cancellation privileges. However, the directive in 985-605-25-37

> *(... Fees from licenses with cancellation privileges expiring ratably over the license period are considered to become determinable ratably over the license period as the cancellation privileges lapse ...)*

is encompassed in IAS 18.19 to 21 that refer to the matching of revenue and expenses and the use of the percentage-of-completion method, provided that the stage of completion and the associated costs can be reliably measured:

> 19 *Revenue and expenses that relate to the same transaction or other event are recognized simultaneously; this process is commonly referred to as the matching of revenues and expenses. Expenses, including warranties and other costs to be incurred after the shipment of goods, can normally be measured reliably when the other conditions for the recognition of revenue have been satisfied. However,*

revenue cannot be recognized when the expenses cannot be measured reliably; in such circumstances, any consideration already received for the sale of the goods is recognized as a liability.

Rendering of Services

20 When the outcome of a transaction involving the rendering of services can be estimated reliably, revenue associated with the transaction shall be recognized by reference to the stage of completion of the transaction at the end of the reporting period; the outcome of a transaction can be estimated reliably when all the following conditions are satisfied:

(a) The amount of revenue can be measured reliably

(b) It is probable that the economic benefits associated with the transaction will flow to the entity

(c) And the stage of completion of the transaction at the end of the reporting period can be measured reliably

(d) The costs incurred for the transaction and the costs to complete the transaction can be measured reliably*

* See also SIC-27, **Evaluating the Substance of Transactions Involving the Legal Form of a Lease***, and SIC-31,* **Revenue—Barter Transactions Involving Advertising Services.***

21 The recognition of revenue by reference to the stage of completion of a transaction is often referred to as the percentage-of-completion method. Under this method, revenue is recognized in the accounting periods in which the services are rendered. The recognition of revenue on this basis provides useful information on the extent of service activity and performance during a period. IAS 11 also requires the recognition of revenue on this basis. The requirements of that Standard are generally applicable to the recognition of revenue and the associated expenses for a transaction involving the rendering of services.

985-605-25-32.d is concerned with fiscal funding clauses, that is, arrangements with government agencies where the contract is deemed cancellable until funds are appropriated. Per the paragraph, revenue is not recognizable until the uncertainty of budget approval is removed. A later paragraph requires that the same treatment is applied with nongovernmental agencies if the circumstances about budget approval are the same.

IFRS does not address cancellable sales agreements directly. However, IAS18.18 uses a similar situation to 985-605-25-32.d:

*18 Revenue is recognized only when it is probable that the economic benefits associated with the transaction will flow to the entity. In some cases, this may not be probable until the consideration is received **or until an uncertainty is removed**. For example, it may be uncertain that a foreign governmental authority will grant permission to remit the consideration from a sale in a foreign country. When the permission is granted, the uncertainty is removed and revenue is recognized.*

It is reasonable that the preceding paragraph could be applied to a contract with customer cancellation privileges. Furthermore, IAS 17, *Leases*, and IAS 37, *Provisions*, both address the impact of cancellable agreements. IAS 17 specifies that only the noncancellable portion of a lease agreement is included in minimum lease payments, although the standard does require inclusion of the lease term periods for which the lessee has an option and it is reasonably certain. IAS 37 includes a sentence that the noncancellable portion must be considered when measuring an onerous contract. Given the fact that gain contingencies under IFRS, like US GAAP, must have a higher degree of certainty to be recognized, it is likely that most entities would not recognize revenue until a cancellation clause has expired. For entities adopting IFRS that want to minimize the changes in accounting policy, this is an area where the US GAAP method fits within the *IFRS Framework* and is not contradicted by other IFRS Standards.

UNITS OF ACCOUNT

Both IFRS and US GAAP require either the combination or division of contractual terms of sales when the substance of a transaction or set of transactions are in substance dependent or independent, respectively of each other. One example would be the construction of a large real estate complex where parts are ready for use before other portions. Both standards would require that the completed section of the project be separated for revenue recognition purposes.

However, there are potential differences with regard to more complex arrangements involving multiple-element arrangements or (MEA). An example of this would be software sale and support, or sale and an upgrade arrangement. The key activity in such an agreement is about the allocation of revenue to the different components of the transactions. IFRS does not have an extensive guidance for MEAs, but it does have the basic principles that are equivalent to US GAAP. However, IAS 8, *Accounting Policies,* permits an entity to apply the current standards of another standard setter, provided that the standard has a framework similar to IFRS. Many software companies (for which MEAs are common) use the US GAAP guidance for MEAs (formerly known as SOP 97-2).

The table below summarizes the timing of recognition under US GAAP for some of the common units of account defined in US GAAP (primarily ASC 985).

US GAAP—Multiple-Element Arrangement Revenue Recognition Matrix (MEARRM)

#	*Unit of account*	*Defer*	*At once*	*Over time*	*Loss*
1	MEA—VSOE		x		
2	MEA—Undelivered				x
3	MEA—VSOE-does not exist for delivered item	x	x		
4	MEA-only postcontract support			x	
5	MEA arrangement is in substance a subscription-unspecified future products	x		x	
6	MEA—Fixed fee for two or more products-per product delivered [Note 1]	x	x		
7	MEA—VSOE does not exist for **any** of the products				
8	Delivery agents	x	x		
9	Authorization keys [Note 2]		x		

#	*Unit of account*	*Defer*	*At once*	*Over time*	*Loss*
10	Upgrade rights—no VSOE	x	x		
11	MEA—Allocation of discounts				

VSOE—Vendor Specific Objective Evidence
Note 1: Because of the circumstances, allocation cannot be made.
Note 2: Software must be fully functional, payment not contingent on delivery of keys, history of collecting.

The MEARRM does not address the measurement of the amount allocated to each unit account. This will be covered later in the chapter.

The acronym VSOE stands for vendor-specific objective evidence. In short, VSOE is a technique to approximate the relative sales value of a component to other components of an MEA. The two-pronged approach defines VSOE as the stand-alone selling price (preferred) or a price decided by the relevant pricing authority in the entity. For instance, if a software company sells a package of two software programs at a discount, and one is delivered within a different accounting period than the other, and both were sold separately for $200 and $300, respectively, the first unit would be assigned 2/5 of the package price, and unit B the remainder (e.g., package price = $400, A price = $160, and B = $240).

If VSOE does not exist for a delivered item in an MEA, but does for undelivered components, the revenue allocation is the total sales price less the VSOE of the undelivered items. This is termed the *residual method*.

IFRS requires that revenue be measured at fair value. Likewise, components of revenue must be allocated using fair value. Presently, IFRS and US GAAP have separate definitions for fair value. However, the IASB and FASB issued a joint standard on fair value (IFRS 13 and ASU 2011-04 for topic 820) in 2011. IFRS 13 is mandatory at January 1, 2013. Earlier application is permitted. Until the effective date, or prior to adoption, all items dealing with fair value will have an inherent difference. However, the basic definition of revenue in US GAAP does not refer to fair value, and the definition of VSOE is based on selling price. The present definition of fair value under IFRS is the amount for which an asset could be exchanged or a liability settled between knowledgeable, willing parties in an arm's-length transaction. This definition renders fair value under IFRS compatible with the US GAAP definition used for vendor-specific objective evidence. However, US GAAP specifies that the allocation of VSOE among multiple elements be done according to the fair value. A joint revenue standard is being reexposed in 2011. The goal of that standard is to converge revenue recognition, at which point the semantic differences between the basis for measurement of revenue will likely be eliminated.

The comparison table on the previous page conveys the timing and method of recognition. The following section compares the relevant US GAAP paragraphs that underpin this table to the IFRS revenue recognition guidance.

Scenario 1

Scenario 1 covers the general concept of the amount of revenue to be allocated to elements of an MEA. Since the current definition of fair value under IFRS is compatible with the definitions and usage in the US GAAP guidance for MEA (ASC 620-25-30), there is no practical difference between the two. US GAAP requires revenue to be allocated on a relative selling price. The relative selling price amount is VSOE. If VSOE is not available, then the third-party selling price of a similar product can be used:

ASC 605-25-30

> *6B Third-party evidence of selling price is the price of the vendor's or any competitor's largely interchangeable products or services in stand-alone sales to similarly situated customers.*

Note that there is a customer-specific element to the above definition—"… similarly situated customers …"   The present fair value definition under IFRS does not include this aspect. However, the representational faithfulness characteristic demanded by the *IFRS Framework* would compel an entity to use the most likely customer, which would be their typical customers, and thus likely align with ASC 605-25-30-6B. In any case, using this US GAAP definition fits within *The Framework*.

Scenario 2

Scenario 2 deals with probable losses on a component of a MEA. ASC 985-605-25-7 directs that amounts allocated to undelivered elements are fixed, and that an expected loss on that component is recognized immediately. IFRS 11, *Construction Contracts,* and IAS 18, *Revenue*, which can be applied to MEAs, specify that when components of a transaction are independent of each other, they must be recognized separately:

IAS 18

> *13 The recognition criteria in this Standard are usually applied separately to each transaction. However, in certain circumstances, it is necessary to apply the recognition criteria to the separately identifiable components of a single transaction in order to reflect the substance of the transaction. For example, when the selling price of a product includes an identifiable amount for subsequent servicing, that amount is deferred and recognized as revenue over the period during which the service is performed. Conversely, the recognition criteria are applied to two or more transactions together when they are linked in such a way that the commercial effect cannot be understood without reference to the series of transactions as a whole. For example, an entity may sell goods and, at the same time, enter into a separate agreement to repurchase the goods at a later date, thus negating the substantive effect of the transaction; in such a case, the two transactions are dealt with together.*

> *36 An entity discloses any contingent liabilities and contingent assets in accordance with IAS 37, **Provisions, Contingent Liabilities and Contingent Assets**. Contingent liabilities and contingent assets may arise from items such as warranty costs, claims, penalties or possible losses.*

The above guidance from IAS 18 makes two important parallels to the ASC 985 paragraph for recognizing losses on a component of an MEA: (1) Contracts are split when there are in substance more than one transaction, and (2) An expected loss on a contract must be accrued immediately.

Note that the portion of IAS 37 that is applicable is *onerous contracts*. Contracts are onerous when the costs of fulfilling or cancelling them exceed the expected benefit. The amount that must be accrued is the difference between the lower of the costs to fulfill or cancel, and expected value of the contracts; applying this concept to a sales contract, the value is the sales price allocated to the component, and the costs would be the costs of the product and any direct costs attributed to it.

Neither IAS 18 nor IAS 11 mentions that the allocated prices to components cannot be changed. However, the requirement to allocate based on fair value would lead to the same conclusion, that the amount allocated cannot be changed, at least without good reason.

Scenario 3

Scenario 3 directs that if VSOE does not exist for the delivered item, but does for the undelivered item, that the difference between the total contract price and the VSOE of the undelivered item must be allocated to the delivered item (the residual method). While many software companies reporting under IFRS do adopt ASC 985, if an entity were to apply IFRS in this circumstance, it is likely that the amount allocated to the delivered item would differ. Since IFRS requires revenue to be measured at fair value, and there are very few exceptions to when fair value is permitted to be bypassed, the entity would need to use a reasonable, consistently applied method to estimate fair value. The residual method, following IFRS strictly, would not be allowed. However, since many IFRS companies use ASC 985, it's likely that the differences are not material. However, the management and auditors would need to be comfortable with the materiality of any variance from fair value. Under US GAAP, when using the residual method, materiality is moot since the standard is followed.

Scenario 4

This scenario specifies that under US GAAP, postsales support is to be recognized separately from the delivery of the product and recognized over the life of the contract. IAS18.13 offers this as an example. The following paragraph also lends support to consistent treatment with US GAAP for postsales support:

IAS 18

> 25 *For practical purposes, when services are performed by an indeterminate number of acts over a specified period of time, revenue is recognized on a straight-line basis over the specified period unless there is evidence that some other method better represents the stage of completion. When a specific act is much more significant than any other acts, the recognition of revenue is postponed until the significant act is executed.*

Accordingly, the recognition pattern for postsales support under IFRS and US GAAP is generally compatible. However, US GAAP does offer bright-line guidance for when postsales (the term used in the ASC is postcontract) revenue can be recognized immediately:

ASC 985-605-25

71 Postcontract customer support revenue may be recognized together with the initial licensing fee on delivery of the software if all of the following conditions are met:

   a. The postcontract customer support fee is included with the initial licensing fee.
   b. The postcontract customer support included with the initial license is for one year or less.
   c. The estimated cost of providing postcontract customer support during the arrangement is insignificant.
   d. Unspecified upgrades or enhancements offered during postcontract customer support arrangements historically have been and are expected to continue to be minimal and infrequent.

IFRS has no specific equivalent language to this effect. The guidance in IAS18.25 would apply to the arrangement in 985-605-25-71. However, the clause in IAS18.25 "…unless there is evidence that some other method better represents the stage of completion…" together with an assessment of materiality and cost benefit considerations may enable an entity to apply 985-605-25-71. However, the substance of the transaction would need to be reflected and the entities' management and auditors would need to be comfortable with the accounting procedure. Disclosure of this policy would most likely be required because it involves the entity's application of an IFRS statement.

The telephone support referred to in 985-605-25-74 applies the same concept as 25-71, and thus the comparison with IFRS is the same.

ASC 985-605-25-74 addresses postcontract support to resellers with regard to upgrade and enhancements. In essence, the guidance specifies that a vendor needs to look through the legal arrangement and apply the general guidance regarding VSOE. As covered in earlier sections, since VSOE does not exist in IFRS, if a reasonable estimate of fair value for the postcontract support could be calculated, the revenue would be recognized ratably over the period of the support. If VSOE does not exist for which IFRS fair value does, IFRS would recognize the revenue for the support sooner than under US GAAP. This is because IFRS does not include a definition of VSOE. Fair value is the basis on which multiple elements of a contract are measured.

Scenario 5

Scenario 5 involves agreements in which entities offer future or unspecified software:

ASC 985-605-25

58 As part of a multiple-element arrangement with a user, a vendor may agree to deliver software currently and to deliver unspecified additional software products in the future (including unspecified platform transfer rights that do not qualify for exchange accounting as described in paragraphs 985-605-25-60 through 25-65). For example, the vendor may agree to deliver all new products to be introduced in a family of products over the next two years. These arrangements are similar to arrangements that include postcontract customer support in that future deliverables are unspecified. Nevertheless, they are distinguished from arrangements that include postcontract customer support because the future deliverables are products, not unspecified upgrades or enhancements.

59 *The software elements of the kinds of arrangements discussed in paragraph 985-605-25-58* shall be accounted for as subscriptions. *No allocation of revenue shall be made among any of the software products, and all software product-related revenue from the arrangement shall be* recognized ratably over the term of the arrangement beginning with delivery of the first product. *If the term of the arrangement is not stated, the revenue shall be recognized ratably over the estimated economic life of the products covered by the arrangement, beginning with delivery of the first product.* An intent on the part of the vendor not to develop new products during the term of the arrangement does not relieve the vendor of the requirement to recognize revenue ratably over the term of the arrangement, beginning with the delivery of the first product.

IAS 18 and IAS 11, as covered earlier in the chapter, require that components of a contract that are in substance separate agreements must be accounted for separately. IAS 18 includes references in the appendix (not authoritative but nonetheless illustrative of how to apply the IAS 18 concepts) to account for subscriptions. Although these examples do not relate to software, the concept is that subscriptions should be recognized ratably over time, just as US GAAP requires.

What is less clear concerning Scenario 5 with regard to IAS 18 versus ASC 985 is the commencement and time over which revenue is recognized. ASC 985-605-25-29 specifies that the revenue recognition commences with the delivery of the first product and continues throughout either the term of the agreement, or, if none is specified, the estimated economic life of the products subject to the agreement. IFRS does not specifically address MEAs, as mentioned earlier in the chapter. An examination of the revenue recognition policies of public software companies using IFRS indicates that revenue for unspecified upgrade rights is generally recognized over time, although not necessarily the term of the contract. The lack of this specificity leaves open the possibility of using some other term. However, the representational faithfulness characteristic in *The Framework* would cause the term to gravitate towards the term of the contracts (probably using a composite life for cost benefit, although this is not condoned by IFRS; reference IAS39/IFRS 9, *Financial Instruments'* requirement to account for certain aspects of instruments on an instrument-by-instrument basis and IAS 16, *Property Plant, and Equipment*'s use of component depreciation. However, IAS 2, *Inventories,* permits grouping of like items of inventory).

The "intent" clause of ASC 985-605-25-59 is not addressed in IAS 18. Regarding the term of the recognition for unspecified software, nothing in IFRS prohibits an entity from making a judgment at a point in time that the likelihood of delivering additional software is not probable, and thus the entire contract is earned. However, the entity would need a policy and consistency.

Scenario 6

Scenario 6 describes arrangements where a fixed fee covers two or more un-specified products. Under US GAAP, when products in a contract are not specified at the inception of the agreement, a measurement of VSOE cannot be made, and thus revenue is not recognized until either VSOE exists or all the products are delivered. However, 985-605-25-52 specifies that if a fixed-fee contract is for a maximum number of copies, the entity can recognize revenue per product delivered, at a rate that assumes the maximum number will be conveyed.

IAS 18 does not address this circumstance directly. Revenue for components of a contract is to be allocated at fair value. However, the measurement of recognition method in 95-605-25-52 is within both *The Framework* and the principles in IAS 18. The simple division of the contract price over the maximum number of products is supported by

IAS 18

> *11 In most cases, the consideration is in the form of cash or cash equivalents and the amount of revenue is the amount of cash or cash equivalents received or receivable...*

This is permitted despite the overall concept that fair value is the measurement basis. Measurement at fair value would be considered if nonmonetary assets were exchanged. IAS 18.11 also requires that where material, the time value of money must be incorporated into the recognition of revenue. (The discount would be recognized over time as interest expense).

Scenario 7

Scenario 7 covers allocation of revenue to elements of an MEA when VSOE does not exist for delivered nor undelivered items. ASC 985-605-25-49 is clear that in this circumstance, revenue is deferred until either VSOE is determined or all the products are delivered. Since IAS 18 does not include the concept of VSOE, but allocates revenue to MEAs based on fair value, there could be many circumstances that revenue for a delivered portion could be recognized, provided the measurement was reliable. Reliability of measurement of revenue is a core principle of IFRS revenue recognition. However, an examination of public filings of software companies using IFRS reveals that some of these entities do follow ASC 985-605-25-49; even though that section is not specifically quoted, some entities do. This policy needs to be based on the substance of the transactions. For instance, if history demonstrates that the entity provides refunds if the second product is not delivered, or this is in the contract under the IFRS concept that it must be probable that revenue will flow to the entity would intercede and require that revenue is deferred until the second products is transferred.

In summary, if there is absent contractual or customary practice to refund advances if the remaining products are not delivered, entities using IFRS are not prohibited from recognizing revenue if VSOE does not exist, provided the fair value of the delivered item can be reliably measured.

Scenario 8

The accounting for sales through delivery agents is nearly identical between IFRS and US GAAP. While US GAAP offers some examples, both standards require selling through to the end user for recognition if the nature of the relationship is consignment. Both include very similar assessments of whether the recipient of the good is an agent or principal.

Scenario 9

ASC 985-605-25-27 to 29 details revenue recognition when authorization codes (or keys) are used or needed by the customer to activate the software. If keys are used only to enforce payment terms or are otherwise incidental to the functioning of the software, revenue is recognized when the key is delivered. IFRS does not address authorization keys, but it does consider the impact of relatively insignificant elements of an arrangement on revenue recognition:

IAS 18

17 *If an entity retains only an insignificant risk of ownership, the transaction is a sale and revenue is recognized. For example, a seller may retain the legal title to the goods solely to protect the collectability of the amount due. In such a case, if the entity has transferred the significant risks and rewards of ownership, the transaction is a sale and revenue is recognized. Another example of an entity retaining only an insignificant risk of ownership may be a retail sale when a refund is offered if the customer is not satisfied. Revenue in such cases is recognized at the time of sale provided the seller can reliably estimate future returns and recognizes a liability for returns based on previous experience and other relevant factors.*

IAS 18.IE17 (a) installation and inspection.

(a) *Revenue is normally recognized when the buyer accepts delivery, and installation and inspection are complete. However, revenue is recognized immediately upon the buyer's acceptance of delivery when*

(i) *The installation process is simple in nature, for example the installation of a factory tested television receiver which only requires unpacking and connection of power and antennae.*

(ii) *The inspection is performed only for purposes of final determination of contract prices, for example, shipments of iron ore, sugar, or soybeans.*

The accounting for authorization keys specified in ASC 985-605 is compatible with IFRS.

Scenarios 10 and 11

ASC 985-605-25-44 to 46 covers the accounting for upgrade rights. Upgrade rights that are part of an MEA are allocated based on either the fee charged separately to existing users or for items not yet sold separately, the price set by management with the relevant authority. Further, discounts on an MEA including upgrade rights are not to be allocated to the rights. Any VSOE about the percentage of customers that do not take advantage of upgrade rights shall be considered in the allocation of revenue.

This guidance also directs that where VSOE does not exist for the upgrade right, the revenue is deferred until the earlier of when VSOE exists or all the elements have been delivered. This clause can defer the revenue on a product that was otherwise delivered. Because IAS 18 does not use VSOE, but rather fair value (which can be estimated using a variety of techniques), products containing upgrade rates would likely always be recognized sooner than under US GAAP. Since the upgrade right is available over time, IFRS would permit this portion of the revenue to be recognized ratably over the time period that the customers are expected to use it. IAS18.13 uses an example of postcontract support allocated over time.

Concerning the use of VSOE to alter the allocation revenue to upgrade rights for discounts covered in ASC 985-605-25-45, IFRS would permit this method since it is consistent with allocation based on fair value, and, as discussed earlier in this chapter, practically speaking, IFRS would use selling price in determining fair value. Additionally, concerning including forfeitures of upgrade rights by customers, IAS 37, *Provisions,* and IAS 19, *Employee Benefits,* both require estimates of forfeiture to influence measurement, this concept is pervasive throughout IFRS and thus aligned with the *IFRS Framework.*

ASC 985-605-25

> 45 *If a multiple-element arrangement includes an upgrade right, the fee shall be allocated between the elements based on vendor-specific objective evidence of fair value. The fee allocated to the upgrade right is the price for the upgrade or enhancement that would be charged to existing users of the software product being updated. If the upgrade right is included in a multiple-element arrangement on which a discount has been offered (see paragraph 985-605-25-8), no portion of the discount shall be allocated to the upgrade right. If sufficient vendor-specific evidence exists to reasonably estimate the percentage of customers that are not expected to exercise the upgrade right, the fee allocated to the upgrade right shall be reduced to reflect that percentage. This estimated percentage shall be reviewed periodically. The effect of any change in that percentage shall be accounted for as a change in accounting estimate.*

The nonallocation of discounts to upgrade rights per ASC 985-605-25-44 is very prescriptive and not aligned with IFRS principles. Unless immaterial, entities would be expected to allocate discounts to all elements of an MEA.

EXCHANGES AND RETURNS OF SOFTWARE

ASC 985-605-25-60 to 65 describes various circumstances under which a return of software for another is accounted for as a return or an exchange. US GAAP and IFRS are generally consistent in accounting for both returns and exchanges for all products. In summary, an exchange of similar products does not produce revenue. Exchanges of products that are dissimilar produce revenue. Also, both standards specify that that revenue measured for nonmonetary consideration is measured at the value of the products received, but, if not reliable nor determinable, the value given up. IFRS refers to exchange of dissimilar products as one that contains commercial substance. Commercial substance is present when a transaction changes the amount, timing, or risk of cash flows because changes in these factors alter the predictive and informational value of the entities' financial statements.

IAS 18

> 12 *When goods or services are exchanged or swapped for goods or services which are of a similar nature and value, the exchange is not regarded as a transaction which generates revenue. This is often the case with commodities like oil or milk where suppliers exchange or swap inventories in various locations to fulfill demand on a timely basis in a particular location. When goods are sold or services are rendered in exchange for dissimilar goods or services, the exchange is regarded as a transaction which generates revenue. The revenue is measured at the fair value of the goods or services received, adjusted by the amount of any cash or cash equivalents transferred. When the fair value of the goods or services received cannot be measured reliably, the revenue is measured at the fair value of the goods or services given up, adjusted by the amount of any cash or cash equivalents transferred.*

ASC 985-605-25-60 to 65 provides very specific guidance regarding "platform transfer rights." The ASC defined a platform as

> *The hardware architecture of a particular model or family of computers, the system software, (such as the operating system) or both.*

Platform transfer rights convey to the customer (not a reseller) the right to use software on another platform. If platform transfer rights are for **only** the same product, and do not give the user additional copies, the exercise is accounted for as an exchange (thus no revenue or expense is recognized).

Regarding whether a product is the same product, US GAAP offers the following:

ASC 95-605-25

> 64 *Products are considered to be the same product if there are no more than minimal differences among them in price, features, and functions, and if they are marketed as the same product, even though there may be differences arising from environmental variables such as operating systems, databases, user interfaces, and platform scales. Indicators that products are marketed as the same product include the same product name (although version numbers may differ) and a focus on the same features and functions.*

Because the above US GAAP definition does not conflict with *The Framework*, if a company uses US GAAP as permitted by IAS 8, *Accounting Policies*, an entity reporting under IFRS could use this definition.

Regarding swaps of software products with resellers:

ASC 985-605-25

> 65 *As part of their standard sales terms or as a matter of practice, vendors may grant resellers the rights to exchange unsold software for other software, including software that runs on a different hardware platform or operating sys-*

tem. Because the reseller is not the ultimate customer (see paragraph 985-605-25-61), such exchanges, including those referred to as stock balancing arrangements, shall be accounted for as returns. Arrangements that grant rights to make such exchanges shall be accounted for in conformity with Subtopic 605-15, even if the vendors require the resellers to purchase additional software to exercise the exchange rights.

IAS 18 gives essentially the same guidance for transfers of products to the reseller, namely that if the capability or nature of a relationship with a reseller is such that the risks and rewards of ownership have not passed, revenue is recognized upon transfer to the end user (see section earlier in this chapter). However, prescriptive guidance about returns to resellers is not given.

IAS 18.12 (see full text earlier in the chapter) is clear that a swap of similar goods and services is a transaction that does **not** generate revenue. (Returns are recognized as a reduction of revenue.) IFRS often refers to this as a transaction that lacks commercial substance. Commercial substance is defined in IAS 16, *Property, Plant, and Equipment.*

IAS 16

25 An entity determines whether an exchange transaction has commercial substance by considering the extent to which its future cash flows are expected to change as a result of the transaction. An exchange transaction has commercial substance if

(a) The configuration (risk, timing and amount) of the cash flows of the asset received differs from the configuration of the cash flows of the asset transferred

(b) The entity-specific value of the portion of the entity's operations affected by the transaction changes as a result of the exchange

(c) The difference in (a) or (b) is significant relative to the fair value of the assets exchanged

For the purpose of determining whether an exchange transaction has commercial substance, the entity-specific value of the portion of the entity's operations affected by the transaction shall reflect posttax cash flows. The result of these analyses may be clear without an entity having to perform detailed calculations.

It follows then that an exchange of similar products to a reseller for which an entity recognizes revenue upon delivery to it would account for such a swap according to the substance of the transaction. In this case, the swap would be accounted for as an exchange (no revenue recognized) if it was for a similar product or a return if it was for a dissimilar product.

SOFTWARE SERVICES

ASC 985-605-25-76 to 85 gives specific guidance as to whether services provided in conjunction with the purchase of software must be accounted for separately, and, if so, if that support would be recognized ratably over the support period (as covered in previous sections of this chapter) or, essentially as construction in progress.

Paragraph 78 prescribes the following with regard to the decision of a separate unit of account:

ASC 985-605-25

78 *To account separately for the service element of an arrangement that includes both software and services, sufficient vendor-specific objective evidence of fair value shall exist to permit allocation of the revenue to the various elements of the arrangement (as discussed in paragraphs 985-605-25-6 through 25-7 : and 985-605-25-9 through 25-11). Additionally, both of the following conditions shall be met:*

   a. *The services are not essential to the functionality of any other element of the transaction.*
   b. *The services are described in the contract such that the total price of the arrangement would be expected to vary as the result of the inclusion or exclusion of the services.*

ASC 985-605-81 to 84 distinguishes further between whether services are not a separate unit of account. Paragraph 81 defines off-the-shelf and core software. Services offered for off-the-shelf software are accounted for separately since they are not essential to the functioning of the software. Core software is not usable until substantial configuration or programming is done. These services, under US GAAP, do not qualify as a separate unit of account and would apply contract accounting.

Paragraph 84 offers examples of indications that the services are not a separate unit of account. These examples are all compatible with the IFRS determination of separating or aggregating transactions as specified in IAS 18.13. While IFRS is not prescriptive about services that are the subject of ASC 985-605-76 to 85, the concepts, with the exception of the role of VSOE, fit within *The Framework*.

So, in summary, if the services are not integral to the use of the software, and customers would pay for them, the services are a separate unit of account. Paragraphs 79 and 80 reiterate the VSOE guidance found throughout ASC 985, namely that if VSOE does not exist for the services, they are recognized with the sale of the software, so not a separate unit of account. This would usually result in deferral of all revenue from the arrangement.

SOFTWARE CONTRACT ACCOUNTING

The US GAAP accounting for software contract accounting refers heavily to the general project accounting guidance in ASC 605-35. Likewise, IAS 18, *Revenue*, refers to IAS 11, *Construction Contracts*. Thus, a comparison of the respective standards for software contract accounting must include one that examines construction contracts.

The determination of unit of account is particularly critical for production-type revenue. If disparate projects are grouped together, the revenue and profit of these efforts subsidize each other which can obscure the predictive value of financial statements. However, the separation of a project into artificial units can lead to a premature recognition of revenue and also a subsidization of profitability across projects.

ASC 985-605-91 to 92 refers to 605-35-10 to 14 for the determination of segmentation. These paragraphs define two sets of factors that can be applied. If the first set is met, there is no further consideration needed and the projects are accounted for separately. All of the conditions in the second step must be met before segmentation. Likewise, per ASC 605-35-25 to 29, an entity combines contracts if five conditions can be met.

Under IFRS, while there are similarities with US GAAP for segmenting and combining construction or production type contracts, there are differences.

IAS 11

7 The requirements of this Standard are usually applied separately to each construction contract. However, in certain circumstances, it is necessary to apply the Standard to the separately identifiable components of a single contract or to a group of contracts together in order to reflect the substance of a contract or a group of contracts.

8 When a contract covers a number of assets, the construction of each asset shall be treated as a separate construction contract when

(a) Separate proposals have been submitted for each asset.
(b) Each asset has been subject to separate negotiation and the contractor and customer have been able to accept or reject that part of the contract relating to each asset.
(c) The costs and revenues of each asset can be identified.

However, since each paragraph in IFRS has equal weight, and the underlying substance of a transaction determines the accounting, IAS11.7 must be applied to determine the unit of account for related construction or production contracts.

US GAAP provides the following factor which, if present, requires an entity to segment the projects, provided it has established a policy:

ASC 605-35-25

12 A project may be segmented if all of the following steps were taken and are documented and verifiable:

a. The contractor submitted bona fide proposals on the separate components of the project and on the entire project.
b. The customer had the right to accept the proposals on either basis.
c. The aggregate amount of the proposals on the separate components approximated the amount of the proposal on the entire project.

IAS 11.8(a) and (b) are very similar to 605-35-25-12(a) and (b) and in practice the set of circumstances that would lead this part of US GAAP to be applicable would also result in a segmentation of projects under IFRS. However, 12(c) does not have a counterpart in IAS 11. A possible reason why 12(c) is part of the analysis of this subparagraph is that the combination of contracts subject to such an agreement that had a lower price would indicate that economies of scale can be realized, without which the costs and risk of the project would be different, indicating that the projects are linked in some way to the other projects. IAS 11.7 directs the entity to reflect the substance of transactions. Further, segmentation of projects that had dissimilar risk characteristics, which subparagraph 12(a) alludes to, would not be representationally faithful. Thus, applying 12(c) under IFRS would be a strong indicator, although not definitive, that contracts should be accounted for separately. However, because it is not a requirement of segmentation per IAS 11, the entity's management would need to design and comply with a policy.

US GAAP also requires segmentation if all of the following conditions are met:

ASC 605-35-25-25

13 *A project that does not meet the criteria in the preceding paragraph may be segmented* only *if it meets* all *of the following criteria:*

    a. *The terms and scope of the contract or project clearly call for separable phases or elements.*

    b. *The separable phases or elements of the project are often bid or negotiated separately.*

    c. *The market assigns different gross profit rates to the segments because of factors such as different levels of risk or differences in the relationship of the supply and demand for the services provided in different segments.*

    d. *The contractor has a significant history of providing similar services to other customers under separate contracts for each significant segment to which a profit margin higher than the overall profit margin on the project is ascribed. In applying this criterion, values assignable to the segments shall be on the basis of the contractor's normal historical prices and terms of such services to other customers. A contractor shall not segment on the basis of prices charged by other contractors, because it does not follow that those prices could have been obtained by a contractor who has no history in the market.*

    e. *The significant history with customers who have contracted for services separately is one that is relatively stable in terms of pricing policy rather than one unduly weighted by erratic pricing decisions (responding, for example, to extraordinary economic circumstances or to unique customer-contractor relationships).*

    f. *The excess of the sum of the prices of the separate elements over the price of the total project is clearly attributable to the cost savings incident to combined performance of the contract obligations (for example, cost savings in supervision, overhead, or equipment mobilization). Unless this condition is met, segmenting a contract with a price substantially less than the sum of the prices of the separate phases or elements would be inappropriate even if the other conditions are met. Acceptable price variations shall be allocated to the separate phases or elements in proportion to the prices ascribed to each. In all other situations a substantial difference in price (whether more or less) between the separate elements and the price of the total project is evidence that the contractor has accepted different profit margins. Accordingly, segmenting is not appropriate, and the contracts shall be the profit centers.*

g. *The similarity of services and prices in the contract segments and services and the prices of such services to other customers contracted separately should be documented and verifiable.*

Since neither IAS 11 nor other IFRS guidance defines similar conditions, the concepts paragraph IAS 11.7 must be compared to preceding subparagraphs. 13(a) focuses on the nature of the project and how individual contracts are connected. 13(b) and 13(c) refer to market characteristics. 13(d) and 13(e) give weight to entity-specific outcomes of past similar projects and contracts. 13(f), like 12(c), makes project economics part of the decision process to separate components contracts. 13(g) ensures that the reasons behind segmentation are verifiable.

Under IFRS, not all of the conditions in 605-35-25-13 would need to be met in order to segment a project. However, the nature of the conditions in these subparagraphs is certainly relevant to such a decision under IFRS.

The economics of the projects, the nature, and history of similar projects are all important for this type of decision under IFRS. The economics and nature of the projects would need to be assessed if the substance of the subprojects would be represented faithfully by segmentation. If the risks and cash flows of the projects are significantly different, accounting for them as one unit would not be in compliance with IFRS. The outcome of past, similar transactions would need to be incorporated into how management makes estimates. Ignoring this information would not be permitted. IAS 8, *Accounting Policies,* requires an entity to account for an adjustment as an error if the information should have been known. Obviously, having relevant history would be reasonably expected to be incorporated into a segmentation decision. Finally, having documentation to support estimates is also part of *The Framework*. Financial statement information must be verifiable.

As stated earlier, not all of the conditions of 605-35-25-13 would need to be met in order to segment the accounting under IFRS. Specifically, the clause in subparagraph 12(d) that prohibits entities from using prices charged by other contractors would not be excluded from an analysis using IAS 11. Market indicators are prominent in calculating fair value in IFRS.

COMBINING CONTRACTS

IFRS and US GAAP use very similar criteria for combining construction and production type contracts. Like segmentation, under US GAAP an entity may combine projects if it has an established policy, but it would not otherwise be required to do so. Under IAS 11, if a set of contracts meets the criteria for combination, they must be combined (just as projects must be segmented if they meet the criteria).

Following are the US GAAP paragraphs that address combining construction or production type contracts:

ASC 605-35-25

8 *A group of contracts may be combined for accounting purposes if all the following conditions exist:*

a. *The contracts are negotiated as a package in the same economic environment with an overall profit margin objective. Contracts not executed at the same time may be considered to have been negotiated as a package in the same economic environment only if the time period between the commitments of the parties to the individual contracts is reasonably short. The longer the period between the commitments of the parties to the contracts, the more likely it is that the economic circumstances affecting the negotiations have changed.*

b. *The contracts constitute in essence an agreement to do a single project. A project for this purpose consists of construction, or related service activity with different elements, phases, or units of output that are closely interrelated or interdependent in terms of their design, technology, and function or their ultimate purpose or use.*

c. *The contracts require closely interrelated construction activities with substantial common costs that cannot be separately identified with, or reasonably allocated to, the elements, phases, or units of output.*

d. *The contracts are performed concurrently or in a continuous sequence under the same project management at the same location or at different locations in the same general vicinity.*

e. *The contracts constitute in substance an agreement with a single customer. In assessing whether the contracts meet this criterion, the facts and circumstances relating to the other criteria should be considered. In some circumstances different divisions of the same entity would not constitute a single customer if, for example, the negotiations are conducted independently with the different divisions. On the other hand, two or more parties may constitute in substance a single customer if, for example, the negotiations are conducted jointly with the parties to do what in essence is a single project.*

Contracts that meet all of these criteria may be combined for profit recognition and for determining the need for a provision for losses in accordance with paragraphs 605-35-25-46 through 47. The criteria shall be applied consistently to contracts with similar characteristics in similar circumstances.

9 *Production-type contracts that do not meet the criteria in paragraph 605-35-25-8 or segments of such contracts may be combined into groupings such as production lots or releases for the purpose of accumulating and allocating production costs to units produced or delivered on the basis of average unit costs if both of the following circumstances exist:*

a. *The contracts are with one or more customers for the production of substantially identical units of a basic item produced concurrently or sequentially.*

b. *Revenue on the contracts is recognized on the units-of-delivery basis of applying the percentage-of-completion method.*

IAS 11 has the same requirements for combining contracts, although they are stated more succinctly:

IAS 11

9 *A group of contracts, whether with a single customer or with several customers, shall be treated as a single construction contract when*

(a) The group of contracts is negotiated as a single package.
(b) The contracts are so closely interrelated that they are, in effect, part of a single project with an overall profit margin.
(c) The contracts are performed concurrently or in a continuous sequence.

The language is largely consistent, although the US GAAP guidance is more detailed. However, the guidance fits within *The Framework*. Note that ASC 605-35-25-9 guidance on homogenous units would also be consistent with IFRS.

RECOGNITION PATTERN

The tension between percentage-of-completion and completed-contract methods is that the first invites abuse to record revenue prematurely, whereas the completed contract approach can produce profits that are closer to cash flow than accrual-based income. Manipulating percentage of completion can result in income tax abuse by enabling the shifting of operating income from one year to the next. Consequently, both IFRS and US GAAP provide guideposts to funnel revenue recognition to a method that is most representationally faithful.

Although an entity chooses its method under US GAAP, there is a provision that the choice of completed-contract method must result in income that across accounting periods approximates the percentage-of-completion method.

IFRS does not include the completed-contract method. IAS 11 requires deferral of revenue if the outcome of the contract cannot be estimated reliably. Expenses would be recognized in the period that they occur. If the outcome cannot be determined, but costs incurred are estimated to be recoverable, revenue is recognized only to the extent of these costs. The effect is a net-zero profit margin until the contract is completed. Nonrecoverable costs would be expensed.

Like US GAAP, if an over loss on a contract (unit of account) is probable, the loss must be recognized immediately.

Because the completed-contract method is not permitted under IFRS, all other things being equal, IFRS financial statements would show losses for a project early on, with revenue occurring at the end of the project. However, because IAS 11 is not prescriptive in how to assess the reliability of estimates, more projects may qualify for percentage-of-completion than under US GAAP.

CONTRACT REVENUE

IFRS and US GAAP are generally consistent about what elements of the initial arrangement fee are includable as revenue. In summary, the negotiated price of a contract (or segment) is the potential revenue. However, accounting for revenue for changes in the scope and nature of projects, while similar in concept, differ with regard to conditions needed to recognize the revenue from these changes.

The US GAAP guidance for both priced and unpriced change orders fit within *The Framework*. Thus there would be little if any difference in the accounting. These paragraphs ASC 605-35-25-25 to 28 require the revenue to be probable and measureable.

US GAAP provides specific guidance to determine if additional or optional revenue and costs should be combined with the original contract, and thus included in the measurement of progress of the entire contract, or accounted as a separate profit center.

ASC 605-35-25

29 *An option or an addition to an existing contract shall be treated as a separate contract in any of the following circumstances:*

    a. *The product or service to be provided differs significantly from the product or service provided under the original contract.*

    b. *The price of the new product or service is negotiated without regard to the original contract and involves different economic judgments.*

    c. *The products or services to be provided under the exercised option or amendment are similar to those under the original contract, but the contract price and anticipated contract cost relationship are significantly different.*

Because of the reliance in IFRS upon substance over form, under IAS 11, the above paragraphs describe circumstances which would likely lead to also accounting for the contract separately. In practice, there would little if any difference.

CLAIMS UNDER CONTRACT ACCOUNTING

Claims in the context of construction or production accounting are amounts that a contractor is to receive from the customer or third party as a result of increased cost due to a delay or other event. US GAAP provides prescriptive guidance when to recognize a claim into revenue. These include having a favorable legal basis or legal opinion, not caused by the contractor's performance, costs are estimable, and evidence is objective.

ASC 605-35-25

31 *Recognition of amounts of additional contract revenue relating to claims is appropriate only if it is probable that the claim will result in additional contract revenue and if the amount can be reliably estimated. Those two requirements are satisfied by the existence of all of the following conditions:*

    a. *The contract or other evidence provides a legal basis for the claim; or a legal opinion has been obtained, stating that under the circumstances there is a reasonable basis to support the claim.*

    b. *Additional costs are caused by circumstances that were unforeseen at the contract date and are not the result of deficiencies in the contractor's performance.*

    c. *Costs associated with the claim are identifiable or otherwise determinable and are reasonable in view of the work performed.*

    d. *The evidence supporting the claim is objective and verifiable, not based on management's feel for the situation or on unsupported representations.*

If the foregoing requirements are met, revenue from a claim should be recorded only to the extent that contract costs relating to the claim have been incurred. Costs attributable to claims should be treated as costs of contract performance as incurred. However, a practice such as recording revenues from claims only when the amounts have been received or awarded may be used.

Conversely, IAS 11, while the same in concept, does not provide specific circumstances, although the example in the main paragraph refers to customer (not contractor) delays, which is explicitly stated (although indirectly) in 605-35-25-31(b):

IAS 11

14 *A claim is an amount that the contractor seeks to collect from the customer or another party as reimbursement for costs not included in the contract price. A claim may arise from, for example, customer-caused delays, errors in specifications or design, and disputed variations in contract work. The measurement of the amounts of revenue arising from claims is subject to a high level of uncertainty and often depends on the outcome of negotiations. Therefore, claims are included in contract revenue only when*

(a) *Negotiations have reached an advanced stage such that it is probable that the customer will accept the claim.*
(b) *The amount that it is probable will be accepted by the customer can be measured reliably.*

Paragraph 605-35-25-31(a) requires that a claim must have a legal basis to be recognized in revenue. While this would certainly support recognition under IFRS, IAS 11.14 does not mention that a legal basis is necessary, only that negotiations have reached an advanced stage. There are many examples in IFRS where a probable event need not be legally binding. These include constructive obligations and IAS 12, *Income Taxes,* where, unlike US GAAP, a new tax law does not need to have been completely executed, only enacted. Because of this difference, claims are likely to be booked in revenue sooner than under US GAAP, assuming that a legal process would slow down the determination.

Subparagraph 12(d) specifies that costs must have been unforeseen at the contract date to be recognizable. While this is an obvious attribute of a claim, if delays were possible, but negotiations did not include it in the final agreement, this would not preclude recognizing under IFRS. The absence of this condition in IAS 11 makes it likely that claims would be booked earlier in revenue than under US GAAP, all other things being equal.

The last two subparagraphs are consistent with IFRS and would result in no differences in practice.

The last paragraph of ASC 605-35-25-31 contains two concepts that do not apply under IAS 11. The second sentence prescribes a zero-cost margin accounting for claims that meet the criteria, that is, equal amounts of revenue and costs are recognized until all costs are incurred. Zero-margin accounting under IAS 11 only applies when the profitability of the project is in doubt. The last sentence essentially endorses cash-basis accounting, if done consistently. There is no guidance in IAS 11 that would permit this, as it is counter to accrual accounting. However, IAS 37, *Provisions and Contingencies,* has similar guidance to US GAAP for *contingent assets.* This guidance, under both standards, specifies that these amounts must be virtually certain (as opposed to probable) to be recognized. If the claim were in this state, IAS 11 would require all revenue from the claim to be deferred and costs booked as incurred. However, if the claim was that uncertain to be received, it's likely that the entire contract would be accounted for as such (unless the claim was to be received from a third party).

Other Construction Guidance

The remainder of ASC 605-35-25, paragraphs 45 to 99, are more in the nature of implementation guidance than standards. Because IFRS does not have extensive guidance for application, generally, these paragraphs fall inside of *The Framework* as can be used as supplements to construction accounting per IAS 8, *Accounting Policies*.

MILESTONE METHOD

The milestone method under US GAAP (605-28-25) prescribes the timing and amount of revenue to be recognized when an entity (the vendor) achieves a goal. The goal, termed *the milestone*, is defined in the ASC master glossary as

An event having all of the following characteristics:

> a. *There is substantive uncertainty at the date the arrangement is entered into that the event will be achieved. A vendor's assessment that it expects to achieve a milestone does not necessarily mean that there is no substantive uncertainty associated with achieving the milestone.*
> b. *The event can only be achieved based in whole or in part on either of the following:*
>
>> 1. *The vendor's performance*
>> 2. *A specific outcome resulting from the vendor's performance*
>
> c. *If achieved, the event would result in additional payments being due to the vendor.*

A milestone does not include events for which the occurrence is either of the following:

> a. *Contingent solely upon the passage of time*
> b. *The result of a counterparty's performance*

So a milestone under US GAAP must be based on a vendor's performance.

Additionally, if the agreement that contains the milestone includes conditions under which revenue can be reclaimed by the customer (or presumably a third party), that revenue is deferred, rather than being recognized as a return of revenue at a later date.

What is common under IFRS and US GAAP is that when substantial uncertainty exists, revenue is deferred until that uncertainty is removed. The most direct guidance in IFRS is IAS 18.18.

In comparison to IFRS, there are four issues:

1. Milestone is determined only at the inception of the arrangement
2. The only criteria is vendor performance
3. Milestone must be deferred in its entirety
4. The effect of a clawback

Milestone Determined at the Inception of the Arrangement

ASC 605-28-25 specifies that milestones must be determined at the inception of the arrangement. Presumably the requirement is to avoid "engineering" revenue by setting goals using hindsight or other new information in a way that accelerates recognition.

IFRS contains no such requirement. However, *The Framework* and IAS 11 direct that revenue must reflect the substance of an arrangement, be probable, be able to be measured, and realizable. If the substance of the business transaction is that there is a reasonable basis to believe both parties agree that a particular achievement or event concludes a segment of a deal, revenue should be recognized. In other words, as the work on an arrangement continues, negotiations subsequent to the inception of the agreement can lead to an "earnings point."

Vendor Performance Criteria

The requirement that only vendor performance can be considered in a milestone does not have a parallel in IFRS. In general, it is doubtful under either US GAAP or IFRS that a vendor can recognize additional revenue based on what a customer does. Revenue is earned, so earning based on a customer's actions is counterintuitive. What the exclusive reliance on vendor performance is getting at is that the performance must be completely within the vendor's control, not jointly with another party. Under IFRS, there is no prohibition against recognizing milestone revenue as probable and measureable. An example might be that a vendor outsources part of the work to a subcontractor.

There is no guidance in IFRS that indicates an uncertainty is removed **only** based on a vendor's performance. Certainly vendor performance is a core requirement of revenue recognition under IFRS, and revenue would be deferred under IAS 18.18 if there were significant uncertainty.

Recognition in Entirety

The US GAAP requirement that revenue cannot be recognized in its entirety until the milestone, which is by definition substantive, is connected closely with the first stipulation that milestones can only be set at the inception of the contract. Because IFRS does not encompass this first point, the point is moot for IFRS.

Effect of a Clawback

Milestone guidance under US GAAP employs a very conservative approach when clawbacks are part of an arrangement. In summary, any part of an agreement that conveys a possibility of a return of funds based on future performance precludes revenue from the entire milestone from being recognized. Under IFRS, if the future performance were probable, there is no reason the revenue could be recognized, or perhaps even a portion that could not be returned would be recognized with the remainder deferred, if this reflected the substance of the transaction and was not overly conservative.

Conversely, ASC 605-28-25-1 gives license to entities to defer part of milestone revenue even if all the requirements of recognition are met:

ASC 605-28-25

1   *The guidance in this Subtopic shall be met in order for a vendor to recognize deliverable consideration or unit of accounting consideration that is contingent upon the achievement of a substantive milestone in its entirety in the period in which the milestone is achieved. Other methods that result in the recognition of milestone consideration in its entirety in the period the milestone is achieved are precluded. Even if the criteria in this Subtopic are met,* a vendor is not precluded *from making an accounting policy election* to apply a different policy *that results in the* deferral of revenue *relating to some portion of the milestone consideration.*

Summary of Milestone Revenue Comparison

In summary, the effect of US GAAP milestone accounting compared to IFRS is to defer revenue for a longer period of time given the same set of circumstances. Under IFRS, milestones (although that term is not defined in IFRS) can be set after the inception of the agreement, can be based on any criteria that is probable, reasonable, realizable, and measurable (as opposed to being based on vendor performance only), and can be recognized in entirety, even if a clawback is present in the arrangement, provided that the clawback is not probable. Any clawbacks that materialized would be charged to expense in the period that they occur.

ENTERTAINMENT INDUSTRY

The guidance for the recognition of revenue for the entertainment industry is virtually identical. ASC 928-605 covers this under US GAAP. Example 20 in the Illustrative Examples section of IAS 18 covers license fees in the entertainment industry. Both standards follow the basic concept of revenue recognition, that is, it must be earned and realizable.

Customer Loyalty Programs

The net effect of the accounting for customer loyalty or "points" programs is the same under IFRS and US GAAP. IFRIC 13, *Customer Loyalty Programs,* requires that the fair value of the awards related to the transaction is deferred. Under US GAAP, an accrued liability is made with an offset going to a reduction in revenue. The net effect of both standards is a deferral of revenue.

Recognizing revenue for the estimated unused reward value, termed *breakage* under US GAAP (ASC 605-50-25), is demonstrated in Example 1 in the Illustrative Examples section of IFRIC 13. The Illustrative Examples section is not part of IFRIC 13 (as disclaimed); however, both IAS 37, *Provisions,* and IAS 19, *Employee Benefits,* require that under circumstances where uncertainty is involved in recognizing liabilities, that the measurement must be probability-weighted or reflect the nonuse of benefits.

Per IAS 18 and ASC 605, revenue is recognized as earned, usually upon delivery of the item. However, estimating the use of points as a basis for amortizing revenue is acceptable as long as the basis is reasonable.

IFRIC 13 requires when the unavoidable costs of fulfilling the program exceeds the deferred revenue, an onerous contract is recognized under IAS 37, *Provisions:*

IFRIC 13

9   *If at any time the unavoidable costs of meeting the obligations to supply the awards are expected to exceed the consideration received and receivable for them (i.e., the consideration allocated to the award credits at the time of the initial sale that has not yet been recognized as revenue plus any further consideration receivable when the customer redeems the award credits), the entity has onerous contracts. A liability shall be recognized for the excess in accordance with IAS 37. The need to recognize such a liability could arise if the expected costs of supplying awards increase, for example, if the entity revises its expectations about the number of award credits that will be redeemed.*

IFRIC 13 is silent on the unit of account, but paragraph 9 appears to indicate that all the outstanding awards that offer a particular benefit are evaluated together.

In contrast, US GAAP prohibits recognizing the losses before the sale of the item:

ASC 605-50-25

Sales Incentives That Will Result in a Loss on the Sale of a Product or Service

5   *For sales incentives offered voluntarily by a vendor and without charge to customers that can be used or that become exercisable by a customer as a result of a single exchange transaction, and that will result in a loss on the sale of a product or service, a vendor shall not recognize a liability (see Topic 405) for the sales incentive prior to the date at which the related revenue is recognized by the vendor.*

6   *Paragraph 330-10-35-13 explains that the offer of a sales incentive that will result in a loss on the sale of a product may indicate an impairment of existing inventory under Topic 330.*

However, note that paragraph 605-50-25-6 directs the entity to consider a possible impairment of inventory. While IFRIC 13 does not mention this, application of IFRS 2, *Inventories,* requires impairment of inventories as circumstances indicate.

Other Customer Incentives

ASC 605-50 includes detailed guidance of accounting for cash and noncash consideration given to customers to induce sales of products and services. The primary purpose of the section is to prescribe when an incentive can be presented as a cost rather than a reduction of revenue. Presumably, this guidance is to prevent abuse of revenue recognition in the case of complex customer and vendor relationships.

The main concept of ASC 605-50 is that if a vendor receives a separate identifiable benefit, then the consideration given to the customer is a cost since it in substance represents a separate transaction. More specifically, the characterization of consideration as cost can only be applied if it is the result of a single transaction, not one that a customer has become entitled to as a result of a series of transactions. For example, an auto manufacturer often rebates dealers based on the full year sales of its cars. *Buydowns,* which are arrangements where vendors pay distributors for shortfalls in projected selling prices, are specifically prohibited from being characterized as costs (they must be presented as a reduction of revenue). Similarly, slotting fees also are always presented as a reduction of revenue.

IFRS does not have equivalent guidance. However, IAS 18.13 requires that a transaction must be accounted for separately according to its substance. Because the substance of the US GAAP guidance reflects this concept, it can be applied to entities reporting under IFRS (in accordance with IAS 8, *Accounting Policies*) because its guidance does not contradict other IFRS statements or *The Framework*.

Recognition Pattern of Customer Incentives

The following US GAAP guidance prescribes how revenue is recognized when rewards are earned by customers based on a volume of purchases:

ASC 605-50-25

7 *A vendor may offer a customer a rebate or refund of a specified amount of cash consideration that is redeemable only if the customer completes a specified cumulative level of revenue transactions or remains a customer for a specified time period. The vendor shall recognize the rebate or refund obligation as a reduction of revenue based on a systematic and rational allocation of the cost of honoring rebates or refunds earned and claimed to each of the underlying revenue transactions that result in progress by the customer toward earning the rebate or refund. Measurement of the total rebate or refund obligation shall be based on the estimated number of customers that ultimately will earn and claim rebates or refunds under the offer (that is, breakage should be considered if it can be reasonably estimated). However, if the amount of future rebates or refunds cannot be reasonably estimated, a liability shall be recognized for the maximum potential amount of the refund or rebate (that is, no reduction for breakage shall be made). The ability to make a reasonable estimate of the amount of future rebates or refunds depends on many factors and circumstances that will vary from case to case. However, any of the following factors may impair a vendor's ability to make a reasonable estimate:*

   a. *Relatively long periods in which a particular rebate or refund may be claimed*

   b. *The absence of historical experience with similar types of sales incentive programs with similar products or the inability to apply such experience because of changing circumstances*

   c. *The absence of a large volume of relatively homogeneous transactions*

8 *In some cases, the relative size of the rebate or refund changes based on the volume of purchases. For example, the rebate may be 10 percent of total consideration if more than 100 units are purchased but may increase to 20 percent if*

*more than 200 units are purchased. If the volume of a customer's future pur-
chases cannot be reasonably estimated, the maximum potential rebate or refund
factor shall be used to record a liability (20 percent in the example). In contrast,
if the volume of a customer's future purchases can be reasonably estimated, the
estimated amount to be rebated or refunded shall be recognized as a liability.*

9 *Changes in the estimated amount of rebates or refunds and retroactive changes
by a vendor to a previous offer (an increase or a decrease in the rebate amount
that is applied retroactively) shall be recognized using a cumulative catch-up
adjustment. That is, the vendor would adjust the balance of its rebate obligation
to the revised estimate immediately. The vendor would then reduce revenue on
future sales based on the revised refund obligation rate as computed.*

Paragraph 605-50-25-7 directs that if the value of the incentives that will not be
exercised cannot be estimated, that the maximum amount be accrued over the attributable period. The *IFRS Framework's* definition of neutrality prohibits deliber-
ately conservative estimates of financial statement elements. Thus, unless it can be
deemed immaterial, accruing for the full value of incentives when the certainty is
high that not all of them would be redeemed is not allowable under IFRS.

Airline Industry

ASC 908-605-25 describes both a specific identification and statistical approach
to recognizing revenue from airline flights. Amounts received or receivable are first
recorded as unearned revenue. The following methods are then used to recognize
these amounts as revenue.

The Sales-lift Match Method requires a ticket-by-ticket matching of miles used
by a passenger. This can be analogized to the inventory-specific identification cost
flow. Alternatively, revenue from airline miles can be estimated by sampling tickets
and dividing the value of the tickets by the miles flown. This average is then applied
to all miles flown to determine how much revenue is recognized. The sampling can
also be done to produce an average fare per customer which is applied to the number
of passengers served.

IFRS does not contain any guidance specifically for airlines. Airlines reporting
under IFRS do not typically report using a statistical method but merely state that
revenue is recognized as flights are made. Some entities reporting under US GAAP
describe a statistical method. This suggests that airlines filing under IFRS use the
specific identification method. However, if the sampling method was proven to result in revenue that is not significantly different than specific identification, it could
be employed under IFRS. In any case, the revenue recognized would need to meet
the criteria set forth in IAS 11 for services. In summary, the flows of resources
would need to be reliably estimated, the risk and rewards would need to have been
passed, and the costs incurred would need to be reliably measurable.

FEDERAL GOVERNMENT CONTRACTS

ASC 912-605 prescribes the revenue and cost recognition for projects using a
cost-plus fee arrangement provided to the US federal government. The guidance is

aimed at determining when billed amounts, based on cost incurred to date, can be recognized as revenue instead of on a typical accrual base using perhaps percentage of completion. The guidance emphasizes that a unique aspect of many US federal contracts is the ownership of the constructed project is passed continuously to the government and that payment is virtually assured (negligible credit risk). The decision turns on whether revenue can be recognized before delivery of article or on percentage of completion.

To use costs as the basis for revenue recognition, like all construction or production contacts, the costs attributable to the revenue recognized must be estimable with a reasonable degree of accuracy. The guidance includes example of circumstances that may invalidate this assumed relationship between costs incurred and revenue earned. These include

ASC 912-605-25

10 *Judgment shall be exercised in each circumstance as to whether accrual of the fee when billable is preferable to accrual on the usual basis of delivery or of percentage of completion otherwise determined. While the approval of the government as to amounts billable shall ordinarily be regarded as objective evidence, factors may exist which suggest an earlier or later accrual. Such factors include all of the following:*

   a. *There are indications of substantial difference between estimated and final cost.*
   b. *Preparatory or tooling-up costs were much more than estimated.*
   c. *Raw material needs were greatly and unduly anticipated by advance purchases.*
   d. *Delays in delivery schedules or other circumstances suggest that costs are exceeding estimates.*

In effect, the above examples cite situations in which the relationship between costs and revenue in a cost-plus contract can be distorted.

ASC 912-605-25-17 to 19 specifies that where a contractor is acting as an agent, only the fee is reflected in the contractor's income statements (not the cost).

ASC 912-605-25-20 to 37 focuses on the accounting following a cancellation of a contract by the US federal government. Upon termination, the contractor must recognize all revenue not yet billed and accrue all costs yet recognized. Additionally, formulas in the contracts with the US federal government for determining compensation for terminated contracts may result in claims that produce profits above the formula used during construction. The profit margin can be further increased for costs properly written off in prior periods (because they were not reimbursable, but now are under the termination clauses).

IFRS Comparison

Revenue recognition assumes that the costs related to these inflows can be reliably estimated.

IAS 11 permits using cost as a basis for accruing revenue for cost-plus contracts.

Like US GAAP, costs that are not reimbursable are excluded for the measurement of revenue. IAS 11 does address cost-plus contracts. The guidance is aligned with the language in 905-605-25-9 which permits revenue recognition for cost-plus contracts based on costs incurred:

IAS 11

24 In the case of a cost-plus contract, the outcome of a construction contract can be estimated reliably when all the following conditions are satisfied:

   (a) It is probable that the economic benefits associated with the contract will flow to the entity.
   (b) The contract costs attributable to the contract, whether or not specifically reimbursable, can be clearly identified and measured reliably.

30 The stage of completion of a contract may be determined in a variety of ways. The entity uses the method that measures reliably the work performed. Depending on the nature of the contract, the methods may include

   (a) The proportion that contract costs incurred for work performed to date bear to the estimated total contract costs

Additionally, the following paragraph aligns with the concept underlying 912-605-25-10:

IAS 11

31 When the stage of completion is determined by reference to the contract costs incurred to date, only those contract costs that reflect work performed are included in costs incurred to date. Examples of contract costs which are excluded are

   (a) Contract costs that relate to future activity on the contract, such as costs of materials that have been delivered to a contract site or set aside for use in a contract but not yet installed, used or applied during contract performance, unless the materials have been made especially for the contract
   (b) Payments made to subcontractors in advance of work performed under the subcontract

The examples in ASC 912-605-25-10 all describe circumstances in which cost to date does not reflect the work performed and is not considered when calculating revenue.

Contract Terminations

IFRS does not directly address cancellations of construction-type contracts. However, the guidance in ASC 912-605-25-20 to 37 is a more detailed explanation of accrual accounting. In summary, the concept that if contract's clauses specifically define the rights and obligations when it is cancelled, general recognition principles are applied to reflect the substance of the event. The references to the accounting for claims stemming from the cancellation are aligned with the guidance in IAS 11.14 that claims are recognized as revenue when the amount can be reliably estimated and when negotiations are advanced enough so that it is probable that the claim will be accepted. If a contract specifies the claims process, then the stage of negotiation is moot, unless there is a dispute.

ENTERTAINMENT INDUSTRY: FILMS AND REVENUE RECOGNITION

ASC 926 specifies incremental guidance particular to the entertainment industry. IFRS does not have guidance specific to the film industry. However, IAS 18 does cover licensing.

The guidance on revenue recognition, ASC 926-605, for the most part follows the core principles of revenue recognition, which IFRS and US GAAP share (please refer to the beginning of this chapter). The topics cover recognition of flat fee and variable fee arrangements, as well arrangements that encompass multiple films. Under US GAAP, the revenue allocable to the films is based on the fair values. This is consistent with IAS 18.13 for contracts with multiple deliverables. Until IFRS 13, *Fair Value*, is effective (January 1, 2013), the definitions of fair value differ between IFRS and US GAAP, and there would be an inherent measurement disparity between the amounts allocated to the different films within an agreement. However, to the extent that each method produces the same relative values, the allocation of the revenue may not be material.

Below is example 20 from IAS 18 that specifically mentions motion pictures.

IAS 18, Illustrative Examples section:

INTEREST, ROYALTIES AND DIVIDENDS

20 License fees and royalties

> *Fees and royalties paid for the use of an entity's assets (such as trademarks, patents, software, music copyright, record masters and motion picture films) are normally recognized in accordance with the substance of the agreement. As a practical matter, this may be on a straight-line basis over the life of the agreement, for example, when a licensee has the right to use certain technology for a specified period of time.*

> *An assignment of rights for a fixed fee or nonrefundable guarantee under a noncancellable contract which permits the licensee to exploit those rights freely and the licensor has no remaining obligations to perform is, in substance, a sale. An example is a licensing agreement for the use of software when the licensor has no obligations subsequent to delivery. Another example is the granting of rights to exhibit a motion picture film in markets where the licensor has no control over the distributor and expects to receive no further revenues from the box office receipts. In such cases, revenue is recognized at the time of sale.*

> *In some cases, whether or not a license fee or royalty will be received is contingent on the occurrence of a future event. In such cases, revenue is recognized only when it is probable that the fee or royalty will be received, which is normally when the event has occurred.*

While this guidance is not part of IAS 18, it does accompany it. Since the example relates directly to motion pictures, it is particularly comparable to ASC 926.

The only aspect of revenue recognition in ASC 926 which, at least in theory, is counter to IFRS is 926-605-25-1(c) which states that revenue from film licensing agreement cannot be recognized until

> c.   *The license period of the arrangement has begun and the customer can begin its exploitation, exhibition, or sale*

Under IFRS and, in general, US GAAP, if there are no further costs that that an entity needs to incur, nor any contingency, revenue is recognized in full when the revenue is measureable and collection is reasonably assured. This may be an area where revenue is recognized under IFRS before it is under US GAAP.

ENTERTAINMENT INDUSTRY: CASINOS AND REVENUE RECOGNITION

ASC 924-605 describes incremental revenue recognition guidance. IFRS has no specific guidance for casinos.

The following US GAAP paragraph directs that revenue is a net figure of gaming wins and losses:

ASC 924-605-25

> 1   *Casino revenue shall be reported on an accrual basis. Revenue recognized and reported by a casino is generally defined as the win from gaming activities, that is, the difference between gaming wins and losses, not the total amount wagered.*

Under IFRS, the closest guidance is in IAS 18.10 which prescribes that trade discounts reduce net revenue.   Additionally, IAS 1 offers the following guidance with regard to offsetting:

> 3   *An entity reports separately both assets and liabilities, and income and expenses. Offsetting in the statements of comprehensive income or financial position or in the separate income statement (if presented),* except when offsetting reflects the *substance* of the transaction or other event, *detracts from the ability of users both to understand the transactions, other events and conditions that have occurred and to assess the entity's future cash flows.*

The question in applying IFRS to casinos is whether it is more representationally faithful to record gaming losses as expense or net against revenues.

Discounts, which are netted against revenue, are not expenses because the discount would never be an inflow of resources, the entity would never have the claim to it, and thus not have the resources to expend.

An expense, under both US GAAP and IFRS, is characterized by the reduction of assets or the incurrence of liabilities. A person at a slot machine who wins pulls is not clearly an expense to the casino. The entity does not incur a liability (the gambler already has the cash, or tokens readily convertible into cash). Nor is it assured that that the casino would need to use its assets since some of the cash was likely put in by the gambler (and others). Since casinos are typically open continuously, there is no traditional end to a transaction. The closest set of events that approximates a transaction is the time between when a gambler enters a casino and when he or she leaves. It is also likely prohibitively expensive to track losses and gains. The clearest measure of what a casino takes in is the counting of cash at the end of the prescribed period (perhaps just before an armored car pickup). In this sense, cost-benefit constraints would likely prohibit separate tracking of gambling gains and losses.

While not prescribed anywhere, following US GAAP for revenue of casinos falls within *The Framework*.

OIL & GAS INDUSTRY—REVENUE RECOGNITION

ASC 932-605-25 contains only one paragraph specific to the oil & gas industry:

Take-or-Pay Contracts

2   *Sometimes gas producers and purchasers execute agreements whereby a purchaser agrees to take or pay for a minimum quantity of gas per year. Usually, any amount paid in excess of the price of gas taken is recoverable from future purchases in excess of minimum quantities. If the purchaser is not allowed to make up deficiencies, it is appropriate for the producer to record revenues to the extent of the minimum contracted quantity, assuming payment has been received or is reasonably assured. If deficiencies can be made up, receipts in excess of actual sales shall be recorded as deferred revenues until production is actually taken or the right to make up deficiencies expires.*

The above treatment falls within *The Framework* because it recognizes the substance of the transaction and is in line with the general principles for revenue recognition which are virtually identical between IFRS and US GAAP.

BROKERS AND DEALERS—REVENUE RECOGNITION

ASC 940-605 contains the following four paragraphs that provide incremental guidance of revenue recognition for brokers and dealers of securities:

Underwriting

25-1   *A broker-dealer may underwrite a security offering by contracting to buy the issue either at a fixed price or a price based on selling the offering on a best-effort basis. The difference between the price paid by the public and the contract price less the related expenses represents the underwriting income or loss.*

25-2   *The fee revenue relating to the underwriting commitment shall be recorded when all significant items relating to the underwriting cycle have been completed and the amount of the underwriting revenue has been determined. This will generally be the point at which all of the following have occurred (which may or may not be before the settlement date of the issue):*

   a.   The issuer's registration statement has become effective with the Securities and Exchange Commission (SEC), or other offering documents are finalized (as opposed to the closing or settlement date).

b. *The broker-dealer has made a firm commitment for the purchase of the shares or debt from the issuer.*

c. *The broker-dealer has been informed of the exact number of shares or the principal amount of debt that it has been allotted (if it is not the lead underwriter of an undivided offering).*

Mutual Fund Distribution

25-3 *A front-end commission shall be recorded in full by the broker-dealer at the time it is earned (the trade date).*

25-4 *With respect to 12b-1 fees and deferred sales charges, the broker-dealer generally shall defer its incremental direct costs associated with the selling of the fund shares (such as sales representatives' commissions and direct marketing costs) and shall amortize these costs over the period in which the fees from the fund or fund shareholders are expected to be received. Indirect costs associated with selling the fund shares shall be expensed as incurred.*

Generally, paragraphs 25-1 and 25-2 align with the IFRS revenue recognition principles which for services states that to be recognized as revenues, fees from services must be reliably measurable, probable that the amount will flow to the entity, the costs incurred can be reliably measured, and stage of completion can be reliably measured (the last two are applicable to services that have multiple stages or are deliverable over a significant period of time). Additionally, if any uncertainties must be removed prior to having the right to receive the fee, that uncertainty must be removed since until then it is not probable that the economic benefits will flow to the entity (IAS 18.18)

ASC 940-605-25-2(a) aligns with IAS 18.18 since until registration statements are accepted, it is not certain that the revenue will be realized. The firm commitment required by 25-2(b) is a major component of both the demonstration that services are rendered and are measureable (as required by IAS 18.21 which states that revenues are recognized in the period that the services are rendered. Obviously, for an offering of securities, it is necessary to commit to tender the instruments to render the main service. 25-2(c) is necessary for either measurement of revenue in the case of a best-efforts arrangement since this information is needed to calculate the fees receivable. In a fixed-fee arrangement, if there is some minimum requirement of securities, and the number of shares is below that amount, further negotiation would be needed to determine if it can fulfill the agreement.

In the absence of any connection to receiving the fee to the number of securities, Illustrative Example 14 of IAS 11, captioned *Financial Service Fees,* offers some guidance:

(c) *Fees that are earned on the execution of a significant act.*

The fees are recognized as revenue when the significant act has been completed, as in the examples below.

(i) *Commission on the allotment of shares to a client.*

Note that IAS 11.IE.14(c)(i) specifies that commission is recognized when shares are allotted to a client, not the broker or dealer. However, it is conceivable that the shares *received* from the issuer would be necessary to know how many shares it could deliver to a buyer (the client). In this case, deferral of revenue until this information is known is aligned with IFRS.

The difference with US GAAP would occur if the information on the number of shares per 25-2(c) was received in a later accounting period than information pursuant to the subparagraphs 25-2(a) and (b) and there was no connection with revenue probability or measurement.

Paragraphs 940-605-25-3 and 4 concerning mutual fund fees are within the *IFRS Framework*.

FINANCIAL SERVICES—INVESTMENT COMPANIES AND REVENUE RECOGNITION OF FEES

Cost Deferral

ASC 946-605 contains guidance of limited scope to fees received by investment companies. All other general requirements of US GAAP revenue recognition apply.

Following is ASC 946-605-25 regarding deferral of costs:

Investment Adviser's Offering Costs when Both 12b-1 Fees and Contingent-Deferred Sales Fees Are Not Received

1   *Paragraph 946-605-25-8 provides guidance on accounting by investment advisers who are reimbursed for offering costs paid through both 12b-1 fees and contingent-deferred sales fees. Accordingly, the accounting by those investment advisers for fees and offering costs are outside the scope of the guidance in paragraphs 946-605-25-2 through 25-3.*

2   *Benefits expected from the expenditures paid by an investment adviser in connection with the distribution of shares of a fund in circumstances in which the investment adviser does not receive both 12b-1 fees and contingent-deferred sales fees do not meet the definition of an asset of the investment adviser as provided in FASB Concepts Statement No. 6, **Elements of Financial Statements**. Accordingly, such offering costs paid by the investment adviser shall be expensed as incurred. Initial offering costs paid by an investment adviser that does not receive both 12b-1 fees and contingent-deferred sales fees are start-up costs of the investment adviser, which should be accounted for in accordance with Subtopic 470-20.*

3   *The guidance in the preceding paragraph applies also to distribution plans of open-end investment companies permitted under Rule 12b-1. Some closed-end interval funds incur distribution-related fees (similar to 12b-1 fees) and impose early withdrawal charges (similar to contingent-deferred sales fees) pursuant to exemptive orders issued under the Investment Company Act of 1940. In addition, certain offshore funds not subject to regulation under the Investment Company Act of 1940 also may incur fees and impose charges that are substantially the same as 12b-1 fees and contingent-deferred sales fees, respectively. In such instances, it would be appropriate to account for offering costs incurred for distribution of those funds in a manner similar to the accounting for distribution fees specified in paragraph 946-605-25-8.*

ASC 946-605-25-1 to 3 draws a bright line as to whether costs incurred by an investment advisor are able to be deferred onto the balance sheet. The message is clear: if both 12b-1 contingent deferred sales fees (fees that are collected upon redemption but can be decreased and even eliminated over time) are not received, costs are expensed.

IFRS has no specific guidance regarding these fees. However, it is unlikely that such prescriptive language could be applied without further analysis of the substance of the agreement. If it were probable that the fees would be recovered and a reliable estimate could be made, the fees could be deferred up to the amount expected to be recovered. These costs would need to be evaluated each period for write-down.

IAS 18.IE14

(iii) Investment management fees

> *Fees charged for managing investments are recognized as revenue as the services are provided.*
>
> *Incremental costs that are directly attributable to securing an investment management contract are recognized as an asset if they can be identified separately and measured reliably and if it is probable that they will be recovered. As in IAS 39, an incremental cost is one that would not have been incurred if the entity had not secured the investment management contract. The asset represents the entity's contractual right to benefit from providing investment management services, and is amortized as the entity recognizes the related revenue. If the entity has a portfolio of investment management contracts, it may assess their recoverability on a portfolio basis.*

Distribution Fees

ASC 946-605-25-4 to 6 prescribes when 12b-1 fees and contingent-deferred sales fees are recognized by a distributor. A distributer in this context is a principle that makes the market for the securities in question and carries the risks and rewards of ownership.

Distributor Transfer of Rights to Certain Future Distribution Fees

4   *Revenue recognition is appropriate when cash is received from a third party for the rights to 12b-1 fees and contingent-deferred sales fees if the distributor has neither continuing involvement with the transferred rights nor recourse. The distributor has neither continuing involvement nor recourse if neither the distributor nor any member of the consolidated group that includes the distributor does any of the following:*

> a. *Retains any disproportionate risks or rewards in the cash flows of the transferred rights*
> b. *Guarantees or assures in any way the purchaser's rate of return or return on investment related to the transferred rights*
> c. *Restricts the ability of the consolidated group or the mutual fund independent board to remove, replace, or subcontract any of the service providers of the fund.*

5　*Deferred costs for the shares sold to which the transferred rights pertain should be expensed concurrent with the recognition of revenue consistent with the guidance in paragraph 946-605-25-8.*

6　*This guidance does not address the accounting for the rights to 12b-1 fees and contingent-deferred sales fees by a mutual fund, an investor in a mutual fund, or a third-party investor that obtains the rights to 12b-1 fees and contingent-deferred sales fees. For guidance to be applied by mutual funds, see Subtopic 946-20.*

IAS 39, *Financial Instruments—Recognition and Measurement* which provides guidance to determine whether the risks or rewards of ownership of a financial asset are passed and qualifies as a sale, can be used to determine if ASC 946-605-25-4 to 6 could be used under IFRS. IAS 39 includes references to all three of the sub-paragraphs in 25-4 as indicators of a sale of a financial instrument. Consequently, any fees associated with such a transfer would be recognizable as revenue.

Franchises—Revenue

ASC 952-605 covers recognition of revenue by a franchisor for service and goods transferred to a franchisee. All the guidance fits within the guidance of IAS 18, *Revenue*. IAS 11.IE18 contains guidance that is very similar to ASC 952-605-20.

Health-Care Entities—Revenue Recognition

ASC 954-605 provides incremental guidance for revenue recognition by a health-care entity. The guidance fits within *The Framework* and is aligned with IAS 18, *Revenues*.

Not-for-Profit Entities—Revenue Recognition

ASC 958-605 defines the revenue recognition for nonprofit entities. IFRS has no guidance specifically for nonprofit entities. However, one of the core principles under ASC 958-605, that receipt of assets whose use is not restricted by a donor is recognized revenue, does have some parallels in IFRS.

The *IFRS Framework* specifies that there is not necessarily a connection between expenditures and assets. If an entity controls resources, and it meets the definition of an asset, it is accounted for as an asset.

IFRS Framework (2010) - 4.14

There is a close association between incurring expenditure and generating assets but the two do not necessarily coincide. Hence, when an entity incurs expenditure, this may provide evidence that future economic benefits were sought but is not conclusive proof that an item satisfying the definition of an asset has been obtained. Similarly the absence of a related expenditure does not preclude an item from satisfying the definition of an asset and thus becoming a candidate for recognition in the balance sheet; for example, items that have been donated to the entity may satisfy the definition of an asset.

Also, IFRIC 18, *Transfers of Assets from Customers*, contains guidance that when a customer provides control of an asset to a vendor (for the purposes of procuring the goods or services of that vendor) the asset is recognized by the vendor and classified in the income statement as revenue.

The guidance in ASC 958 adheres closely to the principles of revenue recognition, which IFRS and US GAAP, in effect, share (see the first section of this chapter for a comprehensive comparison). Consequently, the guidance in ASC 985-605 fits within the *IFRS Framework.*

LAYAWAY SALES

Layaway sales, that is, arrangements where a retailer holds goods until a customer has paid the full purchase price, can result in revenue being recognized earlier under IFRS. Example 3 in the IAS 18 Illustrative Examples section states that, in line with IFRS revenue recognition concepts, when goods are available and a significant amount of the deposit is received, revenue can be recognized because the follow of resources to the entity is probable.

> 3   *Layaway sales under which the goods are delivered only when the buyer makes the final payment in a series of installments.*
>
> *Sale of Goods—Layaway: Revenue from such sales is recognized when the goods are delivered. However, when experience indicates that most such sales are consummated, revenue may be recognized when a significant deposit is received provided the goods are on hand, identified and ready for delivery to the buyer.*

However, US GAAP provides a strict interpretation, at least for public companies.

> *605-10-Question: In the staff's view, when may Company R recognize revenue for merchandise sold under its layaway program?*
>
> *Interpretive Response: Provided that the other criteria for revenue recognition are met, the staff believes that Company R should recognize revenue from sales made under its layaway* program upon delivery of the merchandise to the customer. *Until then, the amount of cash received should be recognized as a liability entitled such as "deposits received from customers for layaway sales" or a similarly descriptive caption. Because Company R retains the risks of ownership of the merchandise, receives only a deposit from the customer, and does not have an enforceable right to the remainder of the purchase price, the staff would object to Company R recognizing any revenue upon receipt of the cash deposit. This is consistent with item two (2) in the Commission's criteria for bill-and-hold transactions which states "the customer must have made a fixed commitment to purchase the goods."*

CHAPTER SUMMARY

Despite the numerous exceptions to revenue recognition principles under US GAAP, the core concepts are nearly identical to IFRS. Significant differences regarding timing of revenue recognition are prominent for multiple-element arrangements, construction contracts, and research and development revenue.

11 INCOME TAXES

Accounting for income taxes is one of the more pervasive areas under either US GAAP or IFRS. Income taxes touch almost every other area of accounting because results of an entity, except not-for-profits, incur tax liability. Furthermore, income tax strategies and planning occupy the time and budgets of most entities except perhaps for the very smallest. The basic concept underlying income tax is a simple one: to recognize the income tax attributed to the current period's results. Unfortunately, the inherent differences between income for book and tax bases complicate the measurement of tax expense and balance sheet attributes.

The two drivers of these differences are timing and characterization. Timing refers to the disparity between the periods an item of income or expense is recognized for tax purposes and when it is included in taxable income. Characterization refers to the rate at which an item is taxed, including those items that are excluded from taxable income, which can be looked at as having a rate of zero. The interaction of timing and characterization can also render certain items of income or expense effectively excluded from taxable income. An example is the need to offset capital gains with capital losses. Capital losses go unused if they cannot be matched with a capital gain before a certain time period.

IFRS and US GAAP both use a balance sheet approach to recognizing income tax expense. In other words, tax expense or benefit is merely an outcome of recognizing and measuring correct balance sheet amounts—current tax payable, current tax receivable, deferred tax assets, deferred tax liabilities, and tax contingencies.

Because in many tax jurisdictions income is always taxed, but losses are limited, the right to receive credits for taxes paid or credits earned, referred to as deferred tax assets, must be evaluated for realization each period. In essence, a deferred tax asset is a receivable from a taxing jurisdiction for taxes paid in advance, the collectability of which is dependent on having enough future taxable income to deduct them from. Additionally, both deferred tax assets and deferred tax liabilities resulting from prior periods can be adjusted in a current period pursuant to applicable future tax rate changes, characterization, changes in forecasts, or other changes.

After the balance sheet amounts are appropriately recognized and measured, and the total income tax expense computed, an entity must allocate the expense to different parts of comprehensive income. Comprehensive income is used because under both IFRS and US GAAP, certain financial items such as cumulative translation adjustments (due to foreign currency effects) and hedging, are included in other comprehensive income (OCI).

After the income statement, balance sheet, statement of equity, and statement of cash flows are complete, an entity must provide extensive disclosure concerning how the balance sheet and income statement elements of income tax were calculated, what their composition is, when they are expected to be realized, and where they are reflected in the financial statements.

INCOME TAX RECOGNITION

Income tax in its simplest form is income multiplied by the tax rate. The income against which a rate is applied however, is usually different than the income determined under either IFRS or US GAAP. The rest of this chapter, except where specifically stated, assumes that income under IFRS and US GAAP for a particular period is equal. This assumption is used to isolate the differences between IFRS and US GAAP owing solely to the difference in accounting for income tax.

Both IFRS and US GAAP use the statutory (US GAAP) or applicable (IFRS) tax rate multiplied by the taxable income to compute tax expense for ordinary income (e.g., not an item that is subject to another rate, such as capital gains in the United States). Both standards require reconciliation between book income multiplied by the applicable statutory rate to the tax expense reflected in the income statement.

Taxable income differs from book income by the effect of timing or exclusions from taxable income. This is a matter of fact according to the tax rules of the jurisdiction(s) in which an entity produces taxable income. In case of timing difference, taxable income will, all other things being equal, book income either in a prior period or a future period. A common timing difference is an allowance by a taxing jurisdiction of accelerated depreciation for property, plant, and equipment. The rate of depreciation permitted by the tax code is decided by law to achieve a certain political or economic effect. The rate compares to useful life in a financial book sense usually only in orders of magnitude. For instance, accelerated depreciation schedules for buildings are usually based on a longer period than is used for machinery. Consequently, there is almost always a difference between tax and book depreciation. And the difference almost always results in an entity receiving a tax deduction in an earlier period than would be the case using book income.

DEFERRED TAX LIABILITY COMPUTATION

The difference between the carrying values for tax and book produces a *basis* difference. Under both IFRS and US GAAP, with some exceptions unique to each standard, a deferred tax asset or liability is created when the tax and book bases of balance sheet items are different. The basic difference is multiplied by the tax rate that is expected to be in effect when the item will enter into taxable income. Using the example from the previous paragraph, since the entity will use up the tax deduction for depreciation sooner than for book purposes, the entity has a deferred tax liability:

Cost: 100 USD   Year 1 Depreciation: Tax: 34, book 20

At the end of year one, the difference between the carrying value of tax and book is 14 (Book = 80, Tax = 66). The 14 carrying value difference multiplied by the rate expected to be in effect when the liability will be paid is the deferred tax liability. If the rate is 40%, the deferred tax liability is 5.6 (40% × 14).

While the deferred tax liability would have been identical had the difference in profit and loss, 14, been used rather than the difference in carrying values, the basis differences are used. This is because it is sometimes the case that not all, or more than, the item amount will be included in taxable income. This could be the case for share-based compensation. Some proportion of the book or tax expense will be excluded from the other because of the inherent differences in the way share-based compensation is calculated. These are referred to as *permanent differences*. Permanent differences always result in an incremental difference between the statutory or applicable rate and the effective rate. The effective rate is the tax expense/benefit divided by pretax income/loss.

Another aspect of deferred tax computation that gives rise to differences between tax expense and book income multiplied by the tax rate is that that the tax rates can be different in the future. If we change the prior example and propose that tax rates in four years will be 45%, the deferred tax liability would be 14 × 45%, or 6.3 since in years four and five, when the book expense is recognized, the tax rate applied to taxable income, which will "lack" the deduction for depreciation since it has been fully recorded in the tax return as of year 3, will be 45%. Since the offset for the recognition of the deferred tax liability is tax expense, **net** income is different than what would be recorded if book income were multiplied by the tax rate.

DEFERRED TAX ASSET COMPUTATION

The same mechanics apply to cases in which taxable income is higher in the current period, which produces a deferred tax asset. If an entity must include a deposit received from a customer (unearned income) in year one, but will recognize the revenue in year two, the deferred tax asset will equal the balance in unearned income multiplied by next year's tax rate. If the deposit is $200 USD, and the tax rate for the following year is expected to be 40%, the deferred tax asset will be $80 USD. If in year two the revenue is still not completely earned (for instance if the deposit relates to a multiple deliverable arrangement), the deferred tax asset will be the remaining balance multiplied by the tax rate for year three. If the unearned income is $100 USD at the end of year three, and the tax rate is expected to hold steady at 40%, the deferred tax asset is $40 USD. To effect this change, the entity would credit deferred tax assets and debit income tax expense. This has the effect of "normalizing" the effective tax rate since the lower taxable income would produce tax expense that is lower than book income multiplied by the tax rate. The debit to deferred tax expense "trues up" the tax rate.

The reduction in future taxable income that is measured by the deferred tax asset will only be realized if the entity can ultimately obtain a refund from the tax jurisdiction. This in turn depends on whether an entity can deduct a future loss, since most jurisdictions, to protect tax revenues, will only refund taxes to an entity to the extent it has paid taxes in the past.

This uncertainty of realizing the deferred tax assets requires entities, under both IFRS and US GAAP, to formally assess each period the likelihood that deferred tax assets will be credited to the entity.

TAX RATES

The tax rates applied to timing differences, for both IFRS and US GAAP, are those that are expected to apply when the items will enter into taxable income. For US GAAP, only enacted rates are permitted. IFRS requires either enacted or *substantially enacted* rates.

ASC 740-10-30

Tax Rates

Applicable Tax Rate Used to Measure Deferred Taxes

8   *Paragraph 740-10-10-3 establishes that the objective is to measure a deferred tax liability or asset using the enacted tax rate(s) expected to apply to taxable income in the periods in which the deferred tax liability or asset is expected to be settled or realized. Deferred taxes shall not be accounted for on a discounted basis.*

9   *Under tax law with a graduated tax rate structure, if taxable income exceeds a specified amount, all taxable income is taxed, in substance, at a single flat tax rate. That tax rate shall be used for measurement of a deferred tax liability or asset by entities for which graduated tax rates are not a significant factor. Entities for which graduated tax rates are a significant factor shall measure a deferred tax liability or asset using the average graduated tax rate applicable to the amount of estimated annual taxable income in the periods in which the deferred tax liability or asset is estimated to be settled or realized. See Example 16 (paragraph 740-10-55-136) for an illustration of the determination of the average graduated tax rate. Other provisions of enacted tax laws shall be considered when determining the tax rate to apply to certain types of temporary differences and carryforwards (for example, the tax law may provide for different tax rates on ordinary income and capital gains). If there is a phased-in change in tax rates, determination of the applicable tax rate requires knowledge about when deferred tax liabilities and assets will be settled and realized.*

The following is excerpted from IAS 12:

Measurement

46   *Current tax liabilities (assets) for the current and prior periods shall be measured at the amount expected to be paid to (recovered from) the taxation authorities, using the tax rates (and tax laws) that have been enacted or substantively enacted by the end of the reporting period.*

47   *Deferred tax assets and liabilities shall be measured at the tax rates that are expected to apply to the period when the asset is realized or the liability is settled, based on tax rates (and tax laws) that have been enacted or substantively enacted by the end of the reporting period.*

However, IAS 12.48 puts specific context around the use of substantially enacted rates:

> 48 *Current and deferred tax assets and liabilities are* usually *measured using the tax* rates *(and tax laws)* that have been enacted. *However, in some jurisdictions, announcements of tax rates (and tax laws) by the government have the substantive effect of actual enactment, which may follow the announcement by a period of several months. In these circumstances, tax assets and liabilities are measured using the announced tax rate (and tax laws).*

IAS 12 does not contain examples or guidance of whether substantially enacted rates are applied to only those countries for which announcement is equivalent to enactment, or for any country. Previous IFRS and US GAAP convergence efforts (which have been stalled indefinitely) for income taxes produced discussion on clarifying what *substantially enacted* means. This indicates that there was some diversity in practice. Nonetheless, if an entity has a reasonable expectation based on sound facts that a tax rate will change because legislation has advanced far enough to warrant a high degree of probability of enactment, that rate can be used. This difference underscores a key philosophical difference between US GAAP and IFRS. On the balance scale between relevance and reliability, IFRS weighs on the relevance side. US GAAP, conversely, emphasizes reliability and legal certainty.

When graduated rates are a significant element in an entity's tax calculation, both IFRS and US GAAP require factoring this into the applied rate. US GAAP specifically directs users to use the rate applicable to the average income for the years projected. IAS 12 does not include specific guidance, but requires the use of average rates. Because US GAAP guidance about calculating average rates is intuitive and falls within the *IFRS Framework*, there is no difference between IFRS and US GAAP, when, given fully enacted rates, graduated rates are a significant factor in computing tax liabilities. Because both standards have similar definitions of materiality, this concept would not produce any divergence.

TAX RATES: MANNER OF RECOVERY OR SETTLEMENT

The tax rate applicable to certain items of comprehensive income depends in many jurisdictions on the manner in which the deferred tax is recovered. One such instance is when earnings retained in a foreign subsidiary are subject to excess profits tax. IFRS clearly defines the treatment for this circumstance. US GAAP guidance is largely implicit with regard to accounting for manner of recovery. There is direct guidance concerning dividends from foreign subsidiaries, but this guidance on accounting for special credits indirectly prohibits recognition of different tax rates for the same asset or liability depending on the manner in which it is realized.

IFRS requires that the tax rate applied in these circumstances to calculate deferred tax assets or liabilities are consistent with the manner of recovery:

IAS 12

> 51 *The measurement of deferred tax liabilities and deferred tax assets shall reflect the tax consequences that would follow from the manner in which the entity*

expects, at the end of the reporting period, to recover or settle the carrying amount of its assets and liabilities.

52 *Example A: An asset has a carrying amount of 100 and a tax base of 60. A tax rate of 20 percent would apply if the assets were sold and a tax rate of 30 percent would apply to other income.*

The entity recognizes a deferred tax liability of 8 (40 at 20 percent) if it expects to sell the asset without further use and a deferred tax liability of 12 (40 at 30 percent) if it expects to retain the asset and recover its carrying amount through use.

US GAAP does not employ this concept. The effective tax rate applied is gross of any tax credits to be received and the credit is recognized upon remittance, although the valuation of deferred tax assets may result in partial recognition of the difference in tax rates. The paragraph that most closely demonstrates this is 740-10-30-13:

ASC 740-10-30

13 *As required by paragraph 740-10-25-37, the tax benefit of special deductions ordinarily is recognized no earlier than the year in which those special deductions are deductible on the tax return. However, some portion of the future tax effects of special deductions are implicitly recognized in determining the average graduated tax rate to be used for measuring deferred taxes when graduated tax rates are a significant factor and the need for a valuation allowance for deferred tax assets. In those circumstances, implicit recognition is unavoidable because those special deductions are one of the determinants of future taxable income and future taxable income determines the average graduated tax rate and sometimes determines the need for a valuation allowance.*

The above paragraph assumes that the IFRS example IAS 12.52 A is a tax credit, which is reasonable given the description.

With regard to dividends, however, in certain circumstances, a lower, distributed earnings rate may apply for US GAAP:

ASC 740-10-5

41 *The accounting required in the preceding paragraph may differ in the consolidated financial statements of a parent that includes a foreign subsidiary that receives a tax credit for dividends paid, if the parent expects to remit the subsidiary's earnings. Assume that the parent has not availed itself of the exception for foreign unremitted earnings that may be available under paragraph 740-30-25-17. In that case, in the consolidated financial statements of a parent, the future tax credit that will be received when dividends are paid and the deferred tax effects related to the operations of the foreign subsidiary shall be recognized based on the distributed rate because, as assumed in that case, the parent is not applying the indefinite reversal criteria exception that may be available under that paragraph. However, the undistributed rate shall be used in the consolidated financial statements to the extent that the parent has not provided for deferred taxes on the unremitted earnings of the foreign subsidiary as a result of applying the indefinite reversal criteria recognition exception.*

This guidance limits the application of a different rate based on manner of recovery only in the context of consolidated financial statements. However, if an entity using IFRS was also not providing for income taxes because it had the ability to control dividends and the dividends would not be remitted in the foreseeable future (IAS 12.39), then the decision of what rate to use would be moot.

DEFERRED TAX VALUATIONS

Both US GAAP and IFRS required deferred tax assets to be evaluated for realization each period. US GAAP requires full recognition and a valuation allowance to the extent that deferred tax assets are not deemed realizable for the current reporting period. IFRS prohibits recognition for deferred tax assets if their realization is not probable. The practical effect of this difference is not substantive. Both standards require disclosures about tax expense or benefit related to deferred tax assets (this will be covered in detail later in the chapter). Also, in practice, an inventory of tax attributes must be maintained to measure the net deferred tax assets that are reflected in the balance sheet. Consequently, there is no difference in an entity's day-to-day tax planning and accounting with regard to deferred tax assets.

Both standards identify four classes of future taxable income against which deferred tax assets can be recognized, which are subject to varying degrees of certainty.

1. The reversal of deferred tax liabilities will result in highly certain taxable income. Absent any other elements, reversal of deferred tax liabilities will result in taxable income, which can be used to offset deferred tax assets. In summary, these amounts are based on events that have already occurred.
2. Future taxable income exclusive of the reversal of deferred tax liabilities. This is basically future book income that will result in cash inflows.
3. Taxable income in taxable carryback years. Where allowable by the jurisdiction, current income can be reduced by past losses, up to a certain number of years (i.e., three years)
4. Tax planning strategies. These involve accelerating or delaying income or expenses includable in taxable income.

While worded differently, under both US GAAP and IFRS an entity must have convincing evidence that a reduction in deferred tax assets is not needed in the presence of recent or projected losses. Factors that may support this assertion are the significance of recent one-time losses or a substantial backlog of recent orders.

ASC 740-10-55-13 to 22 includes guidance on the level of detail that should be used to compute a valuation allowance. In summary, this subsection recommends that scheduling can be minimized as long as the method for doing so is logical, systematic, and bases conclusions on enacted tax law. While IFRS does not include this type of guidance, the underlying premise contained in the *IFRS Framework* that financial statement elements must be representationally faithful would likely entail some sort of scheduling to calculate materially correct positions.

ASC 740-10-30-28, like IAS 12.29(b) permits entities to include the effect of tax planning strategies in determining valuation allowances for deferred tax assets. Both standards have similar guidance that provide examples of tax strategies. Both specify that tax planning strategies are actions where the only purpose is to increase the realization of deferred tax assets. However, US GAAP specifically directs that the cost of these strategies reduce the deferred tax assets that might otherwise be realized:

ASC 740-10-30

19 This Subtopic refers to those actions as tax-planning strategies. An entity shall consider tax-planning strategies in determining the amount of valuation allowance required. Significant expenses to implement a tax-planning strategy or any significant losses that would be recognized if that strategy were implemented (net of any recognizable tax benefits associated with those expenses or losses) shall be included in the valuation allowance.

IFRS does not include such guidance. It follows that only the net effect of tax savings would be included in the calculation of deferred tax assets to be recognized. However, IAS12.9(b) conceptually would include the cost of tax planning in the valuation of deferred tax assets:

IAS 12

9 When there are insufficient taxable temporary differences relating to the same taxation authority and the same taxable entity, the deferred tax asset is recognized to the extent that

a. It is probable that the entity will have sufficient taxable profit relating to the same taxation authority and the same taxable entity in the same period as the reversal of the deductible temporary difference (or in the periods into which a tax loss arising from the deferred tax asset can be carried back or forward). In evaluating whether it will have sufficient taxable profit in future periods, an entity ignores taxable amounts arising from deductible temporary differences that are expected to originate in future periods, because the deferred tax asset arising from these deductible temporary differences will itself require future taxable profit in order to be utilized.

b. Tax planning opportunities are available to the entity that will create taxable profit *in appropriate periods.*

IAS12.9(b) specifies the valuation of deferred tax assets includes incremental taxable profit, a net figure. Consequently, it stands to reason that the cost of tax planning strategies is deducted from the valuation of deferred tax assets.

TAX POSITIONS

US GAAP ASC 740 contains specific guidance regarding the measurement and recognition of liabilities that represent amounts for tax deductions taken on a tax return that are likely to be settled unfavorably. This is regarded as a *tax position*. US GAAP defines a tax position as follows:

A position in a previously filed tax return or a position expected to be taken in a future tax return that is reflected in measuring current or deferred income tax assets and liabilities for interim or annual periods.

A tax position can result in a permanent reduction of income taxes payable, a deferral of income taxes otherwise currently payable to future years, or a change in the expected reality of deferred tax assets. The term tax position also encompasses, but is not limited to

a. *A decision not to file a tax return*
b. *An allocation or a shift of income between jurisdictions*
c. *The characterization of income or a decision to exclude reporting taxable income in a tax return*
d. *A decision to classify a transaction, entity, or other position in a tax return as tax exempt*
e. *An entity's status, including its status as a pass-through entity or a tax-exempt not-for-profit entity*

The guidance requires an entity to first determine whether a settlement of the tax position is more likely than not (50% or greater) to be required. In other words, it is more likely that not than a tax position will **not** be sustained upon examination. If a tax position is more likely than not to require settlement, it recognizes a liability for the amount as the one that has a minimum cumulative probability over 50% of being assessed by the tax jurisdiction in question.

Here is an example:

#	Probability	Settlement amount	Expected value	Cumulative USD	Cumulative probability
1	0.07	3,000	210	210	0.07
2	0.15	2,000	300	510	0.22
3	0.15	1,500	225	735	0.37
4	0.18	1,000	180	915	0.55
5	0.20	750	150	1,065	0.75
6	0.25	500	125	1,190	1.00

In this example, row 4 indicates that there is a 55% probability that the settlement amount will be $915 USD. Consequently $915 USD will be recognized as the liability since 55% is the first cumulative percentage that is higher than 50%, or more likely than not.

An entity must determine if a tax position is more likely than not to be sustained based on the following assumptions:

ASC 740-10-5

7 *In making the required assessment of the more-likely-than-not criterion:*

a. *It shall be presumed that the tax position will be examined by the relevant taxing authority that has full knowledge of all relevant information.*
b. *Technical merits of a tax position derive from sources of authorities in the tax law (legislation and statutes, legislative intent, regulations, rulings, and case law) and their applicability to the facts and circumstances of the tax position. When the past administrative practices and precedents of the taxing authority in its dealings with the entity or similar entities are widely un-*

derstood, for example, by preparers, tax practitioners, and auditors, those practices and precedents shall be taken into account.

c. *Each tax position shall be evaluated without consideration of the possibility of offset or aggregation with other positions.*

The assumptions in 740-10-5-7 are designed to bring a measure of objectivity to the determination of whether an amount will be required for settlement of the position.

ASC 740 also contains reconciliation requirements that break down the movements in an unrecognized tax position into flows that demonstrate the manner and timing in which an unrecognized tax position is recognized and derecognized, either fully or partially. Disclosures also require a sensitivity analysis about tax positions that are likely to change within the following twelve months. Also included are past tax periods that are still subject to review by the relevant tax authorities.

ASC 740-10-50

15 *All entities shall disclose all of the following at the end of each annual reporting period presented:*

a. *Subparagraph superseded by Accounting Standards Update No. 2009-06*

b. *Subparagraph superseded by Accounting Standards Update No. 2009-06*

c. *The total amounts of interest and penalties recognized in the statement of operations and the total amounts of interest and penalties recognized in the statement of financial position*

d. *For positions for which it is reasonably possible that the total amounts of unrecognized tax benefits will significantly increase or decrease within 12 months of the reporting date:*

   1. *The nature of the uncertainty*

   2. *The nature of the event that could occur in the next 12 months that would cause the change*

   3. *An estimate of the range of the reasonably possible change or a statement that an estimate of the range cannot be made.*

e. *A description of tax years that remain subject to examination by major tax jurisdictions.*

15A *Public entities shall disclose both of the following at the end of each annual reporting period presented:*

a. *A tabular reconciliation of the total amounts of unrecognized tax benefits at the beginning and end of the period, which shall include at a minimum:*

   1. *The gross amounts of the increases and decreases in unrecognized tax benefits as a result of tax positions taken during a prior period*

   2. *The gross amounts of increases and decreases in unrecognized tax benefits as a result of tax positions taken during the current period*

   3. *The amounts of decreases in the unrecognized tax benefits relating to settlements with taxing authorities*

   4. *Reductions to unrecognized tax benefits as a result of a lapse of the applicable statute of limitations.*

    b. *The total amount of unrecognized tax benefits that, if recognized, would affect the effective tax rate.*

IAS 37, *Provisions and Contingencies,* is the relevant standard under IFRS to account for tax positions.

14 A provision shall be recognized when

    a. *An entity has a present obligation (legal or constructive) as a result of a past event.*
    b. *It is probable that an outflow of resources embodying economic benefits will be required to settle the obligation.*
    c. *A reliable estimate can be made of the amount of the obligation.*

If these conditions are not met, no provision shall be recognized.

Provisions are measured as the best estimate of the expenditure required to settle the present obligation at the end of the reporting period.

In the context of tax positions that are likely to require a settlement, the liability is measured like any other provision as prescribed by IAS 37. This means that in many cases, the amount of liability for tax positions will be different than the prescriptive method required for US GAAP. Additionally, because neither IAS 37 nor IAS 12 addresses uncertain tax positions, it is not necessary for an entity to adhere to the assumptions in ASC 740-10-5-7. Consequently, if an entity believes, based on past experience, that a tax position is not "more likely than not" to result in a settlement, it would not accrue an amount. Likewise, an entity may consider the offsetting nature of other tax positions, unlike the directive in 740-10-5-7(c).

However, because the subparagraph IAS 37.14(b) specifies that for a provision to be recognized it must be probable that economic resources will be required to settle the obligation, the positions that are recognized will in many cases be the same under US GAAP and IFRS, although the amount will likely be different.

Since IAS 37 is followed for accounting for uncertain tax positions, the disclosure also needs to be in accordance with this standard. Following are the disclosures for IAS 37:

IAS 37

84 For each class of provision, an entity shall disclose

    a. *The carrying amount at the beginning and end of the period*
    b. *Additional provisions made in the period, including increases to existing provisions*
    c. *Amounts used (i.e., incurred and charged against the provision) during the period*
    d. *Unused amounts reversed during the period*
    e. *The increase during the period in the discounted amount arising from the passage of time and the effect of any change in the discount rate*

Comparative information is not required.

85   An entity shall disclose the following for each class of provision:

    a.   A brief description of the nature of the obligation and the expected timing of any resulting outflows of economic benefits.

    b.   An indication of the uncertainties about the amount or timing of those outflows. Where necessary to provide adequate information, an entity shall disclose the major assumptions made concerning future events, as addressed in paragraph 48.

    c.   The amount of any expected reimbursement, stating the amount of any asset that has been recognized for that expected reimbursement.

86   Unless the possibility of any outflow in settlement is remote, an entity shall disclose for each class of contingent liability at the end of the reporting period a brief description of the nature of the contingent liability and, where practicable

    a.   An estimate of its financial effect, measured under paragraphs 36-52

    b.   An indication of the uncertainties relating to the amount or timing of any outflow

    c.   The possibility of any reimbursement

87   In determining which provisions or contingent liabilities may be aggregated to form a class, it is necessary to consider whether the nature of the items is sufficiently similar for a single statement about them to fulfill the requirements of paragraphs 85(a) and (b) and 86(a) and (b). Thus, it may be appropriate to treat as a single class of provision amounts relating to warranties of different products, but it would not be appropriate to treat as single class amounts relating to normal warranties and amounts that are subject to legal proceedings.

88   Where a provision and a contingent liability arise from the same set of circumstances, an entity makes the disclosures required by paragraphs 84-86 in a way that shows the link between the provision and the contingent liability.

Below is a tabular comparison of the disclosure requirements for tax positions:

Tax Position Disclosure Comparison

#	ASC 740-10-50-15	IAS 37	Analysis
1.	1. The gross amounts of the **increases** and **decreases** in unrecognized tax benefits as a result of tax positions taken during a **prior** period 2. The gross amounts of increases and decreases in unrecognized tax benefits as a result of tax positions taken during the **current** period 4. Reductions to unrecognized tax benefits as a result of a lapse of the applicable statute of limitations	84(b) additional provisions made in the period, including increases to existing provisions 84(d) unused amounts reversed during the period 85 An entity shall disclose the following for each class of provision: (a) A brief description of the nature of the obligation and the expected timing of any resulting outflows of economic benefits	The requirement of IAS 37 is aligned with those of ASC 740-10-5-7, provided that an entity defines a tax position as a "class" of provision. This is likely since an amount owed to a government body is a different nature and risk than, for example, a trade obligation. While IAS 37 would not require an analysis of the effect that current or prior year positions had on the balance, doing so may be necessary for the financial statement user to understand the risks and nature per IAS 1, *Financial Statements*, paragraphs 125 to 133. See Note 1 at the bottom of this table.

#		ASC 740-10-50-15	IAS 37	Analysis
2.	3.	The amounts of decreases in the unrecognized tax benefits relating to settlements with taxing authorities	84(c) amounts used (i.e., incurred and charged against the provision) during the period	The amounts paid against the provisions would likely be disclosed as a "class" of provisions.
3.	e.	A description of tax years that remain subject to examination by major tax jurisdictions.	N/A	There is nothing in either IAS 37 or IAS 12 that requires disclosure of tax years that are open. If open tax years were a source of significant uncertainty, per IAS 1.125, that fact would need to be disclosed, if material.
	c.	The total amounts of interest and penalties recognized in the statement of operations and the total amounts of interest and penalties recognized in the statement of financial position	N/A	There is nothing in either IAS 37 or IAS 12 that requires disclosure of interest and penalties as a result of tax positions. There also is no specific requirement to accrue interest and penalties if it were not reasonably expected to be part of a settlement. If interest and penalties were a source of significant uncertainty, per IAS 1, that fact would need to be disclosed, if material.
4.	d.	For positions for which it is reasonably possible that the total amounts of unrecognized tax benefits will significantly increase or decrease within 12 months of the reporting date: 1. The nature of the uncertainty 2. The nature of the event that could occur in the next 12 months that would cause the change 3. An estimate of the range of the reasonably possible change or a statement that an estimate of the range cannot be made	N/A	IAS 1 would require some disclosure similar to 740-10-5-7(d) but only if significant.

Note 1: IAS 1.125 An entity shall disclose information about the assumptions it makes about the future, and other major sources of estimation uncertainty at the end of the reporting period, that have a significant risk of resulting in a material adjustment to the carrying amounts of assets and liabilities within the next financial year. In respect of those assets and liabilities, the notes shall include details of their nature and their carrying amount at the end of the quarter.

Overall, the disclosures for uncertain tax positions are much greater under US GAAP than IFRS.

INCOME TAX INTEREST AND PENALTIES

ASC 740-10-45-25 permits entities to make a policy election to classify interest on uncertain tax positions as either a tax expense or an interest expense. This paragraph also permits an entity to present penalties as a tax expense or other expense. There is no guidance in IFRS concerning these classifications. Consequently, per IAS 1, *Financial Statements*, the inclusion of interest and penalties for tax positions is a policy or practice choice that is consistent with *The Framework*.

PROFIT AND LOSS PRESENTATION

Both IFRS and US GAAP require overall income tax expense to be allocated to continuing operations and other components of comprehensive income. These components include discontinued operations, change in accounting policies that, for practical purposes, are all recognized in the current period, and other comprehensive income (i.e., hedging effect). US GAAP also includes extraordinary items (amounts that are both unusual and infrequent) to which initial income tax expense is allocated. US GAAP terms this process *intraperiod tax allocation*.

ASC 740-20 contains explicit guidance and examples regarding intraperiod allocation. The basic concept is that both current and deferred tax expense must be allocated to continuing operations without consideration of tax expense related to other components of profitability, such as discontinued operations or extraordinary items. The main component is simply operating income multiplied by the effective tax rate. However, changes in valuation allowances that relate to prior years with respect to future years, with some specific exceptions, regardless of the component of comprehensive income to which they relate, are also included in a tax on continuing operations. Conversely, the effect of valuation allowance on current year tax expense related to another component of comprehensive income is allocated to that component. In other words, it is only prior year tax effects that are recognized in a tax on continuing operations, with the following exceptions:

ASC 740-20-45

11   *c. An increase or decrease in contributed capital (for example, deductible expenditures reported as a reduction of the proceeds from issuing capital stock).*

   d. Expenses for employee stock options recognized differently for financial reporting and tax purposes as required by Subtopic 718-740. An employee stock ownership plan and a stock option plan are analogous. Both are compensatory arrangements and both sometimes result in tax deductions for amounts that are not presently recognized as compensation expense in the financial statements under existing generally accepted accounting principles (GAAP). The tax benefits of both are reported as a credit to shareholders' equity.

   e. Dividends that are paid on unallocated shares held by an employee stock ownership plan and that are charged to retained earnings. This is different from a tax deduction received for the payment of dividends on allocated shares held by an employee stock ownership plan that

> *represents, in substance, an exemption from taxation of an equivalent amount of earnings for which the tax benefit shall be recognized as a reduction of tax expense and shall not be allocated directly to shareholders' equity.*
>
> *f. Deductible temporary differences and carryforwards that existed at the date of a quasi reorganization.*

US GAAP prescribes that the following are also reflected in income from continuing operations:

ASC 740-20-45

> 8 *The amount allocated to continuing operations is the tax effect of the pretax income or loss from continuing operations that occurred during the year, plus or minus income tax effects of*
>
> a. *Changes in circumstances that cause a change in judgment about the realization of deferred tax assets in future years (see paragraph 740-10-45-20 for a discussion of exceptions to this allocation for certain items)*
> b. *Changes in tax laws or rates (see paragraph 740-10-35-4)*
> c. *Changes in tax status (see paragraphs 740-10-25-32 and 740-10-40-6)*
> d. *Tax-deductible dividends paid to shareholders (except as set forth in paragraph 740-20-45-11(e) for dividends paid on unallocated shares held by an employee stock ownership plan or any other stock compensation arrangement).*
>
> *The remainder is allocated to items other than continuing operations in accordance with the provisions of paragraphs 740-20-45-12 and 740-20-45-14.*

Conversely, IAS 12 does not contain any exceptions to allocating changes in valuation allowance compared to initial recognition. Both the original tax effect and subsequent changes in measurement of deferred tax assets and liabilities are allocated to the same component of other comprehensive income.

IAS 12

> 63 *In exceptional circumstances it may be difficult to determine the amount of current and deferred tax that relates to items recognized outside profit or loss (either in other comprehensive income or directly in equity). This may be the case, for example, when*
>
> a. *There are graduated rates of income tax and it is impossible to determine the rate at which a specific component of taxable profit (tax loss) has been taxed.*
> b. *A change in the tax rate or other tax rules affect a deferred tax asset or liability relating (in whole or in part) to an item that was previously recognized outside profit or loss.*
> c. *An entity determines that a deferred tax asset should be recognized, or should no longer be recognized in full, and the deferred tax asset relates (in whole or in part) to an item that was previously recognized outside profit or loss.*
>
> *In such cases, the current and deferred tax related to items that are recognized outside profit or loss are based on a reasonable pro rata allocation of the*

current and deferred tax of the entity in the tax jurisdiction concerned, or other method that achieves a more appropriate allocation in the circumstances.

INTRAPERIOD ALLOCATION TO OTHER THAN CONTINUING OPERATIONS

As covered in the previous section, US GAAP establishes precedence with regard to intraperiod allocation. Specifically, total tax expense or benefit is first allocated to income from continuing operations. The remainder is attributed to other components of comprehensive income.

ASC 740-20-45

Single Item of Allocation Other Than Continuing Operations

12 If there is only one item other than continuing operations, the portion of income tax expense or benefit for the year that remains after the allocation to continuing operations shall be allocated to that item.

Multiple Items of Allocation Other Than Continuing Operations

14 If there are two or more items other than continuing operations, the amount that remains after the allocation to continuing operations shall be allocated among those other items in proportion to their individual effects on income tax expense or benefit for the year. When there are two or more items other than continuing operations, the sum of the separately calculated, individual effects of each item sometimes may not equal the amount of income tax expense or benefit for the year that remains after the allocation to continuing operations. In those circumstances, the procedures to allocate the remaining amount to items other than continuing operations are as follows:

a. Determine the effect on income tax expense or benefit for the year of the total net loss for all net loss items.

b. Apportion the tax benefit determined in (a) ratably to each net loss item.

c. Determine the amount that remains, that is, the difference between the amount to be allocated to all items other than continuing operations and the amount allocated to all net loss items.

d. Apportion the tax expense determined in (c) ratably to each net gain item.

ASC Section 740-20-55 contains several examples of applying the above allocation methods.

IFRS does not contain this primacy of income from continuing operations. There is nothing in either IAS 12 or the *IFRS Framework* that would support the concept in ASC 740-20-45-12 to 14. The allocation of expense to the various components of comprehensive income must be made on detailed calculations, or, where the cost to do so is prohibitive, a pro rata allocation.

BALANCE SHEET PRESENTATION

US GAAP requires that deferred tax balances that are related to a current or noncurrent asset be classified the same way. For example, if a deferred tax asset is related to a provision for doubtful accounts, it must be classified as current assets, since trade accounts receivable are current assets.

IFRS specifically requires that all deferred tax assets and liabilities are classified as noncurrent:

IAS 15

> 6 *When an entity presents current and noncurrent assets, and current and noncurrent liabilities, as separate classifications in its statement of financial position, it shall not classify deferred tax assets (liabilities) as current assets (liabilities).*

Both IFRS and US GAAP permit offsetting of deferred assets and liabilities only when they are with the same jurisdiction and can be legally offset with each other. IFRS further directs that where only certain tax-deferred tax assets and liabilities can be offset (for example, those for a single tax year), the remaining balances must be presented gross.

EXCEPTIONS TO TAX RECOGNITION—INVESTMENTS IN SUBSIDIARIES

IFRS and US GAAP both require an entity to not recognize deferred tax positions in subsidiaries under certain circumstances. For IFRS, the scope of deferral is all subsidiaries, meaning the subsidiary does not need to be foreign. However, this is the most likely case since it is usually the case that a subsidiary in the same country as the parent would likely not be able to defer taxation.

IAS 39

> *An entity shall recognize a deferred tax liability for all taxable temporary differences associated with investments in subsidiaries, branches and associates, and interests in joint ventures, except to the extent that both of the following conditions are satisfied:*
>
> > a. *The parent, investor, or venturer is able to control the timing or the reversal of the temporary difference.*
> > b. *It is probable that the temporary difference will not reverse in the foreseeable future.*

The exception under US GAAP is more specifically defined. It is only applicable for a greater-than-50%-owned investee or joint venture that requires unanimous consent of its investors, and it must be either a foreign or a domestic subsidiary that was in place before a certain date:

ASC 740-30-25

> 18 *As indicated in paragraph 740-10-25-3, a deferred tax liability shall not be recognized for either of the following types of temporary differences unless it becomes apparent that those temporary differences will reverse in the foreseeable future:*

> a. *An excess of the amount for financial reporting over the tax basis of an investment in a foreign subsidiary or a foreign corporate joint venture that is essentially permanent in duration*
> b. *Undistributed earnings of a domestic subsidiary or a domestic corporate joint venture that is essentially permanent in duration that arose in fiscal years beginning on or before December 15, 1992. A last-in, first-out (LIFO) pattern determines whether reversals pertain to differences that arose in fiscal years beginning on or before December 15, 1992.*

IAS 12.39 is aligned with 740-30-25-18 since the requirements for nonrecognition rest on the probability that the earnings will not be remitted soon and controlled. Note however, that the paragraph does not indicate control needs to be as is defined in IFRS statements for consolidation. While that type of relationship would be strongly indicative, agreements connected with the investee must be considered. Indeed, IAS 12.42 indicates that an equity-accounted subsidiary will refrain from recognition of a deferred-tax position if there is an agreement in place that gives control of dividends to the investor:

IAS 12

> 42 *An investor in an associate does not control that entity and is usually not in a position to determine its dividend policy. Therefore,* in the absence of an agreement requiring that the profits of the associate will not be distributed in the foreseeable future, *an investor recognizes a deferred tax liability arising from taxable temporary differences associated with its investment in the associate.*

The above indicates that the control of the remittance is the criteria that must be satisfied in order to not recognize deferred-tax balances. Consequently, in the case of less-than-50%-owned investee with an agreement about remittance of dividends, US GAAP will require recognition of the deferred tax positions, but IFRS would prohibit such recognition.

GENERAL DISCLOSURES

Both IFRS and US GAAP required extensive disclosures for income taxes. Both require analysis of tax expense, reconciliation of the effective tax rate with the statutory rate. US GAAP requires significant disclosures for uncertain tax positions, whereas IFRS requires only a roll forward of deferred tax assets. While the contents differ, the disclosures vary with the difference between the two standards.

CHAPTER SUMMARY

Accounting for income taxes is very similar under US GAAP and IFRS. Both require a balance sheet approach, measurement of deferred positions based on tax rates that will be in effect at the time of reversal, and valuation of deferred tax assets. Differences include the criteria for deferral in deferred taxes for investments in subsidiaries as well as accounting and disclosures of uncertain tax positions.

12 INVESTMENTS IN SUBSIDIARIES

Consolidation, or presenting the results, cash flow, and financial position of many entities as a single one, is a key tool for users of financial statements to understand the amount, timing and risks to the cash flows that are under the purview of a management. Consolidation allows a user, say an investor, to evaluate the kind of job that current management is doing with the resources entrusted to it. It provides a bird-eye view of the entity's assets, obligations, and equity. Without consolidation, someone wanting to assess the performance of the company with multiple divisions would have to lay out all the financial results of subsidiaries, determine how much business the companies did with each other, whether that business was done at arm's length, and put all those together to present one picture of the financial performance of the company.

The principles used in consolidation are designed to do the above for the user. But the first question that must be asked about whether an entity is consolidated is whether the management of that entity can effectively influence the results of another entity. If entities over which a manager did not have effective control were consolidated, the manager would either get credit for good results that were not his/her doing, or get unfairly tainted by poor performance that he/she was not responsible for. In either circumstance, an investor's assessment of the skill of the manager would be skewed and not from the basis of a solid judgment from which it could decide whether to continue its interest in the entity.

In many cases, who controls an entity is clear. The simplest situation is a company with one class of equity, minimal debt, and a traditional corporate structure. This may be the case of a vertically integrated manufacturer of steel. A steel producer may own an iron mine, for example. The company that owns the mine extracts the ore and sells it to the steel company. The steel company owns 100% of the stock. The steel company obviously controls the mine company and it must be consolidated.

In some cases, who controls the mine might not be clear. What if the steel company in the above example sold a 50% share in the mining company? Should the steel company consolidate the mining company? Depending on which standard, IFRS or US GAAP, is used, the answer can be different depending on the circumstances. What if the steel company sells only a 40% share? Again, the answer can be different between US GAAP and IFRS.

CONSOLIDATION UNDER IFRS

In May 2011, the International Accounting Standards Board released IFRS 10, *Consolidated Financial Statements.* IFRS 10 is effective January 1, 2013, but can be adopted early. While the overarching principle is the same as the predecessors, IFRS 10 unified IAS 27, *Consolidated and Separate Financial Statements,* and SIC 13, addressing traditional and risk-and-rewards circumstances, respectively into a single model. The most analogous US GAAP equivalent of SIC 13 was accounting for variable interest entities (ASC 840, formerly FIN 45[R]).

In contrast to US GAAP, IFRS 10 applies a single concept with three significant parts to any consolidation situation. US GAAP has numerous exceptions depending on the type of entity. Moreover, IFRS considers the parent company's potential ownership stakes (e.g., options, contracts to acquire shares) in the assessment of whether an entity controls another.

IFRS 10

At its core, IFRS 10 defines when an entity must consolidate the financial statements of another entity. The standard's edifice is the definition of control. As defined by IFRS 10, control is the ability of an entity to direct the relevant activities of an entity whose return is exposed and entitled to, and for which it can affect the variability of those returns.

Under IFRS 10, control has three components:

1. Power over the investee
2. Exposure or rights to variable returns
3. The ability to effect the variability of those returns

A relationship between the entity and a potential subsidiary must have **all** of the above to consolidate an entity.

POWER

IAS 27 requires consolidation when an entity "… has the power to govern the financial and operating policies of an entity so as to obtain benefits from its activities." IFRS 10 defines power as "An investor has power over an investee when the investor has existing rights that give it the current ability to direct the relevant activities, that is, the activities that significantly affect the investee's returns."

The main reason for the change in defining power was that the IAS 27 definition could require consolidation when an entity only controlled *administrative* activities (i.e., choosing a lender, selecting auditors), ones that did not significantly affect the returns. This led to distortions in applying the principle of including results in an entity that controls it, with all the deficiencies in assessing management performance that accompanies this circumstance. IFRS 10, instead, focuses more on the substance of the relationship than the form. Obviously the intent of IAS 27 was also substance over form—a pervasive constant underlying IFRS. The issue was that policies and the management use of them were not clearly defined from entity to entity. To remedy this disparity, IFRS 10 requires identification of relevant activities.

The focus on relevant activities does not mean that ownership of instruments of a potential subsidiary is unimportant. IFRS 10 does spend considerable time on describing the significance of an entity controlling more than 50% of another's equity instruments. In fact, it also takes into account existing rights to acquire more equity shares, even though they remain unexercised (this will be covered later in the chapter).

Like US GAAP, under IFRS, owning more than 50% of the equity interests is a strong indicator of control. However, IFRS requires considering whether that majority interest is substantive, that it confers the ability to affect the relevant activities that affect returns. In the absence of other factors that give the other party existing rights to control the potential subsidiary, it is assumed that majority interests in voting equity shares give the entity control.

However, when other financial instruments or contracts are involved in relevant activities of the entity, the majority equity stake must be challenged as evidence of control. IFRS 10 requires that the purpose and design of the potential subsidiary be considered in assessing power. The design of the entity's control structure is necessary to understand which party controls the **most** significant part of the relevant activities. So the assessment of power is relative. Other parties may have power, but the party that exercises the most power is the one that has control.

An entity's major activities may be governed by a contractual arrangement among several companies or entities, as would be the case for a receivables servicing company where collections operations are on "autopilot" until an infrequent event occurs (e.g., a large default). Another instance would be where a debt holder has a significant say in the day-to-day operations, perhaps monitoring working capital.

The purpose of the potential subsidiary must also be determined. Without knowing the mission or objective of the entity's existence, it is not possible to determine what activities are relevant.

IFRS 10 uses the example of an investee that conducts the research, development, and marketing of regulated products. One investor has unilateral control for research and development (R&D), the other for manufacturing and marketing. In this example, a judgment must be made about which activities, the R&D or distribution *most* affects returns.

In practice, and alluded to in the example, this decision would involve many subjective and estimated factors. For instance, regulatory approval of a product in the United States can take years, even a decade. Once approved, intellectual property laws give the owner of the product a monopoly for a period of years. Obviously this market position can produce extraordinary profits, which indicates that the R&D activities are relevant and significant to the returns of the entity.

Conversely, a patent on a new product is worthless if it is not marketable, or cannot be distributed or manufactured. One could not argue that making and selling of the product is not integral to the entity's activities. So which set of activities is more relevant? IFRS 10 does not venture an answer but offers factors that would be considered

1. The purpose and design of the investee
2. The factors that determine the profit margin, revenue, and value of the investee as well as the value of the medical product
3. The effect on the investee's returns resulting from each investor's decision-making authority with respect to the factors in 2.
4. The investors' exposure to variability of returns

In this particular example, the investors would also consider

5. The uncertainty of, and effort required in, obtaining regulatory approval (considering the investor's record of successfully developing and obtaining regulatory approval of medical products)
6. Which investor controls the medical product once the development phase is successful

Note that 5. and 6. are forward looking, strongly indicating that the financial projections and forecasts of the investee need to be considered in assessing the impact of relevant activities on returns.

Following are some possible scenarios, keeping in mind that the example refers only to the significance of the activities to the investee, not the investor.

Since both investors have unilateral decision-making authority over each segment, the decision rests on which segment is more significant. Let's assume that the purpose of the entity is to both develop and market the medical products. This removes the "purpose" factor from the analysis.

If we assume that one of the reasons for forming a separate entity to undertake several projects is to leverage fixed costs and property, plant, and equipment (PP&E), the amortization of those costs decreases volatility of returns. Conversely, the number of projects undertaken will likely drive variable costs, which would increase the volatility of and decrease the profitability of the R&D function. Also, the success of regulatory approval determines if there will be any sales at all, which would certainly increase volatility of returns.

Manufacturing returns depend on the costs of equipment, materials, labor and licensing. Marketing returns depend on access to markets and promotion and advertising budgets. The economies of scale achieved by spreading fixed overhead over several product lines would decrease volatility of returns. However, because new medical devices generally generate inelastic demand—the users will pay virtually any price they can to get the benefit from it—in this case, access to markets would likely drive the returns, whether high or low.

	R&D and approval	**Manufacturing & marketing**
Moderating variables	Leverage of research facilities	Leverage of manufacturing facilities
	Management experienced in securing approval	Management experienced in marketing channels
Volatile variables	Approval of a device	Demand inelasticity

The next question in the analysis could be which of the volatile variables has more risk. Put another way, which one will have a greater effect on *expected* returns.

The next step would likely be a scenario of forecasted financial performance on which to make a quantitative decision.

For the purposes of this analysis, let's assume that regulatory approval of devices is determined to be the activity that affects returns the most. The last piece of the assessment of control is which investor is most exposed to the returns. For this purpose, assume that the investors share equally in the profits of the investee. This would eliminate exposure as a variable.

In summary, the preceding analysis results are that the R&D investor has the ability to direct the most relevant activities (regulatory approval) that affect returns and is most exposed to them (50/50). The likely accounting decision would be for the R&D investor to consolidate the investee.

REASSESSMENT

IFRS requires an investor to reassess if it should consolidate an investee when circumstances change that could affect the determination of power. Markets and operations of the investee can change in response to either the business environment or changes in the relative rights of the investors. In the above example of a medical device entity, the maturing of the investee's business could trigger a reassessment. For example, as the number of devices produced by the investee increases, the success of a single regulatory approval will have a successively smaller impact on returns because of the increasing revenues of approved devices. At a certain point, the strategy of management may shift to extracting cash from the investee to fund other ventures. At this point, the margins on the marketed devices would most affect the returns of the entity.

Likewise, each investor's goals can change causing it to seek more, say in the direction of the investee. This could be accomplished by purchasing options on equity shares or seeking contractual changes to the governance of the entity, or the outright purchase of more shares.

RIGHTS

IFRS 10 states that power comes from *substantive* rights. Consequently, both IFRS 10 and IAS 27 place equal emphasis on voting and nonvoting influence. IAS 27 defines control as the power to direct the financial and operating policies of the investee. IFRS 10 takes this concept further by enumerating examples of this influence.

Examples of rights that, either individually or in combination, can give an investor power include but are not limited to

1. Rights in the form of voting rights (or potential voting rights) of an investee
2. Rights to appoint, reassign or remove members of an investee's key management personnel who have the ability to direct the relevant activities
3. Rights to appoint or remove another entity that directs the relevant activities

4. Rights to direct the investee to enter into, or veto any changes to, transactions for the benefit of the investor
5. Other rights (such as decision-making rights specified in a management contract) that give the holder the ability to direct the relevant activities

Generally, when an investee has a range of operating and financing activities that significantly affect the investee's returns and when substantive decision making with respect to these activities is required continuously, it will be voting or similar rights that give an investor power, either individually or in combination with other arrangements or relevant activities.

The above excerpt from IFRS 10 describes a common situation in a simple structure where the investors are more than passive but not directly involved in day-to-day decision making. In this instance, it will likely be clear which investor should consolidate.

However, in the absence of such a straightforward situation, according to IFRS 10, "… In such cases, to enable the assessment of power to be made, the investor shall consider evidence of whether it has the practical ability to direct the relevant activities unilaterally." This includes evidence that an investor has the practical ability, in the **absence** of contractual rights to appoint managers who direct relevant activities, to dominate elections of the investee's governing body, and enter into significant transactions without threat of veto, or have common officers between the investor and investee.

IFRS 10 requires further consideration of any "special relationships," including, but not limited to, former employees in the investee or investor in key, substantive roles, economic dependence of important resources such as scarce materials, know-how, intellectual property, or funding.

IFRS 10 creates, in effect, a continuum of rights using substantive direct voting rights as the initial evaluation concept supplemented by nonvoting influence factors. To say that voting rights are "primary" does not take into account that other influencing factors can, under certain circumstances, be the basis of the assessment of control. This multi-faceted consideration is not a hierarchy, but an enumeration of indicators, with one, if present, providing an anchor for considering the other indications.

US GAAP CONTROL

US GAAP, conversely, does not take into account potential voting rights when determining whether an investor has control. While the concepts of control by those that do not hold a majority voting right as discussed above are considered in much the same way, under US GAAP they can only be used to rebut the presumption of control or determine control for an entity with voting interests.

However, US GAAP does require an assessment of control by nonvoting means when voting interest are not conclusive in determining if an investor has control. US GAAP addresses this by defining variable interest entities (VIEs). Like IFRS, US GAAP requires an investor to assess whether it has the power to direct the activities that most significantly affect the investee's economic performance, as well as its obligation and rights to absorb losses and benefit from returns, respectively.

Role of Derivatives in Analyzing Variability

US GAAP (ASC 810-10-25-34 to 36) specifically addresses how a derivative held by the investee should be considered as a creator of variability.

ASC 810-10-25

35 *The following characteristics, if both are present, are strong indications that a derivative instrument is a creator of variability:*

   1. *It's underlying an observable market rate, price, index of prices or rates, or other market observable variable (including the occurrence or nonoccurrence of a specified market observable event).*
   2. *The derivative counterparty is senior in priority relative to other interest holders in the legal entity.*

A derivative with the above characteristics, according to US GAAP, demonstrate that market risk is being eliminated for a senior investor, thereby transferring the risk to the remaining stakeholders and thus producing variability for those investors.

IFRS does not address the role of derivative in assessing control. However, including such an assessment is within the scope of evaluating the purpose and design of the investee in determining if an investor has exposure to variable returns.

INTEREST RECEIPTS AND PAYMENTS

US GAAP specifically addresses how interest receipts and payments are to be considered in variability analysis:

ASC 810-10-25

33 *Periodic interest receipts or payments shall be excluded from the variability to consider if the legal entity was not designed to create and pass along the interest rate risk associated with such interest receipts or payments to its interest holders.* However, interest rate fluctuations also can result in variations in cash proceeds received upon anticipated sales *of fixed-rate investments in an actively managed portfolio or those held in a static pool that, by design, will be required to be sold prior to maturity to satisfy obligations of the legal entity. That variability* is strongly indicated as a variability *that the legal entity was designed to create and pass along to its interest holders.*

IFRS 10 does not directly address this but does allude to the same treatment prescribed by US GAAP in Example 11 after paragraph B53:

An investee's only business activity, as specified in its founding documents, is to purchase receivables and service them on a day-to-day basis for its investors. The servicing on a day-to-day basis includes the collection and passing on of principal and **interest** payments *as they fall due. Upon default of a receivable the investee automatically puts the receivable to an investor as agreed sepa-*

rately in a put agreement between the investor and the investee. The only relevant activity is managing the receivables upon default *because it is the only activity that can significantly affect the investee's returns. Managing the receivables before default is not a relevant activity because it does not require substantive decisions to be made that could significantly affect the investee's returns—the activities before default are predetermined and amount only to collecting cash flows as they fall due and passing them on to investors. Therefore, only the investor's right to manage the assets upon default should be considered when assessing the overall activities of the investee that significantly affect the investee's returns.*

IFRS 10 Example 11 is saying the same as US GAAP but in a different way — via example. The second underlined sentence that singles out managing the receivables upon default necessarily excludes the receipt of interest payments and receipts as a factor in variability. It should be noted that Appendix B is specifically referenced as being part of the standard, so the example has equal weight as the rest of the standard.

The analogous passages in the standards, however, are careful to qualify the role of interest payments and receipts in determining variability. Both allude to the fact that the individual circumstances must be considered.

Specific US GAAP Guidance on Consolidation

Since IFRS has a single model for consolidation, the following is a comparison of the specific US GAAP guidance for certain legal forms compared to IFRS.

Partnerships

While the concepts of ASC 810-10-25 concerning general partnerships and similar entities is consistent with the general US GAAP consolidation guidance with regard to kick-out and participating rights and their effect on overcoming the presumption of control of a general partner in a limited partnership, paragraph 10 prescribes the accounting of the general partners whose presumption of control is rebutted:

ASC 810-25-25

10 *If, based on the preceding evaluation, the limited partners possess substantive kick-out rights, presumption of control by the general partners would be overcome and each of the general partners would account for its investment in the limited partnership* using the equity method *of accounting. Topic 323 provides guidance on the equity method of accounting.*

While applying IFRS in this circumstance may in fact result in equity method accounting for the general partners, IFRS 10 requires an assessment by investors as to which investor has the greatest relative control. However, while IFRS 10 explicitly provides that there could be an outcome in which no entity controls the investee, this cannot be presumed and result in "automatic" equity accounting.

PROTECTIVE RIGHTS

Both IFRS and US GAAP recognize that protective rights are not enough to overcome the presumption of control by the controlling party. US GAAP enumerates examples of protective rights of limited partners:

ASC 810-20-25

19 *Limited partners' rights (whether granted by contract or by law) that would allow the limited partners to block the following limited partnership actions would be considered protective rights and would not overcome the presumption of control by the general partners:*

  a. *Amendments to the limited partnership agreement*
  b. *Pricing on transactions between the general partners and the limited partnership and related self-dealing transactions*
  c. *Liquidation of the limited partnership initiated by the general partners or a decision to cause the limited partnership to enter bankruptcy or other receivership*
  d. *Acquisitions and dispositions of assets that are not expected to be undertaken in the ordinary course of business (Limited partners' rights relating to acquisitions and dispositions that are expected to be made in the ordinary course of the limited partnership's business are participating rights. Determining whether such rights are substantive requires judgment in light of the relevant facts and circumstances.)*
  e. *Issuance or repurchase of limited partnership interests.*

The above examples are consistent with the general section 810 and with IFRS, although IFRS does not specifically list these events.

PARTICIPATING RIGHTS

Both IFRS and US GAAP specify that the ability of noncontrolling parties (limited partners in section 810-10-20) to participate in decisions related to the ordinary course of business are sufficient to overcome the presumption of power by the controlling investor, consider the facts and circumstances of the situation (so not automatic). IFRS and US GAAP also agree that participation rights need not convey the ability to initiate decisions to be substantive; the ability to block relevant decisions made in the ordinary course of business can be substantive and therefore overcome the presumption of power by the controlling investor.

Kick-Out Rights

Kick-out rights refer to the ability of an investor to remove a controlling investor and thus impact the power of the controlling investor. US GAAP specifically addresses kick-out rights in 810-10-20. Under US GAAP, if limited partners in a limited partnership are able to kick out the general partner under feasible circumstances, the presumption of control by the general partner(s) is overcome and the general partners would account for their interest under the equity method. US GAAP provides examples of when kick-out rights would **not** be feasible, including conditions that make it unlikely they will be exercisable:

- Financial penalties or operational barriers associated with dissolving the limited partnership or replacing the general partners
- Absence of an adequate number of qualified replacement or the lack of adequate compensation to attract a replacement partner
- Absence of an explicit, reasonable mechanism in the limited partnership agreement or in the applicable laws or regulations to affect the rights
- The inability of the limited partners holding the rights to obtain the information necessary to exercise them

IFRS does address removal or kick-out rights, but only in the context of agency (covered later) and in the Basis of Conclusions of IFRS 10. Under agency, the practical ability for another party to remove a decision maker is an indicator of an agency relationship and thus hinders the ability of the decision maker to exercise power. In the IFRS 10 BC, kick-out rights are referred to by this term (not removal rights).

Paragraph BC46 explains that kick-out rights are not included in the general criteria for control since this would be inconsistent with the ability-to-control approach, versus the legal or contractual view. The finality of kick-out rights, in essence, would preclude an investor from having power under the legal approach because it would mean that the major investor does not have the unassailable legal right to control every decision in all cases even if it were contrary to every other holder of interests in the investee. The ability-to-control view, in contrast, considers a spectrum of decisions concerning relevant activities and whether the investor has the current ability with existing rights (including potential rights flowing from options to gain more voting power) to kick out another investor. However, BC106 indicates that kick-out rights must be considered with all other factors in assessing the power to direct the relevant activities. BC121 further adds that kick-out rights in and of themselves do not preclude another investor from having power because the time and feasibility to effect the kick-out rights must be considered, thus assessing whether the investor has the **current** ability to direct relevant activities. If a noncontrolling investor was able to effectively assert the kick-out rights within the time frame it needs to be used to affect the relevant activity, then the kick-out rights would prevent the major investor from concluding it has control.

In summary, US GAAP states that feasible, substantive, kick-out rights of limited partners **automatically** overcome the general partners' ability to control the investee and thus require that that the general partners account for the investment using the equity method. Conversely, IFRS considers kick-out rights as one of a number of rights that must be considered in the assessment of power.

Boundary of Ordinary Course

US GAAP also places boundaries around when participation in decisions in the ordinary course of business can covet substantive rights. Section 810-10 indicates that if an "ordinary course" decision being taken is remote, the right is not substantive:

ASC 810-20-25

20(d)Certain limited partners' rights may provide for the limited partners to participate in significant decisions that would be expected to be made in certain business activities in the ordinary course of business; however, the existence of such limited partners' rights shall not overcome the presumption that the general partners have control if it is remote that the event or transaction that requires the limited partners' approval will occur.

IFRS does not have an analogous paragraph. The main standard specifies that rights must be substantive to be considered in the assessment of power by either the controlling or noncontrolling interest (when this assessment is used to overcome the presumption of power of a controlling interest). Furthermore, rights must concern the relevant activities of the investee, that is, activities that most significantly affect the returns. However, IFRS in paragraph B53 provides

*...The circumstances or events need not have occurred for an investor with the ability to make those decisions to have power. The fact that the right to make decisions is contingent on circumstances arising or an event occurring does **not**, in itself, make those rights protective.*

The above paragraph is used in the context of determining whether the right of a noncontrolling investor is participating or protective. This combined with the concept in IFRS that **potential** voting rights can be used to determine control over an investee indicates that under IFRS, if an activity is relevant, the fact that its possibility is remote would not disqualify it from determining whether the right is substantive and therefore considered in the assessment of control.

Approval of Acquisitions and Disposals

US GAAP (ASC 810-20-55-2) specifically addresses whether the ability of limited partners' ability to approve an acquisition or disposal of the investee is a substantive right. The guidance conveys that if these transactions are in the ordinary course of business, then the rights to approve are substantive, and not substantive if these transactions are not done in the ordinary course of business.

IFRS does not explicitly consider acquisitions and disposals in assessing control. However, if in a particular circumstance the ability to acquire or dispose of assets was a relevant activity (that is, one that significantly effects returns), then it would be considered substantive. Likewise, if acquiring or disposing of assets was not considered a relevant activity, it would not be substantive.

In summary, there could be differences in the determination of control if, for instance, the acquisition and disposal of assets was in the ordinary course of business, but it was not a relevant activity (under IFRS). In this case, all other things being equal, the entity would be consolidated under IFRS, but not consolidated using US GAAP.

Dividends

US GAAP specifically discusses how the ability of limited partners to block dividends can affect the determination if the right is substantive:

ASC810-20-55

4   *The rights of the limited partners relating to dividends or other distributions may be protective or participating and should be assessed in light of the available facts and circumstances. For example, rights to block customary or expected dividends or other distributions may be substantive participating rights, while rights to block extraordinary distributions would be protective rights.*

IFRS does not directly address this issue. However, if the ability to block dividends would substantively affect the general partner(s) ability to have power over the relevant activities, depending on the circumstances of the particular situation, it could prevent the general partner from having control. One example could be if a supplier of a scarce resource received dividends in lieu of the market price for the material. The blocking of dividends could consequently negate the general partner from controlling the investee (considering all the facts and circumstances).

Collective Bargaining Agreements

US GAAP addresses when collective bargaining agreements with unions could be a substantive right. However, it provides examples only of when a right would **not** be substantive:

ASC 810-20-55

6   *The rights of the limited partners relating to a limited partnership's negotiation of collective-bargaining agreements with unions may be protective or participating and should be assessed in light of the available facts and circumstances. For example, if a limited partnership does not have a collective-bargaining agreement with a union or if the union does not represent a substantial portion of the limited partnership's work force, then the rights of the limited partners to approve or veto a new or broader collective-bargaining agreement are not substantive.*

Put another way, if the right to affect collective bargaining is not significant to the operations of the investee, it is not substantive and could not, by itself, overcome the presumption of control by the general partner.

IFRS does not mention collective bargaining in the context of consolidation. However, the guidance in IFRS 10 and to some extent IAS 27 would also result in a nonsubstantive right for the example in ASC 810-10-55-6. If collective bargaining was a relevant activity (one that most affects returns), it could be substantive. Consequently, it is conceivable that IFRS and US GAAP would result in the same decision about consolidation, all other things being equal.

Rights to Block Action of General Partner

US GAAP offers a specific example of nonsubstantive limited partner rights:

ASC 810-10-55

7   *Provisions that govern what will occur if the limited partners block the action of the general partners need to be considered to determine whether the rights of the limited partners to block have substance. For example, if both of the following circumstances exist, then the rights of the limited partners to block the approval of the operating and capital budgets do not allow the limited partners to effectively participate and are not substantive:*

    a.   The limited partnership agreement provides that if the limited partners block the approval of operating and capital budgets, then the budgets simply default to last year's budgets adjusted for inflation.

    b.   The limited partnership operates in a mature business for which year-to-year operating and capital budgets would not be expected to vary significantly.

IFRS 10 paragraph B12 specifies that decisions concerning operating and capital budgets are examples of decisions that affect relevant activities. Given IFRS 10's emphasis on defining relevant activities as those most effecting returns of the investee, the provision in a partnership agreement given in 810-10-55-7 would likely lead to the conclusion that the rights to block the budget are not substantive and thus also would not overcome the presumption of control by the general partner.

Rights Relating to the Initiation of a Lawsuit

US GAAP offers implementation guidance related to the limited partners' roles in the initiation or resolution of a lawsuit:

ASC 810-10-55

8   *Limited partners' rights relating to the initiation or resolution of a lawsuit may be considered protective or participating depending on the available facts and circumstances. For example, if lawsuits are a part of, or are expected to be a part of, the limited partnership's ordinary course of business, as is the case for some insurance entities, then the limited partners' rights may be considered substantive participating rights.*

Under IFRS 10, if the settlement of lawsuits is determined to be a relevant activity, if would be considered substantive in determining if the presumption of control of the general partner can be overcome.

INVESTMENT COMPANIES AND BROKER-DEALERS

US GAAP contains explicit exceptions to consolidation for entities that are investment companies or broker-dealers.

ASC 810-10-15-10(a)

2.   *A majority-owned subsidiary in which a parent has a controlling financial interest shall not be consolidated if the parent is a broker-dealer within the scope of Topic 940 and control is likely to be temporary.*

3. *Except as discussed in paragraph 946-810-45-3, consolidation by an invest-ment company within the scope of Topic 946 of a non-investment-company investee is not appropriate.*

Under US GAAP, an investment company is a separate legal entity whose business purpose and activity comprise all of the following:

1. Investing in multiple substantive investments
2. Investing for current income, capital appreciation, or both
3. Investing with investment plans that include exit strategies.

Accordingly, investment companies do not either

1. Acquire or hold investments for strategic operating purposes, or
2. Obtain benefits (other than current income, capital appreciation, or both) from investees that are unavailable to noninvestor entities that are not related parties to the investee.

The main argument under US GAAP to exclude temporarily controlled companies from consolidation is that the fleeting nature of the investment is an indicator of the investor's lack of incentive to integrate decision making from the parent—if control will be temporary, it is not worth changing strategies or processes.

The main argument under US GAAP that noninvestment company investees of investment companies should not be consolidated rests on the notion that the operations are so disparate, that the financial statements would not provide useful information about the timing, risk, and amount of cash flows, the main objective of US GAAP (and IFRS).

IFRS rejects both of these arguments. There are no exceptions to consolidation under IFRS when an investor has the power to affect the returns of the investee and has exposure to them. The Basis for Conclusions in IFRS 10 (some of which were carried over from IAS 27) stated that management's intentions (to only retain control for a temporary period) is not basis for consolidation. Further, segment reporting (IFRS 8) aids users in gaging the diversity of an entity's operations.

The difference in consolidation with regard to investment and broker-dealer companies is illustrative of a fundamental tension between US GAAP and IFRS with regard to exceptions to principals. IFRS stridently adheres to the core principles, whereas US GAAP contains many exceptions.

FRANCHISES

Both IFRS and US GAAP address consolidation of franchises directly. US GAAP offers more examples and necessary references to other ASC paragraphs regarding VIEs (the guidance assumes that that the equity holders of the franchisee have sufficient equity at risk to not cross into the realm of the VIE decision tree). However, both standards agree that typical franchisor rights are skewed to establishing the franchise and not the day-to-day operations.

IFRS 10, paragraphs B29 to B33, cover the same concepts as in US GAAP, referring back to the basic definition of control—the current ability to direct the relevant activities of the investee to significantly affect returns that the investor is exposed to. The guidance concedes that the decisions a franchisor has may be fundamental and important, but that these decisions do not normally prevent another party from making relevant decisions, alluding to the notion that the franchisor rights typically are protective, and thus do not form the basis of control for the franchisor. US GAAP explicitly states that the franchisor rights are usually protective.

Both standards note the fact that the investor enters into the franchise knowing the restrictions of operating under that model is important to the structure of the arrangement. Both IFRS and US GAAP direct the user to consider the initial structure of the entity to determine the purpose and intent of the investee's activities when deciding to consolidate an investee. Thus, this guidance for franchises is consistent with the broad principal of both standards.

It is not expected that in practice, given the same set of circumstances and legal agreements, that the decision to consolidate a franchise would differ between IFRS and US GAAP.

Not for Profit Entities

More than any other topic of consolidations, the published guidance under US GAAP for not-for-profit entities (NFPs) is illustrative of the wide philosophical gulf between IFRS and US GAAP regarding rule versus principal paradigms. The ASC sections for consolidation of NFPs are rife with bright lines. However, the concepts used are consistent with the main consolidation concepts such as voting interests, board of directors' influence, and control of significant assets or funding.

The approach for this section will be to categorically discuss each bright line for NFP consolidations and view each through the lens of IFRS with the goal of drawing as close a comparison as possible.

Under US GAAP, NFP consolidations are roughly divided into two tracks—one for which a for-profit entity is involved, and a second where this is not the case.

IFRS does not have guidance specifically for the not-for-profit sector and generally conveys that all IFRSs are applicable to all entities, including not-for-profit.

One of the ostensible issues with applying IFRS 10/IAS 27/SIC 12 to not-for-profits is the fact that the language of investor/investee in these standards is incongruent with the terms that describe the relationships between NFPs where there are controlling benefactors, donors, and controlling entities. US GAAP has separate guidance presumably because of the different characteristics of transactions executed by NFPs and for-profit entities. On the surface, it can be argued that NFPs do not have returns and thus are not compatible with IFRS. However, like a for-profit entity, an NFP does have a profit objective—to break even and remain solvent in order to serve its clients and communities. This reasoning coupled with the guidance in IAS 8, *Accounting Policies and Errors*, establishes a precedence of applying IFRS:

1. Specific IFRS standards
2. Other IFRS standards by analogy

3. Current pronouncements of other standard setters whose framework is compatible with IFRS and that guidance does not contradict IFRS. In other words, IFRS is not specific for the matter but another standard's guidance can "fit inside" IFRS.

Point 2 above in concert with IFRS's general notion that IFRS applies to all types of entities provides sufficient basis to apply IFRS 10/IAS 27/SIC 12 to NFPs.

FOR-PROFIT ENTITY NOT INVOLVED

ASC paragraph 958-810-55-3 contains a flowchart which is the framework for this section.

Majority Voting Interest

In the case of a majority voting interest through stock ownership, consolidation is required **only** if the holder of the majority voting interest has the ability to **require** those members to serve on the board of the NFP.

ASC 958-810-25

3   *An NFP has a majority voting interest in the board of another entity if it has the direct or indirect ability to appoint individuals that together constitute a majority of the votes of the fully constituted board (that is, including any vacant board positions). Those individuals are not limited to the NFP's own board members, employees, or officers. For implementation guidance on a majority voting interest in the board of another entity, see paragraph 958-810-55-5.*

Continuing to the implantation guidance, section 958 prescribes a situation in which no judgment is applied:

ASC 958-810-55

5   *A majority voting interest in the board of another entity, as referred to in paragraph 958-810-25-3, is illustrated by the following example. Entity B has a five-member board, and a simple voting majority is required to approve board actions. Entity A will have a majority voting interest in the board of Entity B if Entity A has the ability to appoint three or more of Entity B's board members. If three of Entity A's board members, employees, or officers serve on the board of Entity B but Entity A does not have the ability to require that those members serve on the Entity B board, Entity A does not have a majority voting interest in the board of Entity B.*

Under IFRS 10, if Entity A had the current ability to direct the relevant activities of the NFP, and had the power to significantly affect the returns and had exposure to them, it would consolidate, regardless of whether it could legally require the board members to serve. Using IFRS, the entity would need to determine if it had the influence, legal rights being only one factor, to appoint the board members. This type of influence might involve the concept of the "special relationship" referred to in IFRS 10 under which an investor provides critical materials or expertise as a data point in the decision to consolidate. In the case of NFPs, this could include controlling or being able to heavily influence a major donor or government agency that contributes to the NFP. So, for instance, if a board member of a subsidiary NFP was significantly dependent on the continued successful operation of the "subsidiary" NFP, and the parent NFP had decision authority over a major donor's contribution to the subsidiary NFP, the board member may have no other realistic alternative but to serve on the subsidiary NFP board if the parent NFP wanted him/her to serve.

Control or Economic Interest

The next condition in the decision tree in ASC paragraph 958-810-55-3 evaluates if the NFP has control and an *economic interest*. An economic interest is defined in US GAAP as

A not-for-profit entity's (NFPs) interest in another entity that exists if any of the following criteria are met:

    a. *The other entity holds or utilizes significant resources that must be used for the unrestricted or restricted purposes of the NFP, either directly or indirectly by producing income or providing services.*
    b. *The NFP is responsible for the liabilities of the other entity.*

See paragraph 958-810-55-6 for examples of economic interests.
Control is defined as the direct or indirect ability to determine the direction of management and policies through ownership, contract, or otherwise. If the NFP has neither control nor an economic interest, the NFP does not consolidate.

In this circumstance, the conclusion under IFRS is not determinable. The NFP would need to evaluate if it had the present ability to direct the relevant activities that significantly affect the returns of the entity and is exposed to them. In other words, the absence of the two relationship variables in the above paragraph would be taken into account, and would be indicative of not having power, but would not be definitive. However, the above US GAAP guidance is a bright line.

CONTROLLING FINANCIAL INTEREST VIA MAJORITY VOTING INTEREST OR SOLE CORPORATE MEMBERSHIP

Under US GAAP, if an NFP has a controlling financial interest in another NFP through direct or indirect ownership of a majority voting interest or sole corporate membership in that other NFP, it shall consolidate the other NFP, unless control does not rest with the majority owner or sole corporate member (for instance, if the other [membership] entity is in bankruptcy or if other legal or contractual limitations are so severe that control does not rest with the sole corporate member). So, similar to the general guidance on consolidation, circumstance can overcome the presumption of control by the majority holder of interests. The US GAAP implementation guidance indicates that if an NFP requires a supermajority for certain board decisions, the controlling NFP must use judgment to determine if the votes are for significant actions to severely restrict the controlling member from asserting control.

The conclusion under IFRS for and NFP with a controlling financial interest could lead to the decision to consolidate, or not consolidate if the presumption of power is overcome, including the concepts in US GAAP ASC 985-810-25-2, which is covered in the preceding paragraph. However, the NFP would need to determine if it has current ability (power) to direct the significant relevant activities that significantly affect returns exposed to them. Furthermore, the entity would need to consider if other NFPs have more power. Consequently, although this US GAAP guidance includes characteristics that could lead to the decision to consolidate the other NFP, other factors must be considered for IFRS.

CONTROL AND ECONOMIC INTEREST, BUT NO CONTROLLING FINANCIAL INTEREST/CONTROL BY OTHER MEANS

Per US GAAP ASC 985-810-25, if an NFP does not have a controlling financial interest in another NFP, but does have control (as defined by the ASC section as the ability to direct the financial and operating policies) and an economic interest, the entity is encouraged, but not required to consolidate the NFP.

Under IFRS, the NFP would either be required to be consolidated or not. If the parent NFP did not have power defined by IFRS 10 as the current ability to direct the relevant activities which affect returns and is exposed to those returns, it would not be consolidated. However, the NFP may be accounted for under the equity method.

Using this section of ASC, if under US GAAP an NFP chose not to consolidate, but the NFP had power over the other NFP according to IFRS, the accounting treatment and disclosures would be significantly different from IFRS. More specifically, information about the NFP under US GAAP would come solely from disclosures, whereas under IFRS, the NFP would be fully consolidated and be accompanied by the required disclosures.

Conversely, if the entity chose to consolidate under US GAAP, and the entity had power as defined by IFRS over the NFP (see previous paragraph), using either standard would result in consolidation, albeit with different disclosures as defined by the respective standards.

US GAAP affords the same option to consolidate under which control is effected through contractual or other means.

LESS THAN A COMPLETE INTEREST IN THE SUBSIDIARY NFP

For entities that are required or permitted to consolidate an NFP per ASC section 958, and the NFP is not a health-care entity (ASC 954), for a less-than-one-hundred-percent control circumstance, a noncontrolling interest is not to be reported. The rationale is that no other entity controls the NFP.

ASC 958-810-25

6 *An interest by an NFP in another NFP may be less than a complete interest. For example, an NFP may appoint 80 percent of the board of the other NFP. For NFPs other than those within the scope of Topic 954, if the conditions for consolidation in paragraphs 958-810-25-2, 958-810-25-3, or 958-810-25-4 are met, the basis of that consolidation would not reflect a noncontrolling interest*

for the portion of the board that the reporting entity does not control, because there is no ownership

Special-Purpose-Entity Lessors

US GAAP specifically addresses the accounting for NFPs that enter into lease agreements in the context of consolidation. Under IFRS, SIC 12, *Consolidation— Special-Purpose-Entities,* is the closest analogy to the US GAAP guidance. However, IFRS 10, effective January 1, 2013, and eligible for early adoption, incorporates and enhances the evaluation of SPEs for consolidation. IFRS 10 is a comprehensive standard that covers consolidation of any possible type of relationships between entities and thus is the appropriate comparator.

Following is an analysis of US GAAP NFP guidance followed by a section on IFRS and how it aligns, or does not, with US GAAP.

US GAAP—Lease with SPEs

US GAAP ASC 958-810-25-8 sets out conditions of when an NFP should consolidate a special-purpose entity (SPE) from which it leases assets. Consistent with the broad concept of the transfer of risk and rewards providing a strong indicator of the requirement to consolidate another entity under both IFRS and US GAAP, the section requires consolidation when substantially all the assets of the SPE will be leased to a single entity, the expected substantive residual risks and substantially all the residual rewards of the leased asset(s) and the obligation imposed by the underlying debt of the SPE reside directly or indirectly with the NFP, and the owners of record have not made an initial substantive residual equity capital investment that is at risk during the entire lease term.

The last condition above (reference ASC 958-810-25-8 [c]) also includes a bright-line test: this criterion shall be considered met if the majority owner (or owners) of the lessor is not an independent third party, regardless of the level of capital investment.

IFRS—SPEs (in context of US GAAP NFP's leases from an SPE)

Under IFRS, if an investor has the present ability to direct the significant relative activities of an investee (defined as power) to significantly affect the returns of the investee and is exposed to those returns, the investor is required to consolidate the investee. As is covered in the first section of this chapter, IFRS 10 offers indicators of the rights that could give an investor power, but the power conferred by those rights must be compared to the rights of other investors to determine if it has the *most* power.

The US GAAP main points for an NFP consolidating an SPE from which it leases assets that are compatible with IFRS:

1. 958-810-25-7(a): Substantially all the assets of the SPE are leased to a single lessee. This circumstance aligns neatly with IFRS 10's exposure to risks and rewards of the investor NFP. If no other lessees are party to the potential lease of the assets, the NFP has exposure to 100% of the risk and return of the SPE.

2. 958-810-25-7(b): The expected substantive residual risks and substantially all the residual rewards of the leased asset(s) and the obligation imposed by the underlying debt of the SPE reside directly or indirectly with the lessee through means such as any of the following:

   a. The lease agreement
   b. A residual value guarantee through, for example, the assumption of first-dollar-of-loss provisions
   c. A guarantee of the SPE's debt
   d. An option granting the lessee a right to do either of the following:

      (1) To purchase the leased asset at a fixed price or at a defined price other than fair value determined at the date of exercise
      (2) To receive any of the lessor's sales proceeds in excess of a stipulated amount.

While all the relevant terms of the arrangement, lease, and structure of the SPE would need to be assessed under IFRS, the indicators in paragraph (b) are indicative of the rights to direct the relevant activities (in the case of an SPE leasing assets) and exposure to risks and rewards.

3. 958-810-25-7(c): The owner (or owners) of record of the SPE has not made an initial substantive residual equity capital investment that is at risk during the entire lease term. This criterion shall be considered met if the majority owner (or owners) of the lessor is not an independent third party, regardless of the level of capital investment.

The first sentence in (c) aligns with IFRS's substance over form concepts, but IFRS 10's definition of control would require an analysis of whether the owner of the SPE had control even if the time period the investment was at risk was less than the lease term. If, for instance, the owner of record of the SPE had the option to decrease its interest but it could not feasibly be exercised because, for instance, the option was out-of-the-money, or perhaps giving up control would mean a substantial loss. In other words, IFRS would require that the continuous evaluation of the relationship between an entity and other entities, in the case of an option or probable loss affect the decision to consolidate. While US GAAP also requires continual monitoring of the investment, the bright line in 958-810-25-7(c), sentence 1 would not permit, in and of itself, deconsolidation under IFRS.

The bright line alluded to in the second sentence is consistent with IFRS, but not complete for an assessment of control to determine if the NFP has power. Certainly a related party (so not independent) would heavily weight the conclusion to the directive US GAAP guidance, but if the third party was consolidated by another entity because it had greater relative power (in other words, the third party was an agent of another (fourth party), then IFRS could result in a different decision with regard to paragraph (c) circumstances. More specifically, the SPE would not be consolidated.

Further conditions placed on the decision to consolidate an SPE from which an NFP leases assets are added by the following paragraph:

ASC 958-810-25

9   *To satisfy the at-risk requirement in item (c) in the preceding paragraph, an initial substantive residual equity capital investment shall meet all of the following conditions:*

     a.   It represents an equity interest in legal form.
     b.   It is subordinate to all debt interests.
     c.   It represents the residual equity interest during the entire lease term.

The effect of this paragraph further restricts nonconsolidation of a lessor SPE by defining the characteristic of the investment that the owners of the SPE must have to even be considered as at-risk, and thus not eligible for consolidation.

Under IFRS, while the legal form of an investment is an explicit factor for assessment of control, neither the presence nor absence of it would affect a decision on consolidation. However, the subparagraph (b), together with a majority legal interest would be a strong, although not conclusive, indicator of control by the owners of the SPE. A comparison of subparagraph (c) to IFRS is covered in a previous paragraph in this section covering 958-810-25-7(c).

AGENCY

IFRS 10 contains a section about agency, or delegated power and how it is factored into the decision of consolidation (reference B58 – B63). In summary, if an investor is itself controlled by another investor, under certain circumstances, the other investor must consolidate the investee. In short, the rights of both the investor and the other investor must be considered together.

The determination of agency involves qualifying under a base criteria, then an assessment of other parties' removal rights, followed by how the potential agent is compensated, whether that compensation is commensurate with other entities performing the same functions in a nonagency situation, the scope of its rights, and the exposure to variability of returns. The delegated rights do not need to be the subject of a formal contract. An agent acts upon *delegated rights*. An agent may have only some rights conveyed to it. These rights are the scope against which decision-making authority is evaluated.

The boundaries within which an assessment of whether a decision maker is a principal or agent are

1. The terms of the remuneration, and
2. The existence of substantive removal rights

A decision maker cannot be an agent unless

1. The remuneration provided is commensurate with the services provided
2. The remuneration agreement includes only terms, conditions, and amounts that are customarily present in arrangements for similar services and level of skill negotiated on an arm's-length basis

The above conditions are *qualifiers*, not conclusive facts that a decision maker is an agent. In other words if the above conditions are not present in a relationship between a decision maker and another party, the decision maker can be either a principal (consolidates investee) or will not need to consolidate based on the criteria in IFRS 10. The underlying reason why these qualifiers are indicative of an agency relationship is that a principal has no incentive to compensate an agent any more than what is needed to procure the services. If the compensation is not customary (presumably lower than customary since the principal is assumed to want to maximize profit), the agent will want a variable interest to make up for compensation that is not at market rate. In a sense, these criteria are a "floor" on the decision of agency—they are the foundation of the agency decision.

Conversely, regardless of the breadth of control of a decision maker and its exposure to variable returns, a decision maker cannot be a principal if other parties have substantive removal rights. Removal rights are substantive if other parties have the practical ability to remove the decision maker and another party has majority removal rights itself. The more parties that need to be involved to remove the decision maker, the greater the emphasis is placed on the mechanism for enough of the other parties to coordinate removal such as a regular, frequent forum to vote on such matters. If one party can remove the decision maker without cause, this alone is enough to determine that the decision maker is not a principal, thus an agent. The underlying concept of why removal rights are indicative of an agency relationship is that if a decision maker can be removed when its actions are not aligned with the interest of the principal, the agent will act on behalf of the principal. This criterion can be viewed as a "ceiling" to an agent's power.

Like the general concepts of IFRS 10, the assessment of rights against other parties is a continuum. The more dispersed and unorganized the rights of other interest holders, the more likely that an investor is a principal.

De Facto Agents

US GAAP and IFRS have nearly identical guidance with the definition and treatment of the decisions of other entities over an investee. De facto agents are entities that act primarily on the behalf of another entity with regard to decisions the agent makes for an investee. This concept can be thought of as a chain of power. When an entity evaluates its power over investees, it must combine its agents' power with its own. There is no end to this chain. US GAAP specifically addresses which entity in a consolidated group should be the parent.

In summary, a de facto agent is a related party, another investor that depends on the entity for financial support, contributed the interest in the investee for loans or other support, or even common executive leadership. Both IFRS and US GAAP offers these as examples, meaning that other arrangements (i.e., contractual) must be considered when evaluating if a decision maker is a de facto agent.

VIE GUIDANCE

US GAAP bifurcates its general consolidation guidance among control through equity, VIE, and control via contract. IFRS 10 provides a single concept that is applied to all relationships between entities. However, as covered earlier in this chapter, the VIE guidance aligns well with IFRS.

Below is the main section of US GAAP that defines the scope of a VIE (otherwise entities are subject to the other two sections).

810-10-15

*Entity is subject to VIE guidance when **by design any** of the following exits:*

1. *Equity at Risk (EAR) is not sufficient without additional subordinated financial support.*
2. *As a group the holders of the equity investment at risk **lack any** one of the following three characteristics:*

   a. *The power to direct the activities of the legal entity that most significantly impacts the economic performance*
   b. *The obligation to absorb the expected losses*
   c. *The right to receive the expected **residual** returns*

If interests other than the equity investment at risk provide the holders of that investment with these characteristics or if interests other than the equity investment at risk prevent the equity holders from having these characteristics, the entity is a VIE.

3. *The equity investors as a group also are considered to lack the characteristic in 2.a. if both of the following conditions are present:*

   a. *The voting rights of some investors are not proportional to their obligations to absorb the expected losses of the legal entity, their rights to receive the expected residual returns of the legal entity, or both.*
   b. *Substantially all of the legal entity's activities (for example, providing financing or buying assets) either involve or are conducted on behalf of an investor that has disproportionately few voting rights.*

With the exception of the explicit reference to equity at risk, the US GAAP scope for VIEs would not result in an entity with a given control structure to not be subject to the same tests under IFRS. If an entity failed the equity at risk test, it would not be excluded from IFRS guidance since an entity's relationship with another must be assessed for all types of power, not just majority equity. This is why IFRS 10 requires an entity to determine if it is an agent or principal.

DEEMED SEPARATE ENTITIES

IFRS 10 requires an investor to consolidate portions of the investee which have assets and liabilities that are segregated from other assets and liabilities of the investee. The collection of assets and liabilities are referred to as a Deemed Separate Entity (DSE).

Following is paragraph B77 of IFRS concerning deemed separate entities:

An investor shall treat a portion of an investee as a deemed separate entity if and only if the following condition is satisfied:

Specified assets of the investee (and related credit enhancements, if any) are the only source of payment for specified liabilities of, or specified other interests in, the investee. Parties other than those with the specified liability do not have rights or obligations related to the specified assets or to residual cash flows from those assets. In substance, none of the returns from the specified assets can be used by the remaining investee and none of the liabilities of the deemed separate entity are payable from the assets of the remaining investee. Thus, in substance, all the assets, liabilities and equity of that deemed separate entity are ring-fenced from the overall investee. Such a deemed separate entity is often called a "silo."

An investor assesses its relationship with the deemed separate entities according to definition of control (i.e., control of relevant activities, exposure to returns, and the ability to affect those returns). If an investor consolidates the DSE, no other investor may consolidate the assets and liabilities of the DSE.

US GAAP (in the VIE section) specifically excludes consolidating portions of legal entities if the investee is not a VIE itself:

810-10-15

15 Portions of legal entities or aggregations of assets within a legal entity shall not be treated as separate entities for purposes of applying the Variable Interest Entities Subsections unless the entire entity is a VIE. Some examples are divisions, departments, branches, and pools of assets subject to liabilities that give the creditor no recourse to other assets of the entity. Majority-owned subsidiaries are legal entities separate from their parents that are subject to the Variable Interest Entities Subsections and may be VIEs.

Because of the differences, there could be circumstances where IFRS would consolidate assets and liabilities and US GAAP would not.

DEVELOPMENT STAGE ENTITIES

US GAAP specifies that development stage entities are subject to consolidation. US GAAP defines a development stage entity as

An entity devoting substantially all of its efforts to establishing a new business and for which either of the following conditions exists:

    a. Planned principal operations have not commenced.
    b. Planned principal operations have commenced, but there has been no significant revenue therefrom.

ASC 810-10-15-16 states:

Because reconsideration of whether a legal entity is subject to the Variable Interest Entities Subsections is required only in certain circumstances, the initial application to a legal entity that is in the development stage is very important. A development stage entity is a VIE if it meets any of the conditions in paragraph 810-10-15-14.

The ASC paragraph section continues to explain the circumstance when a development stage entity would not be consolidated:

A development stage entity does not meet the condition in paragraph 810-10-15-14(a) if it can be demonstrated that the equity invested in the legal entity is sufficient to permit it to finance the activities it is currently engaged in (for example, if the legal entity has already obtained financing without additional subordinated financial support) and provisions in the legal entity's governing documents and contractual arrangements allow additional equity investments. However, sufficiency of the equity investment should be reconsidered as required by paragraph 810-10-35-4 for example, if the legal entity undertakes additional activities or acquires additional assets.

ASC 810-10-35-4 is covered in the next section.

CONTINUOUS ASSESSMENT

Both IFRS and US GAAP require entities to reevaluate their relationships with other entities.

US GAAP specifies the changes that require a reassessment of control:

ASC 810-10-35

4 *A legal entity that previously was not subject to the Variable Interest Entities Subsections shall not become subject to them simply because of losses in excess of its expected losses that reduce the equity investment. The initial determination of whether a legal entity is a VIE shall be reconsidered if any of the following occur:*

    a. *The legal entity's governing documents or contractual arrangements are changed in a manner that changes the characteristics or adequacy of the legal entity's equity investment at risk.*

    b. *The equity investment or some part thereof is returned to the equity investors, and other interests become exposed to expected losses of the legal entity.*

    c. *The legal entity undertakes additional activities or acquires additional assets, beyond those that were anticipated at the later of the inception of the entity or the latest reconsideration event, that increase the entity's expected losses.*

    d. *The legal entity receives an additional equity investment that is at risk, or the legal entity curtails or modifies its activities in a way that decreases its expected losses.*

    e. *Changes in facts and circumstances occur such that the holders of the equity investment at risk, as a group, lose the power from voting rights or similar rights of those investments to direct the activities of the entity that most significantly impact the entity's economic performance.*

IFRS (IFRS 10 paragraphs B80 to B85), like US GAAP, requires a reassessment of need to consolidate an investee if circumstances change. Under IFRS, any changes in the elements of control are relevant. Consequently, any event that alters the rights over decision making, proportions of investors' interests or share in the returns, or influence over the returns can result in deconsolidation (or consolidation) of an investee. However, IFRS is broader in its language, and excludes the consequential language of equity at risk since IFRS does not include this as a specific factor (although insufficient equity is an implicit factor along with others to be considered). Also, because IFRS requires consideration of potential rights, the change in the source of the potential rights (e.g., options) would be a factor that would not be considered under US GAAP.

ACCOUNTING FOR CONSOLIDATION

The accounting for consolidated investees under IFRS and US GAAP is very similar. Both require full consolidation and elimination of intercompany revenue, expenses, assets, and liabilities. However, as was noted earlier in this chapter, IFRS requires consolidation of a deemed separate entity (assets and liabilities that are part of an investee that are specifically ring-fenced for the investor). Both require noncontrolling interests to be presented in the equity section of the balance sheet apart from the equity of the parent. Both specify that items of other comprehensive income (OCI) are split between the parent and noncontrolling interests.

One significant difference, which is consequential as a result of the fact that IFRS considers potential rights (e.g., options) in the assessment of control, and thus may result in consolidation of investee under IFRS but not US GAAP, is that results attributable to the parent (as opposed to the noncontrolling interests) are only for **present** interests. For example, if an investor owns a 40% interest in an investee, but consolidates it because it controls the entity due to equity options, the investor attributes only 40% of comprehensive income to the parent interest, not the 40% plus the potential ownership.

IAS 8, *Accounting Policies and Errors,* requires consistent accounting policies and periods for all subsidiaries, which is not the same as US GAAP. Consequently, given the same earnings over a period of time, if the fiscal year of the investee is different than the parent, the US GAAP parent could include a different time period of results than IFRS (e.g., April 1 to March 30), which would require compiling results for the parent fiscal year (e.g., January 1 through December 31).

NONCONTROLLING INVESTMENTS

Under both IFRS and US GAAP, when an entity has significant influence over another entity, it must account for the investment under the equity method, unless unanimous consent by controlling parties is required for decisions. Significant influence is defined in both standards (ASC section 323 and IAS 28) as the ability to exercise significant influence over the financial and operating policies of the other entity.

Both standards also employ virtually identical examples of when an entity has significant influence:

1. Representation on the board of directors or equivalent body
2. Participation in policy making
3. Material transactions between the two entities
4. Interchange of managerial personnel
5. Dependency on the investee's technical information
6. Relative influence as compared to other interest holders

There are slight differences in the wording:

IAS 2

6   *The existence of significant influence by an entity is usually evidenced in one or more of the following ways:*

   (a) Representation on the board of directors or equivalent governing body of the investee
   (b) Participation in policy-making processes, including participation in decisions about dividends or other distributions
   (c) Material transactions between the entity and its investee
   (d) Interchange of managerial personnel
   (e) Provision of essential technical information

ASC 323-10-15

Significant Influence

6   *Ability to exercise significant influence over operating and financial policies of an investee may be indicated in several ways, including the following:*

   a. Representation on the board of directors
   b. Participation in policy-making processes
   c. Material intra-entity transactions
   d. Interchange of managerial personnel
   e. Technological dependency
   f. Extent of ownership by an investor in relation to the concentration of other shareholdings (but substantial or majority ownership of the voting stock of an investee by another investor does not necessarily preclude the ability to exercise significant influence by the investor).

While paragraph 6 of IAS 28 (2011) does not enumerate consideration of relative concentration of ownership, paragraph 5 contains

A substantial or majority ownership by another investor does not necessarily preclude an entity from having significant influence.

The clause of IAS 28 together with the general premise in IAS 28 to consider all facts and circumstances indicate that given the same contracts, ownership profile and concentration, and business relationships, the decision to account for an investment under equity or costs method would not be different under IFRS and US GAAP, in the absence of potential voting rights (covered in the next paragraph).

However, IAS 28 explicitly directs that currently exercisable potential voting rights are assessed when determining significant influence. US GAAP specifically prohibits potential voting rights, which is also the case for consolidated entities. Like IFRS 10, IAS 28 refers to the role of potential voting rights:

IAS 28 (2011)

7 *An entity may own share warrants, share call options, debt or equity instruments that are convertible into ordinary shares, or other similar instruments that have the potential, if exercised or converted, to give the entity additional voting power or to reduce another party's voting power over the financial and operating policies of another entity (i.e., potential voting rights). The existence and effect of potential voting rights that are currently exercisable or convertible, including potential voting rights held by other entities, are considered when assessing whether an entity has significant influence. Potential voting rights are not currently exercisable or convertible when, for example, they cannot be exercised or converted until a future date or until the occurrence of a future event.*

When potential voting rights are present, IAS 28 (2011) prescribes how the share of income (and losses that do not exceed the basis of the investment) is computed

12 *When potential voting rights or other derivatives containing potential voting rights exist, an entity's interest in an associate or a joint venture is determined solely on the basis of existing ownership interests and does not reflect the possible exercise or conversion of potential voting rights and other derivative instruments, unless paragraph 13 applies.*

13 *In some circumstances, an entity has, in substance, an existing ownership as a result of a transaction that currently gives it access to the returns associated with an ownership interest. In such circumstances, the proportion allocated to the entity is determined by taking into account the eventual exercise of those potential voting rights and other derivative instruments that currently give the entity access to the returns.*

14 *IFRS 9, **Financial Instruments**, does not apply to interests in associates and joint ventures that are accounted for using the equity method. When instruments containing potential voting rights in substance currently give access to the returns associated with an ownership interest in an associate or a joint venture, the instruments are not subject to IFRS 9. In all other cases, instruments containing potential voting rights in an associate or a joint venture are accounted for in accordance with IFRS 9.*

Because of the possible inclusion of income from the eventual exercise of instruments that give the investor potential voting rights, IFRS will result in a different share of the investee's income than under US GAAP in these circumstances.

PRESUMPTIONS

Both IFRS and US GAAP contend that ownership of 20% (or more) of voting rights is indicative of significant influence unless there is evidence to the contrary. Conversely, an entity that holds less than 50% can have significant influence depending on the facts and circumstances.

ASC 323-10-15-10 offers examples of indicators that an over-20% investor does not have significant influence (paraphrased):

1. Credible opposition to the investor's influence
2. Standstill agreements
3. Majority ownership by a concentration of other investors that operate the investee without regard to the investor's views
4. Inability of investor to obtain necessary information
5. Investor tries and fails to obtain representation on the investee's board of directors

IAS 28 does not offer examples, but the above circumstances are aligned with IFRS principals. IAS 28 heeds the power of other investors and contractual commitments in the assessment of influence of an investor.

IAS 28 (2011)

8 *In assessing whether potential voting rights contribute to significant influence, the entity examines all facts and circumstances (including the terms of exercise of the potential voting rights and any other contractual arrangements whether considered individually or in combination) that affect potential rights, except the intentions of management and the financial ability to exercise or convert those potential rights.*

INVESTEE COMPREHENSIVE INCOME AND ADJUSTMENTS TO INVESTOR'S SHARE

IFRS and US GAAP require that the proportionate change in the OCI of the investee is reflected in the carrying value of the equity-accounted investment. However, to the extent that the pervasive application IFRS and US GAAP result in different amounts of OCI given the same transactions and events, the adjustment for the investee OCI will differ.

Additionally, acquisition accounting for an equity-accounted investment will under both standards result in adjustments to equity-method profit and loss due to difference in the fair value adjustments to the carrying value of the investee at the time of acquisition. For instance, depreciation on the stepped-up basis of assets will be higher than the historical costs. Both standards also direct that goodwill recognized on acquisition of the equity-method investor is presented and accounted for as part of the investment balance.

EXEMPTIONS FROM THE EQUITY METHOD

Both US GAAP and IFRS require exceptions to apply the equity method of accounting for investees that otherwise meet the criteria. As is the case for consolidation, US GAAP contains an exception based on the combination of the nature of investor and investee. The exceptions under IFRS are consistent with the principals of consolidation and suspend the equity method only when significant influence is curtailed or the information about the investee is provided in other specific financial statements.

Investment Companies

US GAAP requires, and IFRS permits an investment by an investment company to be accounted for at fair value in accordance with their respective standards. The underlying reasoning for this exception is that in this situation, the investments are being managed for a financial return, not for business synergy. Moreover, the investors in these companies have the expectation that their capital can be withdrawn on a shorter timescale than would otherwise be the case. Consequently, for these investments, fair value is a more relevant and useful measure of performance than is the equity method.

ASC 946-323-45

1   *Except as discussed in the following paragraph, use of the equity method of accounting by an investment company of a non-investment-company investee is not appropriate. Investment companies, defined by the Securities Exchange Commission act of 1940 are accounted for at fair value.*

2   *An exception to the general principal in the preceding paragraph occurs if the investment company has an investment in an operating entity that provides services to the investment company, for example, an investment adviser or transfer agent. In those cases, the purpose of the investment is to provide services to the investment company rather than to realize a gain on the sale of the investment. If an investment company holds a non-controlling ownership interest in such an operating entity that otherwise qualifies for use of the equity method of accounting, the investment company should use the equity method of accounting for that investment rather than the fair value of the investee's assets and liabilities.*

IAS 28 (2011) allows the **option** of accounting for investments at fair value through profit and loss in accordance with IFRS 9 when an entity, directly or indirectly, "… is a venture capital organization, or a mutual fund, unit trust and similar entities including investment-linked insurance funds."

IFRS also permits an entity to elect to account for a **portion** of an investment held through a venture capital organization, mutual fund, unit trust, and similar entities at fair value through profit and loss in accordance with IFRS 9. The remainder is accounted for using the equity method.

IFRS

Exemptions from applying the equity method under IFRS are identical to those excluded from preparing consolidation financial statements:

IAS 28 (2011)

17 *An entity need not apply the equity method to its investment in an associate or a joint venture if the entity is a parent that is exempt from preparing consolidated*

financial statements by the scope exception in paragraph 4(a) of IFRS 10 or if all the following apply:

    (a) The entity is a wholly owned subsidiary, or is a partially owned subsidiary of another entity and its other owners, including those not otherwise entitled to vote, have been informed about, and do not object to, the entity not applying the equity method.

    (b) The entity's debt or equity instruments are not traded in a public market (a domestic or foreign stock exchange or an over-the-counter market, including local and regional markets).

    (c) The entity did not file, nor is it in the process of filing, its financial statements with a securities commission or other regulatory organization, for the purpose of issuing any class of instruments in a public market.

    (d) The ultimate or any intermediate parent of the entity produces consolidated financial statements available for public use that comply with IFRSs.

The rationale for the exception under IFRS is that the relevant information is provided for in other reports and accessible by the investor.

IN-SUBSTANCE COMMON STOCK

ASC 323-10-15-13 to 19 defines in-substance common stock (ISCS) as follows:

For purposes of this Topic, in-substance common stock is an investment in an entity that has risk and reward characteristics that are substantially similar to that entity's common stock.

CHANGES IN LEVEL OF INFLUENCE

Increases in Influence

ASC 323-10-35-33. Paragraph 323-10-15-12 explains that an investment in common stock of an investee that was previously accounted for on other than the equity method may become qualified for use of the equity method by an increase in the level of ownership described in paragraph 323-10-15-3 (that is, acquisition of additional voting stock by the investor, acquisition or retirement of voting stock by the investee, or other transactions). If an investment qualifies for use of the equity method (i.e., falls within the scope of this Subtopic), the investor shall adopt the equity method of accounting. The investment, results of operations (current and prior periods presented), and retained earnings of the investor shall be adjusted retroactively on a step-by-step basis as if the equity method had been in effect during all previous periods in which the investment was held. The amount of interest cost capitalized through application of Subtopic 835-20 shall not be changed if restating financial statements of prior periods.

Conversely, IAS 28 does not permit restatement of retained earnings and investment balance upon an increase in the level of influence that causes the investment to fall into the scope of equity accounting.

However, upon qualification of being an associate, the investor recognizes the difference between the cost of the investment and the share of the fair value of the net assets of the investee:

IAS 28 (2011)

> 33   *An investment is accounted for using the equity method from the date on which it becomes an associate or a joint venture. On acquisition of the investment, any difference between the cost of the investment and the entity's share of the net fair value of the investee's identifiable assets and liabilities is accounted for as follows:*
>
> > *(a) Goodwill relating to an associate or a joint venture is included in the carrying amount of the investment. Amortization of that goodwill is not permitted.*
> >
> > *(b) Any excess of the entity's share of the net fair value of the investee's identifiable assets and liabilities over the cost of the investment is included as income in the determination of the entity's share of the associate or joint venture's profit or loss in the period in which the investment is acquired.*

Thus **to the extent** that the change in the underlying fair value of the investment is included in the prior earnings of the formerly-non-equity-invested investee, the IFRS and US GAAP results would be comparable. However, under IFRS the P&L impact from the change in influence is recognized in the current period. Under US GAAP, retained earnings are adjusted.

Decreases in Influence

The accounting for decreases in ownership of an investee when significant influence is lost differs between US GAAP and IFRS. While both discontinue the accrual of income and loss of the investee, the calculation of the gain or loss on disposal and the starting point for the carrying value of the retained interest is different.

Under ASC 323-10-35-35 to 36, the gain or loss is calculated as the proceeds of any sale less the carrying value of the interest disposed. The remaining carrying value of the investment resulting from the application of the equity method prior to the disposition is the starting value for the investment under the subsequent accounting method.

Per IAS 28 (2011) paragraph 22 (b), the gain or loss is the fair value of the retained interest plus any proceeds received, less the carrying value of the portion of investment disposed. In essence, the disposal event is triggering the recognition of a previously unrecognized gain or loss in the fair value of the retained interest. The fair value of the retained interest is the starting position for the investment under the subsequent accounting method.

The treatment of accumulated other comprehensive income (AOCI) upon loss of significant influence is also accounted for differently under IFRS and US GAAP. IFRS recognizes **all** amounts in AOCI (in profit and loss if prescribed by the applicable guidance):

IAS 28

22(c) *When an entity discontinues the use of the equity method, the entity shall account for all amounts previously recognized in other comprehensive income in relation to that investment on the same basis as would have been required if the investee had directly disposed of the related assets or liabilities.*

23 *Therefore, if a gain or loss previously recognized in other comprehensive income by the investee would be reclassified to profit or loss on the disposal of the related assets or liabilities, the entity reclassifies the gain or loss from equity to profit or loss (as a reclassification adjustment) when the equity method is discontinued. For example, if an associate or a joint venture has cumulative exchange differences relating to a foreign operation and the entity discontinues the use of the equity method, the entity shall reclassify to profit or loss the gain or loss that had previously been recognized in other comprehensive income in relation to the foreign operation.*

Conversely, US GAAP offsets AOCI against the carrying value of the investment to the extent the carrying value is not reduced below zero:

ASC 323-10-35

39 *In the circumstances described in paragraph 323-10-35-37, an investor's proportionate share of an investee's equity adjustments for other comprehensive income shall be offset against the carrying value of the investment at the time significant influence is lost. To the extent that the offset results in a carrying value of the investment that is less than zero, an investor shall both*

a. *Reduce the carrying value of the investment to zero*
b. *Record the remaining balance in income*

Consequently, under US GAAP, losses or gains in AOCI are deferred until the complete disposition of the investment. Under IFRS, however, gains and losses are recognized at the time significant influence is lost. This contrast illustrates disparity in the recognition events over the scope cycle of an investment between the two standards. IFRS views the change in the character of the investor's influence as an earnings event, whereas US GAAP views disposition of AOCI as a "cradle to grave" issue—in other words, AOCI is only recycled to profit and loss when the entire earnings process culminates.

CONTRIBUTION OF EQUITY AWARDS

In the circumstances described in the preceding paragraph, a contributing investor shall expense the cost of stock-based compensation granted to employees of an equity method investee as incurred (that is, in the same period the costs are recognized by the investee) to the extent that the investor's claim on the investee's book value has not been increased.

IFRS 11 defines a joint venture, which requires equity accounting, as an interest in the net assets of the investee. Accordingly, since the contribution of stock awards is to the employees of the investee, it would be accounted for in full as part of the investment. There is no theoretical basis in IAS 28 or IFRS 2 to account for a portion of the stock awards that are disproportionate as an expense.

Consequently, in these circumstances, both the carrying value of the investment and the expense associated with the disproportionate share of the stock awards will be different under IFRS than US GAAP. In summary, US GAAP will require a P&L impact, IFRS will not.

EXTRAORDINARY ITEMS

US GAAP requires that investors of equity-accounted investments separate their share of extraordinary items in the financial statements:

ASC 323-10-45

2   *The investor's share of extraordinary items and its share of accounting changes reported in the financial statements of the investee shall be classified separately in accordance with Subtopic 225-20.*

Because IFRS does not include the concept of extraordinary items, this provision would not apply. However, both IAS 8 and IFRS 12 require disclosure of other information to the extent it is necessary to provide a complete picture of the performance of the entity (these standards also require additional information concerning the nature, amount, and timing of cash flows). Knowledge of significant, nonrecurring events does require disclosure under IFRS. Since an extraordinary item includes events that are significant and nonrecurring, an extraordinary item under US GAAP concerning an interest in another entity would require disclosure under IFRS.

LOSSES OF EQUITY-METHOD INVESTEES

IFRS and US GAAP require that recognition of losses on equity-accounted investments be suspended when the investment basis reaches zero. Furthermore, both standards consider extension of other forms of support (e.g., loans) as part of that basis. Additionally, both require recognition of liabilities of the investee to the extent it meets the respective recognition criteria (ASC 450 and IAS 37).

US GAAP includes prescriptive guidance on the precedence of applying losses to carrying values of the components of the investment, in order of liquidation seniority (ASC 323-10-35-23 to 26). IAS 28 (2011) prescribes the same precedence, although the examples are not present. However, other IFRSs would dictate the same accounting treatment as in ASC 323-10-35-23 to 26, except for inherent differences in the accounting for the value of the instruments (e.g., IFRS requires impairment reversals, carrying value differences of investments due to differing treatment of borrowing costs and fair value calculation).

Because IFRS requires reversals of impairments where circumstances indicate, references to the (adjusted) cost basis in ASC 323-10 are not relevant.

US GAAP offers a choice of how to allocate the losses to different components of an investment in an equity-method investee (termed *associates* under IFRS):

ASC 323-10-35

> 28 *In the circumstances described in the preceding paragraph, the investor shall not recognize equity method losses based solely on the percentage of investee common stock held by the investor. Example 5 (see paragraph 323-10-55-48) illustrates two possible approaches for recognizing equity method losses in such circumstances.*

These two methods are based on either investor's proportionate share of the instruments issued by the investee, or the investor's share in the book value of the investee. IAS 28 is silent on the calculation of the share of the loss. Referring to the *IFRS Framework* (per IAS 8), any method that produces a representationally faithful and prudent result is acceptable. Per IAS 8, since ASC 323-10-35-28 does not contradict IFRS (it does not, technically, but may based on the circumstances such as the disparity of the losses on the respective investment instrument), then assuming the entity uses US GAAP as the "other comprehensive standard" that the entity consistently refers to, the investor could apply ASC 323-10-35-28 directly.

ADDITIONAL FUNDING OF EQUITY-METHOD INVESTEES AND SUSPENDED LOSSES

ASC 323-10-35-29 to 30 provides US GAAP guidance on recognition of unrecognized losses (suspended due to losses exceeding the basis of the investment) when additional investments in the investee are procured by the investor (and the additional investment does not change the investor from having significant influence to control). In summary, these paragraphs require the investor to determine if additional investments are funding of prior losses. If prior losses are being funded, then a suspended loss is recognized to the extent of the funding of the prior loss (not the entire investment). The guidance offers examples of when prior losses are funded, but states that all the facts and circumstances must be considered.

The examples include investment acquired from a third party (likely not funding prior losses), disparity in the fair value of the consideration exchanged between the parties (perhaps partial funding of prior losses), the acquisition of an increase in interest in the investee (likely not funding of prior losses), and the relative seniority in case of liquidation (the more junior the instrument acquired, the more likely it is a funding of prior losses). The point is to determine if the additional investment confers upon the investor a greater share of future profits. If not, it is a funding of a prior loss.

IAS 28 (2011) does not address funding of prior losses directly, but implicitly: IAS 28 (2011) paragraph 39:

> *...After the entity's interest is reduced to zero, additional losses are provided for, and a liability is recognized, only to the extent that the entity has incurred legal or constructive obligations or* made payments on behalf of the associate or joint venture.

Under the previous clause (IAS 28) that losses are recognized only up to the investment, and are suspended until basis reaches zero again, and the fact that the

IFRS Framework requires that the accounting for a transaction or event is representationally faithful and prudent, would result in the same result as ASC 323-10-35-29 to 30.

Thus, there would be no difference (except for basis differences in investment from following other applicable IFRSs) in the result of the recognition of suspended losses under IFRS and US GAAP given the same set of circumstances described in ASC 323-10-35-29 to 30. In other words, the difference would be a consequence of the inherent differences between US GAAP and IFRS, not because of the application of the analogous standards.

IMPAIRMENT/OTHER-THAN-TEMPORARY DECREASE IN VALUE

Both IFRS and US GAAP require a write-down of an equity-method investment when circumstances indicate that the carrying value is higher than is justified by the underlying economics concerning the investment. Both standards prohibit impairments of the assets of the investee, although the investor must recognize its share of the investee's impairment for acquisition-accounting fair value step-up. Both standards also require that goodwill is not tested separately, not amortized, but included in the carrying value during impairment testing.

However, since IFRS permits reversals of impairments (IAS 36), all other things being equal, improving economics of an impaired investment in an investee could result in a higher carrying value subsequent to impairment testing.

ASC 323-20-35-31 and 32 provides factors that must be considered to determine if an other-than-temporary decline in value has occurred. The indicators include protracted losses and an expectation that future earnings will not be sufficient to recover the carrying amount. The paragraphs, however, do not provide a method.

For impairments, IAS 28 (2011) refers to IAS 39, *Measurement Financial Instruments*, which in turn refers is IAS 36, *Impairments*, which specifies that the *recoverable amount* must be compared to the carrying value. The recoverable amount is the higher of a present value of cash flows, including estimated proceeds of an eventual disposition, or fair value less costs to sell. See IAS 36 for details (note that IAS 36 applies to long-term assets, goodwill, and investments in associates not accounted for under IFRS 9). In subsequent reporting periods, the entity must assess the impaired asset for recovery. If an assessment's recoverable amount is higher than the carrying value, the impairment must be reversed to being the investment to the recoverable amount.

Practically speaking, the economic distress that underpins recognition of impairment of an equity-accounted investment would likely result in write-downs under both IFRS and US GAAP. However, since IFRS is prescriptive in the method chosen, the same distress may lead to a different resulting carrying amount.

PROPORTIONATE CONSOLIDATION

Despite recent convergence efforts between the IASB and the FASB, US GAAP and IFRS continue to require application of proportionate consolidation under different circumstances. Applying proportionate consolidation under US GAAP, turns largely on industry practice and the legal structure of the investment. IFRS currently has two standards that are effective for proportionate consolidation until January 2013. These standards are IAS 28 (2003) and IAS 28 (2011). The 2011 version was released in May and is eligible for early adoption.

ASC 810-10-45-14 states that proportionate consolidation (or pro-rata consolidation) is only permitted when the investors have an undivided interest (all parties are jointly and severally liable) and the investee is an entity devoted solely to oil and gas exploration or in the construction business.

IAS 28 (2011), referring to IFRS 11, requires proportionate consolidation when investors have stakes in a *joint operation*.

IFRS 11

> 15   *A joint operation is a joint arrangement whereby the parties that have joint control of the arrangement have rights to the assets, and obligations for the liabilities, relating to the arrangement. Those parties are called joint operators.*

A joint arrangement is one which includes both joint operations and joint ventures (where investors have a share in the net assets of the investee rather than the underlying assets and liabilities and the arrangement is accounted for under the equity method). Joint operations exist when the unanimous consent of two or more investors is required for relevant activities. Relevant activities in IFRS 11 have the same meaning as put forth in IFRS 10, *Consolidated Financial Statements*. In summary, relevant activities are those which most impact the financial results of the investee.

The controlling parties report in their financial statements their respective interest in the balance sheet and income statement:

IFRS 11

> 20   *A joint operator shall recognize in relation to its interest in a joint operation:*
>
> *(a) Its assets, including its share of any assets held jointly*
> *(b) Its liabilities, including its share of any liabilities incurred jointly*
> *(c) Its revenue from the sale of its share of the output arising from the joint operation*
> *(d) Its share of the revenue from the sale of the output by the joint operation*
> *(e) Its expenses, including its share of any expenses incurred jointly*

Participants in joint operations that do not share control and have direct interests in the assets, liabilities, revenues, and expenses of the investee also account for their proportionate share. Parties to the arrangement that do not have these interests account for their investments according to IFRS 9, *Financial Instruments*.

Under IFRS 11, the determination of whether an arrangement is a joint operation or joint venture must include an evaluation of all the facts and circumstances. The factors considered are the contracts, agreements, and decision-making structure. In the case of a joint arrangement conducted through a separate vehicle, the legal form (e.g., a corporation) is a factor in the assessment. However, if other agreements alter the rights conferred by the legal form, it could override the judgment of the investees having a share in the net assets.

When assessing the unanimous consent, the relative voting rights of the investees are considered. If the configuration of ownership percentages and the percentage of votes needed to make a decision about relevant activities effectively require agreement from two or more parties, the arrangement is a joint operation.

COTERMINOUS YEAR-ENDS AND INVESTEE ACCOUNTING POLICIES

For both the equity and proportionate consolidation methods of accounting, IFRS requires that financial statements of the investee are as of the same year-end as the investor. If it is not practicable for the associate to prepare financial statements as of the year-end of the investor, the difference cannot be longer than three months and adjustments for significant transactions or events must be made.

Under US GAAP, year-ends are not required to be the same. Please note that ASC 323 refers to ASC 810 for year-end conformity matters for equity-method investees:

ASC 810-10-45

12 *It ordinarily is feasible for the subsidiary to prepare, for consolidation purposes, financial statements for a period that corresponds with or closely approaches the fiscal period of the parent. However, if the difference is not more than about three months, it usually is acceptable to use, for consolidation purposes, the subsidiary's financial statements for its fiscal period; if this is done, recognition should be given by disclosure or otherwise to the effect of intervening events that materially affect the financial position or results of operations.*

Analyzing the difference in the conformity of investee year-ends between IFRS and US GAAP, IFRS **requires** year-ends to be the same unless the effort to do so is not practicable. While practicable is not defined in IFRS, various releases by the IASB and IFRIC have not taken practicability lightly. A high level of effort needed is usually not a valid basis for claiming impracticability, but the availability of information is more relevant. With modern technology and information resources, it would be rare in practice to be able to invoke this practicability exception. Consequently, the nonconformity of year-ends would be much less frequent than under US GAAP, which for all intents and purposes permits year-end differences. ASC 810-10-45-12 also reserves adjustments to **material** effects, not including significant ones. Note that US GAAP also allows disclosure as a substitute for adjustments to an investor's share of investee's results.

Accounting policies for the investees must also be uniform and the same as the investor. Adjustments to the investee's results, assets, and liabilities must be made to conform to the policies of the investor before applying the equity or proportionate consolidation method in the investor's results and financial position. US GAAP has no such requirement for accounting policies.

DISCLOSURES

There are significant differences in the disclosures among IAS 28 (2003), IAS 28 (2011), and ASC 323-10-50.

The next section lists equity-method disclosures subject matter that is common between ASC 323-10-50 and IAS 28 (2003):

1. Investee name and reasons why a greater-than-20% ownership interest is not accounted for under the equity method
2. Investee name and reasons why a less-than-20% ownership interest is accounted for under the equity method
3. For investees for which there is a quoted market price available:

   a. *US GAAP:* Aggregate value of each investment
   b. *IFRS:* Fair value of investment

4. Aggregate financial information for investees: assets, liabilities, results of operations

   a. *US GAAP:* May be needed depending on materiality, aggregated or separately
   b. *IFRS:* For all subsidiaries, whether or not material, can be aggregated based on risk characteristics

US GAAP only:

1. Conversion of outstanding convertible securities, exercise of outstanding options and warrants, and other contingent issuances of an investee may have a significant effect on an investor's share of reported earnings or losses. Accordingly, material effects of possible conversions, exercises, or contingent issuances shall be disclosed in notes to financial statements of an investor.
2. The difference, if any, between the amount at which an investment is carried and the amount of underlying equity in net assets and the accounting treatment of the difference.
3. The name of each investee and percentage of ownership of common stock.

IAS 28 (2003) only:

1. The nature and extent of any significant restrictions (e.g., resulting from borrowing arrangements or regulatory requirements) on the ability of associates to transfer funds to the investor in the form of cash dividends, or repayment of loans or advances
2. The unrecognized share of losses of an associate, both for the period and cumulatively, if an investor has discontinued recognition of its share of losses of an associate
3. The fact that an associate is not accounted for using the equity method in accordance with paragraph 13 (when nonpublic companies have other financial statements report information)

IFRS 12, issued in May 2011, combined the disclosures for all interests in other entities, consolidated or not. The disclosures are much more extensive than IAS 28 (2003) and other IFRSs and were in response to the recommendations after the 2008 Financial Crisis, specifically the report of the Financial Crisis Advisory Group (FCAG). The FCAG was an international panel convened to investigate how financial reporting could be improved to help prevent a repeat of the global financial market depression that occurred after the failure of Lehman Brothers investment bank.

The objective of IFRS 12 is to disclose information that enables users of its financial statements to evaluate

1. The nature of, and risks associated with, its interests in other entities; and
2. The effects of those interests on its financial position, financial performance and cash flows

Paragraphs 2 to 4 of IFRS 12 are succinct in how an entity must go about complying with its guidance:

Meeting the objective

2   *To meet the objective in paragraph 1, an entity shall disclose*

   (a) The significant judgments and assumptions it has made in determining the nature of its interest in another entity or arrangement, and in determining the type of joint arrangement in which it has an interest (paragraphs 7–9)
   (b) Information about its interests in:

     (i) Subsidiaries (paragraphs 10–19)
     (ii) Joint arrangements and associates (paragraphs 20–23) and
     (iii) Structured entities that are not controlled by the entity (unconsolidated structured entities) (paragraphs 24–31)

3   *If the disclosures required by this IFRS, together with disclosures required by other IFRSs do not meet the objective in paragraph 1, an entity shall disclose whatever additional information is necessary to meet that objective.*

4   *An entity shall consider the level of detail necessary to satisfy the disclosure objective and how much emphasis to place on each of the requirements in this IFRS. It shall aggregate or disaggregate disclosures so that useful information is not obscured by either the inclusion of a large amount of insignificant detail or the aggregation of items that have different characteristics (see paragraphs B2–B6).*

Note that paragraph 3 provides a "catchall" for disclosures. This principal is aimed squarely at giving the management of the entity the responsibility for ensuring users of financial statements have the needed information regarding risks, no matter what form they may take.

Also, unlike US GAAP, even if an investee is accounted for at fair value under IFRS 9, an investor must still make all of the other disclosures as defined in IFRS 12. The Basis of Conclusions of the standard indicated that this is a **measurement** exception, not a scope exclusion. US GAAP conversely does not require expanded disclosures.

IFRS 12 carries over all of the disclosures required by IAS 28 (2003) and includes others regarding, among others, the maximum loss of each investee, and financial support provided to an investee for which it was not contractually obligated to do so.

The most significant difference from earlier standards is the amount of qualitative information regarding the nature of risks of investments. Tabular and qualitative information about investments in unconsolidated *structure entities* (equivalent to VIEs as defined in US GAAP) are also specifically defined.

13 POSTRETIREMENT BENEFITS

This chapter covers the accounting and reporting for pension, postretirement medical plans, and other postemployment benefits, such as long-term disability. Defined contribution plans are treated identically under IFRS and US GAAP, so these will not be covered.

This first section covers the differences between US GAAP and IAS 19 (2003), which is currently effective. The second section will cover IAS 19 (2011), which will be effective January 1, 2013. The revised IAS 19 is substantially different than the currently effective version.

SECTION I—IAS 19 (2003)

The crucial accounting attribute of postretirement benefits plans (PRBs) are that the employer assumes the risk of the cost of the benefits to the employees after retirement or employment, as applicable. This assumption of risk creates the need to recognize a liability for the future cost. In broad strokes, the employer recognizes expense in the current period equal to an amount that is attributed to the service an employee performs in that period. So, essentially, it is accrual accounting (as might be expected).

The complexity with determining how much expense to recognize to profit and loss for PRBs is due to the inclusion of the time value of money, inflation, expected years of benefits used (mortality), and, for plans that are funded by assets in a trust, the amount and return on investment of those assets. Inflation and the time value of money are included in the calculation since the payment of the obligations will occur many years in the future. Mortality is included since the ultimate cost of the benefits provided is largely dependent on the number of years a person will draw on benefits. The return on assets is important since this will pay for some of the costs. Ideally, the entity contributes the present value of those obligations in the current year to the trust in hopes that these assets will pay entirely for the benefits.

However, it is rarely the case that the assets at a given moment equal the benefits payable. It is also rare for the cash payments or asset contributions to a trust to equal the cost of the benefits for a particular period. The equalization of the costs and assets used are dependent entirely on the point in the life cycle of the plan. The point in the life cycle of a plan can be viewed as how far away and on which "side" a plan's funded status (plant assets minus liabilities) is from the point where plan contributions equal outlays for benefits. In the early stages of a plan, there are expenses and no cash or asset contributions or outlays. In the latter stages of a plan, there are no expenses but outlays and contributions.

The estimated nature of the expense and obligation is what makes accounting for pension and postretirement benefits complex and subject to large period-to-period changes.

The conceptual pieces of accounting for postretirement benefits are

1. Understanding of the benefit formula, that is, the benefits offered to the employee upon retirement or termination (e.g., retirement income, medical care, etc.). The benefit formula may be written, oral, or based on past practice, or a combination of all of these mediums.
2. The attribution of postretirement cost to accounting periods. The objective of attribution is to reflect the cost to the entity during the period that the employee is providing eligible service.
3. The timing of benefit payments after termination or retirement. This factor is incorporated into the cost by calculating time value of money via a discount rate.
4. The amount of benefit payments after termination or retirement. The amount payable in a given period may be relatively certain (i.e., a cash-balance plan payment based on an interest crediting rate), or highly uncertain (i.e., cost of medical care consumed by the beneficiary, or dependent [s]). The amount can be offset by contributions from employees, governments (e.g., Medicare in the United States), or insurance payments.
5. For funded plans, the return on plan assets and the effect of insured obligations.
6. The timing and amount of benefit contributions during the current accounting period.

The application of the above concepts is broken down into the following components of net periodic costs (NPC) and balance sheet items:

Net Periodic Costs

1. Service cost, which is the present value of benefits earned by the employee in an accounting period.
2. Interest cost, which is the amount that unwinds the discounted value of the obligation to its present value for the period.
3. Expected return on plan assets. The EROA reduces the NPC by producing assets that will be used to pay the plan benefits.
4. Amortization of actuarial gains and losses. AGLs are the difference between the expected and actual return on plan assets and the actual experience of benefit payments as compared to the estimated amounts.
5. Prior service costs. PSC is the amortization of service costs attributable to past periods as a result of a plan amendment. PSC can be positive or negative for benefit increases or decreases, respectively.

Other costs that can enter into comprehensive income in a period include curtailment and settlement gains or losses. Curtailments occur when a plan sponsor reduces benefits by either significantly reducing the number of beneficiaries in a plan or substantially reducing benefits payable to existing participants. While the overall effect of such an action is to reduce future benefit payouts, the impact may be reflected both in operating income and other comprehensive income(OCI).

Balance Sheet

1. The projected benefit obligation (PBO) is the actuarially determined liability owed to plan participants over the life expectancy of the beneficiaries for benefits earned up to the date of the financial statements. The PBO includes the effects of compensation increases, inflation in medical and other benefit costs, demographics (e.g., age, sex, mortality, expected retirement dates, and others).
2. Plan assets are the investments segregated specifically to pay plan benefits. Usually these assets are in a trust. Plan assets increase with contributions and investment gains, and decrease with payments of benefits, lump-sum distributions, plan expenses, and investment losses. Not all plans are funded. In this case, benefit compensation is paid from the assets of the entity.

The measurement of the PBO is nearly identical under IFRS and US GAAP. However, US GAAP requires the full change in the PBO to be offset in OCI at each measurement date. IAS 19 permits entities to defer the recognition of gains and losses (as a matter of policy choice) in the PBO until the cumulative amount exceeds a "corridor" of 10% of the greater of the PBO or plan assets (using absolute values). US GAAP also permits the identical use of a "corridor" but the offset is recognized in OCI since the change in value has already been offset in OCI. In this sense, under US GAAP, OCI is a "parking lot" for gains and losses.

There are some differences in what is considered a plan asset (mainly regarding insurance policies). The following sections on components of NPC detail the differences, all of which are reflected in the PBO measurement and plan asset measurement.

Plan Assets

IAS 19 requires that plan assets are stated at the fair value at the date of measurement. Under ordinary circumstances, the plan assets and PBO are valued at the fiscal year-end date. Plan curtailments and settlements can require an interim valuation. US GAAP, however, permits an entity to use a *market-related value*. The market-related value according to the ASC Master Glossary is

> *A balance used to calculate the expected return on plan assets. The market-related value of plan assets is either fair value or a calculated value that recognizes changes in fair value in a systematic and rational manner over not more than five years. Different ways of calculating market-related value may be used for different classes of assets (for example, an employer might use fair value for bonds and a five-year moving-average value for equities), but the manner of determining market-related value is required to be applied consistently from year to year for each asset class. For a method to meet the criteria of being systematic and rational, it must reflect only the changes in the fair value of plan assets between various dates.*

The basis for conclusions in the precodification SFAS 87, *Employers' Accounting for Pensions*, indicated that this method was allowed to smooth volatility of pension plan results. IFRS is conceptually opposed to smoothing techniques. The *IFRS Framework*, IAS 1, *Financial Statements*, and IAS 34, *Interim Financial Statements*, all reject the notion of smoothing. However, IFRS does permit the use of the "corridor" method of recognizing actuarial gains and losses in profit and loss.

Profit and Loss and Other Comprehensive Income

Service Cost

Under both IFRS and US GAAP, service cost can be looked at as the amount of benefit that an employee earns in a period if that benefit were to be paid in that current period. In other words, it is the present value of the amount an entity pays to an employee for service in respect of future benefits.

The calculation of the service cost is by its nature an estimate. Retirement income is based on the age, life expectancy, and often salary level either over a beneficiary's service years to the entity, the rate at the end of retirement, or an average over some period. Some plans, such as cash balance plans, are based on a cash-crediting rate based on current interest rates.

Both standards base the attribution of defined benefit cost based on the terms of the plan, whether implicit or explicit. If the plan does not specify attribution, the costs are reflected in a period that reflects the substance of the plan.

IAS 19

Accounting for the Constructive Obligation

52 An entity shall account not only for its legal obligation under the formal terms of a defined benefit plan, but also for any constructive obligation that arises from the entity's informal practices. Informal practices give rise to a constructive obligation where the entity has no realistic alternative but to pay employee benefits. An example of a constructive obligation is where a change in the entity's informal practices would cause unacceptable damage to its relationship with employees.

53 The formal terms of a defined benefit plan may permit an entity to terminate its obligation under the plan. Nevertheless, it is usually difficult for an entity to cancel a plan if employees are to be retained. Therefore, in the absence of evidence to the contrary, accounting for post-employment benefits assumes that an entity which is currently promising such benefits will continue to do so over the remaining working lives of employees.

ASC 715-10-15

3 The guidance in the Compensation—Retirement Benefits Topic applies to the following types of benefit arrangements:

a. Any arrangement that is in substance a pension or other postretirement benefit plan, regardless of its form or the means or timing of its funding

b. Written plans and unwritten plans whose existence is discernible either from a practice of paying pension or other postretirement benefits or from oral representations made to current or former employees

c. *Deferred compensation contracts with individual employees if those contracts, taken together, are equivalent to a plan that provides pension or other postretirement benefits*

d. *Health and other welfare benefits expected to be provided to employees deemed to be on a disability retirement*

Both IFRS and US GAAP treat delayed vesting (i.e., after ten years of service, employee is entitled to a lump sum in the tenth year) the same way. The attribution assumes that beneficiaries will reach the vesting date, taking into account factors such as turnover, mortality, and the like. Both IFRS and US GAAP require the obligation and thus service costs to be based on the number of beneficiaries that are expected to qualify for the benefit:

IAS 19

69 *Employee service gives rise to an obligation under a defined benefit plan even if the benefits are conditional on future employment (in other words they are not vested). Employee service before the vesting date gives rise to a constructive obligation because, at the end of each successive reporting period, the amount of future service that an employee will have to render before becoming entitled to the benefit is reduced.* In measuring its defined benefit obligation, an entity considers the probability that some employees may not satisfy any vesting requirements. *Similarly, although certain post-employment benefits, for example, post-employment medical benefits, become payable only if a specified event occurs when an employee is no longer employed, an obligation is created when the employee renders service that will provide entitlement to the benefit if the specified event occurs. The probability that the specified event will occur affects the measurement of the obligation, but does not determine whether the obligation exists.*

ASC 715-30-35

1A *The projected benefit obligation as of a date is the actuarial present value of all benefits attributed by the plan's benefit formula to employee service rendered before that date. The projected benefit obligation is measured using an assumption as to future compensation levels if the pension benefit formula is based on those future compensation levels. Plans for which the pension benefit formula is based on future compensation are sometimes called pay-related, final-pay, final-average-pay, or career-average-pay plans. Plans for which the pension benefit formula is not based on future compensation levels are called non-pay-related or flat-benefit plans. The projected benefit obligation is a measure of benefits attributed to service to date* assuming that the plan continues in effect and that estimated future events (including compensation increases, turnover, and mortality) occur.

Interest Cost and Discount Rate

Both IFRS and US GAAP define the interest cost as the change in the pension obligation (gross of any plan assets) due to the passage of time. IAS 19 specifically requires the entity to consider material changes of the obligation during the plan year. However, there would likely be no difference in practice in computing the interest rate for a given discount rate.

The discount rate under both standards requires that the discount rate applied to the benefit obligation be that of high-quality corporate bonds that matches the expected cash flows of benefit payments. IAS 19 and ASC 715-30-35 also provide guidance that since maturities of corporate bonds will never match the benefit payments, that the yield curve of high-quality corporate bonds is extrapolated. IAS 19 directs that where a country does not have a deep market for corporate bonds, government bonds are used. IAS 19 adds that the bond yields must be in the same currency as the obligation due to the fact that currency exchange rates often include an element for inflation.

ASC 715-30-35 contains more guidance on determining the discount rate for a plan. Specifically, ASC 715-30-35-43 provides that the discount rate reflect the one at which the obligations could be effectively settled. In service of that goal, the entity is encouraged to look to the yields implicit in annuity contract prices. The paragraph also permits the entity to use the yield on high-quality corporate bonds.

The determination of the discount rates and interest cost are very similar for IFRS and US GAAP and would likely not vary significantly in practice.

Expected Return on Plan Assets

Both IFRS and US GAAP require that the rate used to compute the expected return on assets (EROA) be based on the assets invested or expected to be invested over the term of the obligations. Both standards direct that the EROA for plan year is computed by considering the timing of contributions and payments expected to be made during the plan year, but not in subsequent years. In other words, the calculation is a weighted-average of the amount of plan assets available each month throughout the plan year. EROA is a component of net periodic expense for both IFRS and US GAAP.

Actuarial Gains and Losses

Actuarial gains and losses (AGL) is the difference between the actual and the expected balances of plan assets and plan obligations. Looked at another way, it is the amount by which the actuarial return and cost was greater or less than the actual experience.

IAS 19 (2003) permits an entity to make an accounting policy choice to reflect AGL in either profit and loss or other comprehensive income (OCI). However, if under IAS 19, an entity chooses to reflect AGL in OCI, it must be recognized in full. Since US GAAP requires that change in the value of plan assets and liabilities be offset in OCI, if an entity chooses this method under IAS 19, other things being equal (e.g., PBO, plan asset value), IFRS and US GAAP will result in the same movement of plan assets and PBO being offset in OCI at the measurement date. However, under IAS 19, AGL is recognized in OCI and is **not** later "recycled" or reclassified to profit and loss. Under US GAAP, it must always be reflected at some point in profit and loss.

The practice of **not** reclassifying AGL to profit and loss is different than US GAAP, where all elements of OCI (i.e., changes in fair value of available for sale financial instruments, cash flow hedges) are **always** reclassified to profit and loss.

Because of these significant differences in the treatment of AGL, a defined benefit plan can result in a different net periodic expense in both a current period and over the life of the plan.

Under IAS 19, if an entity recognizes AGL in profit or loss, it can make a policy choice (that is consistent across periods and plans) to recognize AGL in the period it arises. If an entity does not make this choice, there is a minimum amount that must be recognized in profit and loss. This method is identical to the one required under US GAAP. AGL is recognized if the cumulative amount exceeds a "corridor" of 10% of the greater of the PBO or plan assets (using absolute values). The amount exceeding the "corridor" must, at a minimum, be amortized over the remaining working lives of the participants:

IAS 19

93 *The portion of actuarial gains and losses to be recognized for each defined benefit plan is the excess determined in accordance with paragraph 92, divided by the expected average remaining working lives of the employees participating in that plan. However, an entity may adopt any systematic method that results in faster recognition of actuarial gains and losses, provided that the same basis is applied to both gains and losses and the basis is applied consistently from period to period. An entity may apply such systematic methods to actuarial gains and losses even if they are within the limits specified in paragraph 92.*

Under US GAAP, entities can also make a policy choice (that is consistent across periods and plans) to recognize AGL in the period it arises or faster than the "corridor" approach:

ASC 715-30-35

20 *However, immediate recognition of gains and losses as a component of net periodic pension cost is permitted if that method is applied consistently, and is applied to all gains and losses on both plan assets and obligations.*

24 *As a minimum, amortization of a net gain or loss included in accumulated other comprehensive income (excluding asset gains and losses not yet reflected in market-related value) shall be included as a component of net pension cost for a year if, as of the beginning of the year, that net gain or loss exceeds 10 percent of the greater of the projected benefit obligation or the market-related value of plan assets. If amortization is required, the minimum amortization shall be that excess divided by the average remaining service period of active employees expected to receive benefits under the plan. The amortization must always reduce the beginning-of-the-year balance. Amortization of a net gain results in a decrease in net periodic pension cost; amortization of a net loss results in an increase in net periodic pension cost. If all or almost all of a plan's participants are inactive, the average remaining life expectancy of the inactive participants shall be used instead of average remaining service.*

Note, however, that the last sentence in 715-30-35-24 allows an entity to use the average remaining life expectancy of participants if all or almost all of the participants are inactive. This difference means that if two entities had identical plans where all the participants were inactive, the **minimum** recognized under US GAAP will be less than under IFRS since IAS 19.39 does not permit this alternative amortization schedule.

Past or Prior Service Costs (PSC)

Past service costs (the terminology used by IFRS) or prior service costs (as referred to in US GAAP) occurs when a plan increases or decreases benefits for active employees and retirees for past service (not future service, as this is accounted for prospectively in the case of a gain or a curtailment in the case of a decrease in benefits).

IFRS and US GAAP differ significantly in the amount of PSC recognized in profit and loss and the timing of recognition.

IAS 19 requires that an entity recognize PSC in profit and loss. For benefits that are not vested, PSC (whether cost increase or cost reduction) is recognized on a straight-line basis from the date of the amendment to the date the benefits become vested. The PSC effects are recognized immediately in profit and loss for vested participants. Straight-line means that equal amounts per employee are recognized in each year. For example, for a single plan amendment, if employee A vests in 2 years, the PSC is recognized over the next two years. If employee B vests in five years, PSC is vested over the next five years. The effect of this treatment, like that of AGLs, is that the net liability on the balance sheet is different than what it would be using the actual PBO.

Contrary to IAS 19, US GAAP requires that PSC is first recognized in full in the PBO at the date of the amendment (this is consistent with US GAAP's reflection of the entire PBO in the net balance of the plan assets and liabilities). ASC 715-30-35-10 to 17 requires that the effect be recognized in OCI unless it is clear that the entity will receive no future benefit (e.g., the shutdown of a business), in which case the amount is included in profit and loss during the period of amendment). Unless it is clear that the expected benefits to the entity will be for a shorter period, PSC is then amortized over either the remaining working lives of the affected plan participants, or, if all or almost all of the of the participants are inactive, over the remaining life expectancy of the beneficiaries. For PSC gains (reductions in cost), the gain is first offset against any remaining PSC losses in OCI. Consequently, the amount of net PSC costs recognized in a given period can be different than IFRS, which requires a layer of gain or loss to be recognized from the time of recognition through the vesting period.

Example: Comparison of Past/Prior Service Costs		

	IFRS	*US GAAP*
PBO	10,000,000	10,000,000
Plan Assets	7,000,000	7,000,000
Unrecognized Accum (Gain) or Loss*	1,000,000	1,000,000
Past/Prior Service Cost Balance	500,000	500,000
Net PBO*	4,500,000	4,500,000
PCS Amendment Current Year	(400,000)	(400,000)
Amount to be recognized	100,000	(400,000)
Remaining working lives average	15	
Remaining vesting period average		4
Effect on NPPC of current year PSC	6,667	(100,000)
Effect on NPPC of prior year PSC		125,000
Total impact	6,667	25,004

* *Since US GAAP requires the balance sheet to be stated as the actual net balance of PBO and assets, the effect of the gain or loss is in OCI, not the obligation. Under IFRS, the net gain or loss is not recognized in the balance sheet, but is disclosed.*

Carrying Amount of Plan Assets and Liabilities on Sponsor Financial Statements

US GAAP requires that the net obligation or asset of a defined-benefit plan be presented on the balance sheet of the sponsor entity at the measurement date using the full fair value of the plan asset (or market-related value) and full PBO. The offset is recognized in other OCI.

IAS 19, conversely, permits gains and losses and past service costs to be deferred:

> 54 *The amount recognized as a defined benefit liability shall be the net total of the following amounts:*
>
> a. *The present value of the defined benefit obligation at the end of the reporting period (see paragraph 64)*
> b. *Plus any actuarial gains (less any actuarial losses) not recognized because of the treatment set out in paragraphs 92 and 93*
> c. *Minus any past service cost not yet recognized (see paragraph 96)*
> d. *Minus the fair value at the end of the reporting period of plan assets (if any) out of which the obligations are to be settled directly (see paragraphs 102-104)*

Because IAS 19 permits actuarial gains and losses to be deferred, the liability used to compute the net asset or obligation can be different than the actuarial balance of the PBO. Consequently, IFRS limits the carrying value of any net plan asset on the balance sheet of the sponsor entity. The limit is intended to prevent an entity from recognizing a plan asset that is only the result of deferred losses or gains recognized in the current period. Otherwise, an entity can present an asset when the economic reality is that the sponsor is in a net obligation position.

IAS 19

58 *The amount determined under paragraph 54 may be negative (an asset). An entity shall measure the resulting asset at the lower of*

    a. *The amount determined under paragraph 54*
    b. *The total of*

        (1) Any cumulative unrecognized net actuarial losses and past service cost (see paragraphs 92, 93 and 96); and
        (2) The present value of any economic benefits available in the form of refunds from the plan or reductions in future contributions to the plan. The present value of these economic benefits shall be determined using the discount rate specified in paragraph 78.

58A *The application of paragraph 58 shall not result in a gain being recognized solely as a result of an actuarial loss or past service cost in the current period or in a loss being recognized solely as a result of an actuarial gain in the current period. The entity shall therefore recognize immediately under paragraph 54 the following, to the extent that they arise while the defined benefit asset is determined in accordance with paragraph 58(b):*

    a. *Net actuarial losses of the current period and past service cost of the current period to the extent that they exceed any reduction in the present value of the economic benefits specified in paragraph 58(b)(ii). If there is no change or an increase in the present value of the economic benefits, the entire net actuarial losses of the current period and past service cost of the current period shall be recognized immediately under paragraph 54.*
    b. *Net actuarial gains of the current period after the deduction of past service cost of the current period to the extent that they exceed any increase in the present value of the economic benefits specified in paragraph 58(b)(ii). If there is no change or a decrease in the present value of the economic benefits, the entire net actuarial gains of the current period after the deduction of past service cost of the current period shall be recognized immediately under paragraph 54.*

The effect on profit and loss in the current period of NPC is higher or lower than it would be in absence of this limit in the case of actuarial losses or gains, respectively.

The recognition of the full fair value of the plan assets and PBO under US GAAP at the measurement date does eliminate the need to test for a maximum asset as is required for IAS 19. However, the use of a market-related asset value as permitted under US GAAP does alter the normal recognition of gains and losses:

ASC 715-30-35

22 *Asset gains and losses are differences between the actual return on plan assets during a period and the expected return on plan assets for that period. Asset gains and losses include both changes reflected in the market-related value of plan assets and changes not yet reflected in the market-related value (i.e., the difference between the fair value of assets and the market-related value). Gains or losses on transferable securities issued by the employer and included in plan assets are also included in asset gains and losses. Asset gains and losses not yet*

reflected in market-related value are not required to be amortized under paragraphs 715-30-35-24 through 25.

In summary, since US GAAP permits the use of the *market-related* value of plans assets, and IFRS permits deferral of recognition of gains or losses or PSC in the balance sheet, all other things being equal, an entity using US GAAP that employs market-related value and with actuarial gains and losses will have a different net asset value than one using IFRS.

Measurement Date

IFRS and US GAAP require the measurement of plan assets and obligations to be as of the fiscal year of the reporting entity. Additionally, both standards permit earlier estimates of funded status to be used as a basis for projecting year-end balances:

IAS 19

56 *An entity shall determine the present value of defined benefit obligations and the fair value of any plan assets with sufficient regularity that the amounts recognized in the financial statements do not differ materially from the amounts that would be determined at the end of the reporting period.*

ASC 715-30-35

64 *Requiring that the pension measurements be as of a particular date is not intended to require that all procedures be performed after that date. As with other financial statement items requiring estimates, much of the information can be prepared as of an earlier date and projected forward to account for subsequent events (e.g., employee service).*

However, since US GAAP permits subsidiaries that have a fiscal year-end different than the parent to be consolidated as is, the measurement date of the subsidiary's funded status can be different than that of the parent.

ASC 715-30-35

62 *The measurements of plan assets and benefit obligations required by this Subtopic shall be as of the date of the employer's fiscal year-end statement of financial position except in both of the following cases:*

   a. *The plan is sponsored by a subsidiary that is consolidated using a fiscal period that differs from its parent's, as permitted by paragraph 810-10-45-12.*
   b. *The plan is sponsored by an investee that is accounted for using the equity method of accounting under paragraph 323-10-35-6, using financial statements of the investee for a fiscal period that is different from the investor's, as permitted by that Subtopic.*

63 *If the exceptions in the preceding paragraph apply, the employer shall measure the subsidiary's plan assets and benefit obligations as of the date used to consolidate the subsidiary's statement of financial position and shall measure the investee's plan assets and benefit obligations as of the date of the investee's financial statements used to apply the equity method. For example, if a calendar year-end parent consolidates a subsidiary using the subsidiary's September 30*

financial statements, the funded status of the subsidiary's benefit plan included in the consolidated financial statements shall be measured as of September 30.

In practice, the differing treatment for subsidiaries between IFRS and US GAAP for measurement date, over time, is not likely to produce a significant difference in the funded status of otherwise identical plans. It is true, however, that historical stock market values tend to follow seasonal trends and could result in some comparability variances, albeit consistently. A circumstance that can result in material differences would be in the case of sudden changes in market interest rates or investment performance, as could be the case during a financial crisis. This would result in delayed recognition of lower market values under US GAAP than under IFRS, although US GAAP may require subsequent event disclosure.

Curtailments and Settlements

The definition of a curtailment is very similar for US GAAP and IFRS:

IAS 19

11 A curtailment occurs when an entity either

    a. Is demonstrably committed to make a significant reduction in the number of employees covered by a plan

    b. Amends the terms of a defined benefit plan so that a significant element of future service by current employees will no longer qualify for benefits, or will qualify only for reduced benefits

ASC Master Glossary

Plan Curtailment

An event that significantly reduces the expected years of future service of present employees or eliminates for a significant number of employees the accrual of defined benefits for some or all of their future services.

Even though the wording is different, an event that constitutes a curtailment under one standard will likely result in one under the other. Notwithstanding this similarity, the occurrence of a curtailment is a matter of judgment, and that judgment will be influenced by the tendencies of US GAAP and IFRS, respectively. To this point, IFRS requires recognition of the curtailment when the entity is "demonstrably committed" to the plan. The recognition of a liability when a loss is probable is consistent with the *IFRS Framework* of a liability and is also applied to exit costs under IAS 37, *Contingencies,* as well as other IFRS statements. Conversely, US GAAP usually requires that exit costs are recognized only when either employees accept a package or services are rendered if services are required for a period longer than the minimum notification period.

Cash Balance Plans

Cash balance plans are specifically addressed in US GAAP:

ASC 715-30-35

> *71 The benefit promise in a cash balance arrangement for a cash balance plan as described in the definition of the term, is not pay-related, and use of a projected unit credit method is neither required nor appropriate for purposes of measuring the benefit obligation and annual cost of benefits earned under this Subtopic. The appropriate cost attribution approach, therefore, is the traditional unit credit method. See paragraphs 715-30-35-36 through 35-39 and 715-30-55-7 through 55-15 for guidance on attribution approaches.*

> *72 The determination of whether a plan is pay-related and the appropriate benefit attribution approach for a cash balance plan with other characteristics or for other types of defined benefit pension plans depends on an evaluation of the specific features of those benefit arrangements.*

The definition of defined benefit plan in IFRS is a long-term employee benefit plan (payable in more than a year) that is **not** a defined contribution plan. IAS 19 defines a defined contribution plan as

> *Defined contribution plans are post-employment benefit plans under which an entity pays fixed contributions into a separate entity (a fund) and will have no legal or constructive obligation to pay further contributions if the fund does not hold sufficient assets to pay all employee benefits relating to employee service in the current and prior periods.*

Because an entity holds the risk for the funding of a cash balance plan, IFRS would treat it the same as US GAAP, respecting the inherent differences in the two standards.

Transfer of Excess Pension Assets to a Retiree Health-Care Benefits Account

US GAAP provides specific guidance with respect to plan assets contributed to a retiree health account:

ASC 715-30-35

> *73 The transfer of excess pension assets to a retiree health-care account or plan (whether or not the transfer of assets is made pursuant to applicable laws or regulations) shall be recognized as a negative contribution to (withdrawal of funds from) the pension plan and a positive contribution to the retiree health-care plan. No gain or loss arises from the transfer of the excess pension assets.*

IFRS does not address this specifically; however, the definition of plan assets under IAS 19 would not include contributions to an account no longer in control of the plan nor to another entity to be treated as plan assets:

> *Plan assets comprise*
>
> *a. Assets held by a long-term employee benefit fund*
> *b. Qualifying insurance policies*
>
> *Assets held by a long-term employee benefit fund are assets (other than non-transferable financial instruments issued by the reporting entity) that*

   a. Are held by an entity (a fund) that is legally separate from the reporting entity and exists solely to pay or fund employee benefits

   b. Are available to be used only to pay or fund employee benefits, are not available to the reporting entity's own creditors (even in bankruptcy), and cannot be returned to the reporting entity, unless either

     (1) The remaining assets of the fund are sufficient to meet all the related employee benefit obligations of the plan or the reporting entity

     (2) The assets are returned to the reporting entity to reimburse it for employee benefits already paid

Consequently, transfers of assets to a retiree health account, which under the control of the employee, would also be accounted for as a withdrawal under IFRS. In summary, the entity has paid out the benefits when transferred to the control of the employee.

Termination Benefits

Termination benefits are ones paid to employees as a result of a separation from employment of the entity that is not retirement. The measurement of termination benefits are described differently between IFRS and US GAAP, but the results would likely be similar, notwithstanding the inherent differences between the standards.

Recognition is defined differently, however:

IAS 19

133 An entity shall recognize termination benefits as a liability and an expense when, and only when, the entity is demonstrably committed to either

   a. Terminate the employment of an employee or group of employees before the normal retirement date

   b. Provide termination benefits as a result of an offer made in order to encourage voluntary redundancy

134 An entity is demonstrably committed to a termination when, and only when, the entity has a detailed formal plan for the termination and is without realistic possibility of withdrawal. The detailed plan shall include, as a minimum

   a. The location, function, and approximate number of employees whose services are to be terminated

   b. The termination benefits for each job classification or function

   c. The time at which the plan will be implemented. Implementation shall begin as soon as possible and the period of time to complete implementation shall be such that material changes to the plan are not likely.

Consistent with the *IFRS Framework* and IAS 37, *Provisions and Contingencies*, the loss is recognized when there is no realistic alternative for the entity to withdraw from the plan and it can be reliably measured. IAS 19.34(c) is included in the definition to permit recognition of an accrual only when it is difficult to reverse the decision, in other words, the plan is highly likely to be executed. Otherwise, an entity could, in effect, arbitrarily manipulate income. This subparagraph is consistent with a condition in IFRS 5, *Discontinued Operations*.

US GAAP requires noncontractual termination benefits to be recognized when the offer is accepted by the employee. Contractual benefits are recognized when the loss is probable and it can be reasonably estimated.

ASC 715-30-25

10 Termination benefits may take various forms including lump-sum payments, periodic future payments, or both. They may be paid directly from an employer's assets, an existing pension plan, a new employee benefit plan, or a combination of those means. An employer that offers special termination benefits to employees shall recognize a liability and a loss when the employees accept the offer_and the amount can be reasonably estimated. An employer that provides contractual termination benefits shall recognize a liability and a loss when it is probable that employees will be entitled to benefits and the amount can be reasonably estimated.

The above differences mean that the timing of recognition for termination costs can be accrued sooner under IFRS than US GAAP. This disparity aligns with the fundamental tension between IFRS and US GAAP: IFRS favors relevance over reliability when recognizing financial effects, where US GAAP is the opposite.

SECTION 2—IAS 19 (2010)

IAS 19 (2011) represents a significant shift in measurement and recognition of pension and postretirement effect on profit and loss from both US GAAP and the currently effective IAS 19. Regardless, the underlying concepts and much of the wording of IAS 19 (2003) regarding measurement and recognition of plan assets and liabilities remains the same. For this reason, section one of this chapter must be read in conjunction with this section.

The major changes from IAS 19 (2003) are

- Like US GAAP, and unlike current IFRS, the full value of the PBO is reflected in the pension or postretirement net liability or asset at the measurement (or remeasurement) date in the balance sheet of the sponsor. Current IFRS permits an entity to defer actuarial gains and losses and past service costs, resulting in a net position that uses a liability that is greater or less than the current PBO.

- IAS 19 (2011) eliminates the concept of expected return on plan assets reflected in the profit and loss statement. Instead, the effect of the discount rate multiplied by the net asset or liability is included in profit and loss as interest income or expense, respectively. The return on plan assets is included in remeasurements.

- AGLs are reflected only in OCI and **not** recycled to profit and loss. This is different than US GAAP, under which OCI is **always** reclassified into profit and loss at some point.

- Plan amendments and curtailments are included in PSC and recognized at the date of amendment (after remeasurement) in profit and loss. Under the currently effective IAS 19 (2003), PSC that is **not** vested is not recognized in either the net asset or liability nor in profit and loss at time of remeasurement, but is instead amortized over the remaining vesting period. US GAAP also requires amortization of PSC into profit and loss over the remaining service of the participants, or the remaining life expectancy if all or almost all of the participants are retired, but the effect is immediately recognized in the net liability or asset with an offset in OCI.

Interest Costs and Expected Return on Plan Assets

IAS 19 (2011) replaces the concept of return on plan assets with net interest cost or income on the net liability or asset, respectively, presented in profit and loss. Consequently, the variable portion of the return on assets (realizing that all investments have some element of return for the passage of time) is reflected in OCI as part of measurement.

In reaching this conclusion, the IASB chose this method because it presented elements of income with different predictive value separately. This concern weighed on the decision because a main reason for reconsidering the accounting for post-employment benefits was that it was widely regarded as weak in terms of disaggregating the effect on profit and loss of actions management takes in the current period and ones that are largely the result of returns and costs determined by market forces (e.g., returns on equity securities, interest rates).

Because the return on plan assets is usually different than the cost of interest on plan obligations (which is based on the period-end rate of high-quality corporate bonds), all other things being equal, the financing components under US GAAP will vary more year over year than IFRS, given plans with identical assets, demographics, and funded status.

Actuarial Gains/Losses and Past Service Costs

Because US GAAP permits actuarial gains and losses and requires past service costs to be recognized over future service or life expectancy (in the case of inactive plans), and IAS 19 (2011) requires immediate recognition in profit and loss, given the same funded status and portfolio of assets, profit and loss will be less volatile under US GAAP than IAS 19 (2011). However, the net plan liability or asset will be the same under both standards, unless a US GAAP entity uses the market-related value of plan assets (please see Section one for a description).

It is also important to note that while permitted under the current IAS (2003), actuarial gains and losses will always be recognized in OCI and not recycled under IAS 19 (2011). Under US GAAP, gains and losses will always be recognized in profit and loss at some point. This means that over a plan year and the life of the plan, the amount of expense recognized in profit and loss will be different than under US GAAP.

Example: Comparison of Net Periodic Cost between IAS 19 (2011) and US GAAP		
	IAS 19 (2011)	*US GAAP*
PBO	10,000,000	10,000,000
Plan assets (marketed-related value not used for US GAAP)	7,000,000	7,000,000
Actuarial gain or loss	500,000	500,000
Net liability	3,500,000	3,500,000
PSC amendment current year	(400,000)	(400,000)
Amount to be recognized	(400,000)	(400,000)
Remaining working lives average	N/A	15
Effect on NPPC of current year PSC	(400,000)	(26,667)
Amortization of actuarial gain or loss CY	0	33,333
Expected return on plan assets	630,000	
Interest cost (net for IAS 19)	(500,000)	175,000
Service cost	125,000	125,000
Net periodic postemployment cost	(145,000)	306,667

The difference in the profit and loss in the above example would be reflected in OCI because both IAS 19 (2011) and US GAAP require the net asset or liability to be measured at the full value of the PBO less the fair value of plan assets. Entities using US GAAP can use market-related value. Please see Section one or ASC 715-30.

CHAPTER SUMMARY

The differences between the currently effective IAS 19 (2003) and US GAAP are as follows.

Profit and loss. The amortization period of prior/past service cost and actuarial gains and losses are over different time periods. US GAAP permits actuarial gains and losses to be amortized over the remaining working lives of a plan with active participants, or life expectancy of beneficiaries for a substantially inactive plan. IFRS requires gains and losses to be amortized over the remaining vesting period. IAS 19 (2003) requires PSC to be amortized over the remaining vesting period on a straight-line basis, whereas US GAAP uses the same period as is used for actuarial gains and losses. Although neither standard allows immediate recognition of PSC as an option, under currently effective IFRS, if all participants are vested, all PSC costs would be immediately recognized in profit and loss. Both IFRS and US GAAP permit immediate recognition of actuarial gains and losses. Service and financing costs (return and plan assets and interest costs from the unwinding of discounting of the PBO) are accounted for very similarly.

Balance sheet. The currently effective IAS 19 (2003) allows deferrals of actuarial gains and losses and past service costs in measuring the PBO, whereas US GAAP does not. US GAAP permits the use of a market-related value of plan assets, IFRS requires valuation of plan assets at fair value at the (re)measurement date. IAS 19 (2011), like current US GAAP, requires the full value of the PBO to be included in the net asset or liability.

Other comprehensive income. Under US GAAP, all elements of OCI are recycled into profit and loss (please see the paragraph above on profit and loss). IAS 19 (2003) permits an entity to make a policy choice to reflect actuarial gains and losses in OCI. IAS 19 (2011) requires gains and losses to be included in OCI and **not** recycled.

14 IMPAIRMENTS

This chapter covers impairment of property plant, and equipment (PP&E), goodwill, and other intangible assets. Impairment of financial assets and inventory are covered in the respective chapters.

Both IFRS and US GAAP require impairment of assets when their value has diminished. However, there are fundamental differences with regard to recognition, measurement, and subsequent measurement.

IMPAIRMENT TRIGGERS AND TIMING

Both IFRS and US GAAP require that goodwill and indefinite-lived intangible assets be tested for impairment annually at the same time each year. For PP&E and definite-lived intangibles, impairment is assessed only after triggers are identified. The triggers are very similar under both standards. The underlying concept of impairment triggers are conditions and evidence that strongly indicate that the future cash flows will be significantly less than originally planned. Both standards require assessment of triggers for internal and external factors such as changes in focus of the entity, operation issues, adverse changes in the market for an entity's products, and changes in interest rates.

IFRS describes the minimum indications that shall be considered; US GAAP gives examples.

IAS 36

12 *In assessing whether there is any indication that an asset may be impaired, an entity shall consider, as a minimum, the following indications:*

External sources of information

(a) *During the period, an asset's market value has declined significantly more than would be expected as a result of the passage of time or normal use.*

(b) *Significant changes with an adverse effect on the entity have taken place during the period, or will take place in the near future, in the technological, market, economic or legal environment in which the entity operates or in the market to which an asset is dedicated.*

(c) *Market interest rates or other market rates of return on investments have increased during the period, and those increases are likely to affect the discount rate used in calculating an asset's value in use and decrease the asset's recoverable amount materially.*

(d) *The carrying amount of the net assets of the entity is more than its market capitalization.*

Internal sources of information

(e) Evidence is available of obsolescence or physical damage of an asset.

(f) Significant changes with an adverse effect on the entity have taken place during the period, or are expected to take place in the near future, in the extent to which, or manner in which, an asset is used or is expected to be used. These changes include the asset becoming idle, plans to discontinue or restructure the operation to which an asset belongs, plans to dispose of an asset before the previously expected date, and reassessing the useful life of an asset as finite rather than indefinite.*

> ** Once an asset meets the criteria to be classified as held for sale (or is included in a disposal group that is classified as held for sale), it is excluded from the scope of this Standard and is accounted for in accordance with IFRS 5, **Noncurrent Assets Held for Sale and Discontinued Operations.***

(g) Evidence is available from internal reporting that indicates that the economic performance of an asset is, or will be, worse than expected.

US GAAP is as follows:

ASC 360-10-35

21 A long-lived asset (asset group) shall be tested for recoverability whenever events or changes in circumstances indicate that its carrying amount may not be recoverable. The following are examples of such events or changes in circumstances:

a. A significant decrease in the market price of a long-lived asset (asset group)

b. A significant adverse change in the extent or manner in which a long-lived asset (asset group) is being used or in its physical condition

c. A significant adverse change in legal factors or in the business climate that could affect the value of a long-lived asset (asset group), including an adverse action or assessment by a regulator

d. An accumulation of costs significantly in excess of the amount originally expected for the acquisition or construction of a long-lived asset (asset group)

e. A current-period operating or cash flow loss combined with a history of operating or cash flow losses or a projection or forecast that demonstrates continuing losses associated with the use of a long-lived asset (asset group)

f. A current expectation that, more likely than not, a long-lived asset (asset group) will be sold or otherwise disposed of significantly before the end of its previously estimated useful life. The term more likely than not refers to a level of likelihood that is more than 50 percent.

Under IFRS, impairments are to be reversed when circumstances indicate that the conditions that led to an impairment have turned favorable.

The triggers for the reversal of impairments are essentially the same as those that would have given rise to that impairment. The amount of reversal will be covered later in this chapter in the section for recognition of impairments.

In practice, triggers for impairment for PP&E and goodwill are essentially the same between IFRS and US GAAP. Circumstances that are triggers for one standard will be the same under the other. However, as will be covered in the following section, the recognition of impairments is very different between IFRS and US GAAP.

RECOGNITION OF IMPAIRMENTS

If an impairment trigger indicates that an asset may be impaired, the next step is the recognition. IFRS and US GAAP use substantially different processes for recognition of impairments. US GAAP employs a two-step process, whereas IFRS uses a single step.

Under US GAAP, step one is to compare future undiscounted cash flows of the asset(s) (recoverable amount) to the carrying value (cost less accumulated depreciation) at the date of impairment. If the undiscounted cash flows are less than the carrying value, the carrying value is written down to the fair value of asset(s). The impaired value becomes the new cost basis and write-backs are prohibited. The undiscounted cash flows include those expected to be realized for operating and disposal (sales proceeds), but exclude those that would increase the service capacity of the asset(s):

ASC 360-10-35

> *33 Estimates of future cash flows used to test the recoverability of a long-lived asset (asset group) that is in use, including a long-lived asset (asset group) for which development is substantially complete, shall be based on the existing service potential of the asset (asset group) at the date it is tested. The service potential of a long-lived asset (asset group) encompasses its remaining useful life, cash-flow-generating capacity, and for tangible assets, physical output capacity. Those estimates shall include cash flows associated with future expenditures necessary to maintain the existing service potential of a long-lived asset (asset group), including those that replace the service potential of component parts of a long-lived asset (for example, the roof of a building) and component assets other than the primary asset of an asset group. Those estimates shall exclude cash flows associated with future capital expenditures that would increase the service potential of a long-lived asset (asset group).*

IFRS defines the recoverable amount as the **higher** of the fair value less cost to sell or value in use. VIU is essentially a discounted cash flow approach. Because there are two values used for any one impairment, IFRS allows an entity to use the first one measured to be used if it is not likely that the other amount would be higher. Likewise, if the first value calculated exceeds the carrying value, there is no need to calculate the second. This allowance is to bring cost-benefit to the measurement of impairment. IAS 36.21 permits an entity to use only VIU if there is not an active market for the asset. This may be the case for specialized equipment or for which there are not many in existence. IAS 36.21 also permits an entity on grounds of practicality to not calculate VIU if it is not expected that it would exceed fair value less cost to sell.

In summary, IAS 36 allows an entity to use either value without calculating the other if it is likely that the other technique would not produce a materially different value, provided that this does not reasonably prevent an impairment from being recognized, or if the first value indicates no impairment; this is because the **higher** of the values is used.

IAS 36

Measuring Recoverable Amount

18 *This Standard defines recoverable amount as the higher of an asset's or cash-generating unit's fair value less costs to sell and its value in use. Paragraphs 19-57 set out the requirements for measuring recoverable amount. These requirements use the term "an asset" but apply equally to an individual asset or a cash-generating unit.*

19 *It is not always necessary to determine both an asset's fair value less costs to sell and its value in use. If either of these amounts exceeds the asset's carrying amount, the asset is not impaired and it is not necessary to estimate the other amount.*

20 *It may be possible to determine fair value less costs to sell, even if an asset is not traded in an active market. However, sometimes it will not be possible to determine fair value less costs to sell because there is no basis for making a reliable estimate of the amount obtainable from the sale of the asset in an arm's-length transaction between knowledgeable and willing parties. In this case, the entity may use the asset's value in use as its recoverable amount.*

21 *If there is no reason to believe that an asset's value in use materially exceeds its fair value less costs to sell, the asset's fair value less costs to sell may be used as its recoverable amount. This will often be the case for an asset that is held for disposal. This is because the value in use of an asset held for disposal will consist mainly of the net disposal proceeds, as the future cash flows from continuing use of the asset until its disposal are likely to be negligible.*

MEASUREMENT OF IMPAIRMENT

IAS 36 and ASC 360-10-35 both specify that impairment is the amount by which the carrying value of the asset exceeds the recoverable amount. Although IAS 36 specifies that an entity uses the higher of VIU or fair value, US GAAP can also result in the use of either fair value or present value techniques. Consequently, it is necessary to compare both measurement bases.

Nearly identical IFRS and US GAAP standards for fair value measurements will become effective on January 1, 2013 (IFRS 13 and updates to ASC 820). IFRS allows early adoption. However, until that point, IFRS and US GAAP measure fair value differently. US GAAP provides a fair value framework within ASC 820. Currently effective IFRS does not, but defines fair value as the amount that an asset would be exchanged for in an arm's-length transaction. Conversely, US GAAP (both current and not-yet-effective) specifies that fair value is an exit price in an orderly transaction in the most advantageous market for a particular asset reflecting its highest and best use.

Regardless of these differences, application of ASC 360 and IAS 36 can result in an entity using a present value calculation under IFRS or US GAAP. ASC 360-10 refers to the US GAAP fair value measurement framework, but provides that the expected present value model will often be used for PP&E impairment measurement:

ASC 360-10-35

> 36 *For long-lived assets (asset groups) that have uncertainties both in timing and amount, an expected present value technique will often be the appropriate technique with which to estimate fair value.*

A significant issue in using the present value technique (US GAAP) or VIU (IFRS) is composition of the nominal cash flows used in the computation. US GAAP and IFRS use very similar concepts for includable cash flows: those for the asset(s) in its present condition and use, including both operating and terminal flows, realistic assumptions based on past and probable future performance, **exclusion** of financing costs and restructuring programs (although IFRS requires that when an entity has committed to a restructuring plan, as defined in IAS 37, *Provisions*, those cash flows are included). Both standards also use net cash flows (that is, cash inflows and outflows).

IAS 36 and ASC 360-10-35 require that forecasts used to estimate nominal cash flows from use be based on current forecasts that management uses for general management of the business. However, IAS 36 offers more specific guidance that take the form of a default of the maximum number of years that management projections can be used. Forecasts after that minimum are limited to a constant or declining growth rate through the end of life of the asset:

IAS 36

Basis for Estimates of Future Cash Flows

> 33 *In measuring value in use an entity shall*
>
> (a) *Base cash flow projections on* reasonable and supportable *assumptions that represent management's best estimate of the* range of economic conditions that will exist over the remaining useful life of the asset. *Greater weight shall be given to external evidence.*
>
> (b) Base cash flow projections on the most recent financial budgets/forecasts approved by management, *but shall exclude any estimated future cash inflows or outflows expected to arise from future restructurings or from improving or enhancing the asset's performance. Projections based on these budgets/forecasts shall cover a maximum period of five years, unless a longer period can be justified.*
>
> (c) *Estimate cash flow projections beyond the period covered by the most recent budgets/forecasts by extrapolating the projections based on the budgets/forecasts using a steady or declining growth rate for subsequent years, unless an increasing rate can be justified. This growth rate shall not exceed the long-term average growth rate for the products, industries, or country or countries in which the entity operates, or for the market in which the asset is used, unless a higher rate can be justified.*
>
> 35 *Detailed, explicit and reliable financial budgets/forecasts of future cash flows for periods longer than five years are generally not available. For this reason, management's estimates of future cash flows are based on the most recent budgets/forecasts for a maximum of five years. Management may use cash flow projections based on financial budgets/forecasts over a period longer than five*

years if it is confident that these projections are reliable and it can demonstrate its ability, based on past experience, to forecast cash flows accurately over that longer period.

36 *Cash flow projections* until the end of an asset's useful life *are estimated by extrapolating the cash flow projections based on the financial budgets/forecasts using a growth rate for subsequent years. This rate* is steady or declining, unless an increase in the rate matches objective information about patterns over a product or industry lifecycle. *If appropriate, the growth rate is zero or negative.*

ASC 360-10 does not include specific guidance for estimation of future cash flows:

ASC 360-10-35

30 Estimates of future cash flows used to test the recoverability of a long-lived asset *(asset group) shall incorporate the entity's own assumptions about its use of the asset (asset group) and* shall consider all available evidence. *The* assumptions *used in developing those estimates* shall be reasonable in relation to the assumptions used *in developing other information used by the entity for comparable periods,* such as internal budgets and projections, *accruals related to incentive compensation plans, or information communicated to others. However, if alternative courses of action to recover the carrying amount of a long-lived asset (asset group) are under consideration or if a range is estimated for the amount of possible future cash flows associated with the likely course of action, the likelihood of those possible outcomes shall be considered. A probability-weighted approach may be useful in considering the likelihood of those possible outcomes. See Example 2 (paragraph 360-10-55-23) for an illustration of this guidance.*

Considering the above descriptions of US GAAP and IFRS for measuring the recoverable amount, where a circumstance would lead to an impairment under both standards (e.g., for US GAAP the undiscounted cash flows are less than the carrying value), there will be many instances where US GAAP and IFRS each use a present value technique to determine the fair value against which to compare the carrying value. However, IFRS more clearly defines the future cash flows that should be used for assets held for use. Because of the difference in specificity in estimating future cash flows under US GAAP, it is likely that the adoption of IFRS would result in a more structured policy. However, since companies use their internal policies to enforce consistency of application, what is likely to change is not the fact that a policy is prescriptive of the method used to measure cash flows for impairment testing, but that the method used may be changed. This will not likely result in significant changes to process. However, the unit of account, as covered in the next section, can result in significant changes in the way a company assesses impairment of asset groups and goodwill.

UNIT OF ACCOUNT

The definition of the unit of account is relevant when an asset that needs to be tested for impairment does not generate separately identifiable cash flows. An example would be a machine in a plant that is used to produce intermediate products for several finished goods. Both IFRS and US GAAP require that an asset in this circumstance must be tested in combination with other assets that, taken together, represent the lowest level group of assets that produce cash flows that are largely independent of other assets. However, this is where the similarity between IAS 36 and ASC 360-10-35 ends.

In general, US GAAP guidance tends to compel an entity to use greater aggregation for impairment testing than IFRS. This divergence in tendency is rooted in the fundamental tension between IFRS and US GAAP in that IFRS tends to favor relevance of information over reliability, whereas US GAAP tends toward the opposite.

There is a bright line for goodwill where US GAAP prescriptively limits the level at which goodwill can be tested to be the operating segment or one unit below. IAS 36 requires goodwill to be allocated based on the lowest level grouping of assets that produces largely independent cash inflows, which IAS 36 terms cash generating units (CGUs).

IAS 36

6   *A cash-generating unit is the smallest identifiable group of assets that generates cash inflows that are largely independent of the cash inflows from other assets or groups of assets.*

Cash Flows and Liabilities

US GAAP also requires that cash flows (both inflows and outflows) are the measurement attribute to determine independent flows. IAS 36 specifies that cash inflows be used for this purpose, which does not include outflows. Consequently, IFRS uses a model that is simpler to apply and in practice would result in more groups of assets. The number of units would be greater not only because costs allocations are not relevant to determining asset groups (however net cash flows are used for measuring impairment), but also because it is less difficult and would result in, all other things being equal, few groupings to be aggregated on cost-benefit grounds.

Other assets and liabilities are included in the asset grouping for impairment testing under US GAAP.

ASC 360-10-35

23 *For purposes of recognition and measurement of an impairment loss, a long-lived asset or assets shall be grouped* with other assets and liabilities *at the lowest level for which identifiable cash flows are largely independent of the cash flows of other assets and liabilities. However, an impairment loss, if any, that results from applying this Subtopic shall reduce only the carrying amount of a long-lived asset or assets of the group in accordance with paragraph 360-10-35-28.*

IFRS includes only assets and specific liabilities only the obligation is linked closely with the asset groups. This would be the case of an asset retirement obligation.

IAS 36

75 *The carrying amount of a cash-generating unit shall be determined on a basis consistent with the way the recoverable amount of the cash-generating unit is determined.*

76 *The carrying amount of a cash-generating unit:*

(a) *Includes the carrying amount of only those assets that can be attributed directly, or allocated on a reasonable and consistent basis, to the cash-generating unit and will generate the future cash inflows used in determining the cash-generating unit's value in use.*

(b) *Does not include the carrying amount of any recognized liability, unless the recoverable amount of the cash-generating unit cannot be determined without consideration of this liability.*

This is because fair value less costs to sell and value in use of a cash-generating unit are determined excluding cash flows that relate to assets that are not part of the cash-generating unit and liabilities that have been recognized (see paragraphs 28 and 43).

77 *When assets are grouped for recoverability assessments, it is important to include in the cash-generating unit all assets that generate or are used to generate the relevant stream of cash inflows. Otherwise, the cash-generating unit may appear to be fully recoverable when in fact an impairment loss has occurred. In some cases, although some assets contribute to the estimated future cash flows of a cash-generating unit, they cannot be allocated to the cash-generating unit on a reasonable and consistent basis. This might be the case for goodwill or corporate assets such as head office assets. Paragraphs 80-103 explain how to deal with these assets in testing a cash-generating unit for impairment.*

However, in a concession to cost benefit, the following paragraph allows inclusion of other assets and liabilities for practical reasons:

IAS 36

79 *For practical reasons, the recoverable amount of a cash-generating unit is sometimes determined after consideration of assets that are not part of the cash-generating unit (for example, receivables or other financial assets) or liabilities that have been recognized (for example, payables, pensions and other provisions). In such cases, the carrying amount of the cash-generating unit is increased by the carrying amount of those assets and decreased by the carrying amount of those liabilities.*

IMPACT OF IAS 36 — RECOVERABLE AMOUNT DETERMINATION

Because IAS 36 uses the higher of fair value less cost to sell or VIU, the following section of IAS 36 is necessary:

IAS 36

22 *Recoverable amount is determined for an individual asset, unless the asset does not generate cash inflows that are largely independent of those from other assets or groups of assets. If this is the case, recoverable amount is determined*

for the cash-generating unit to which the asset belongs (see paragraphs 65-103), unless either

(a) *The asset's fair value less costs to sell is higher than its carrying amount; or*
(b) *The asset's value in use can be estimated to be close to its fair value less costs to sell and fair value less costs to sell can be determined.*

23   *In some cases, estimates, averages and computational shortcuts may provide reasonable approximations of the detailed computations illustrated in this Standard for determining fair value less costs to sell or value in use.*

In other words, there is an exception for including an asset for and impairment for a GGU if there is relevant information available to calculate a fair-value less-costs-to-sell figure.

Another aspect of impairment testing under IAS 36 which would tend to cause more asset groupings to be tested for impairment is paragraphs IAS 36.70 and 71.

70   *If an active* market exists for the output *produced by an asset or group of assets, that asset or group of assets* shall be identified as a cash-generating unit, *even if some or all of the output is used internally. If the cash inflows generated by any asset or cash-generating unit are affected by internal transfer pricing, an entity shall use management's best estimate of future price(s) that could be achieved in arm's-length transactions in estimating*

(a) *The future cash inflows used to determine the asset's or cash-generating unit's value in use*
(b) *The future cash outflows used to determine the value in use of any other assets or cash-generating units that are affected by the internal transfer pricing*

71   *Even if part or all of the output produced by an asset or a group of assets is used by other units of the entity (for example, products at an intermediate stage of a production process), this asset or group of assets forms a separate cash-generating unit if the entity could sell the output on an active market. This is because the asset or group of assets could generate cash inflows that would be largely independent of the cash inflows from other assets or groups of assets. In using information based on financial budgets/forecasts that relates to such a cash-generating unit, or to any other asset or cash-generating unit affected by internal transfer pricing, an entity adjusts this information if internal transfer prices do not reflect management's best estimate of future prices that could be achieved in arm's-length transactions.*

The illustrative Examples section of IAS 36 includes an example for the situation described in IAS 36.70 and 71.

A third difference that tends to result in more asset groups for IFRS for impairment testing is the way IFRS and US GAAP treat corporate assets. Corporate assets are ones that do not belong to any one business or group of assets but contribute to the operations of the whole entity. Both standards use corporate headquarters as an example.

US GAAP requires that the entity adjust the asset group to encompass the asset, which in some cases, is the entire entity:

ASC 360-10-35

> 24 In limited circumstances, a long-lived asset (for example, a corporate head-
> quarters facility) may not have identifiable cash flows that are largely
> independent of the cash flows of other assets and liabilities and of other asset
> groups. In those circumstances, the asset group for that long-lived asset shall
> include all assets and liabilities of the entity.

> 25 In limited circumstances, an asset group will include all assets and liabilities of
> the entity. For example, the cost of operating assets such as corporate
> headquarters or centralized research facilities may be funded by revenue-
> producing activities at lower levels of the entity. Accordingly, in limited
> circumstances, the lowest level of identifiable cash flows that are largely
> independent of other asset groups may be the entity level. See Example 4
> (paragraph 360-10-55-35).

Conversely, IAS 36 requires that the corporate assets be allocated to the CGU's. If there is a reasonable basis to allocate the corporate asset(s) to a CGU, then that method should be used. If there is not, that CGU is tested without the allocation of the corporate asset. This can result in some CGUs bearing the carrying value of a **particular** corporate asset and others free of a portion.

After the testing of each CGU (including any allocation of corporate assets that have been made on a reasonable basis), the second step is a comparison of the carrying values of all **remaining** CGUs for **other** corporate assets where there is a reasonable basis to allocate to the **remaining** CGUs. The total recoverable amount of **remaining** CGUs including the **other** corporate asset is compared to the carrying value of the remaining CGUs.

Thus, in effect, where a corporate asset does not have a fair value less cost to sell, these assets are allocated into successively smaller pieces until it is tested among a group of CGU's. Illustrative Example 8 in IAS 36 demonstrates this process.

> 102 In testing a cash-generating unit for impairment, an entity shall identify all
> the corporate assets that relate to the cash-generating unit under review. If a
> portion of the carrying amount of a corporate asset

> (a) Can be allocated on a reasonable and consistent basis to that unit, the en-
> tity shall compare the carrying amount of the unit, including the portion of
> the carrying amount of the corporate asset allocated to the unit, with its
> recoverable amount. Any impairment loss shall be recognized in
> accordance with paragraph 104.

> (b) Cannot be allocated on a reasonable and consistent basis to that unit, the
> entity shall

>> (i) Compare the carrying amount of the unit, excluding the corporate
>> asset, with its recoverable amount and recognize any impairment
>> loss in accordance with paragraph 104

>> (ii) Identify the smallest group of cash-generating units that includes the
>> cash-generating unit under review and to which a portion of the
>> carrying amount of the corporate asset can be allocated on a
>> reasonable and consistent basis

> (iii) *Compare the carrying amount of that group of cash-generating units, including the portion of the carrying amount of the corporate asset allocated to that group of units, with the recoverable amount of the group of units. Any impairment loss shall be recognized in accordance with paragraph 104.*

103 *Illustrative Example 8 illustrates the application of these requirements to corporate assets.*

ALLOCATION OF IMPAIRMENTS TO ASSETS IN A CGU OR ASSET GROUP

Both IFRS and US GAAP allocate an impairment loss of a CGU or asset group based on the carrying value of the assets that comprise the group. However, since goodwill is allocated down to a lower level (a CGU) for IFRS than for US GAAP, allocation of impairment to goodwill is part of the guidance for allocation of impairment for CGU. US GAAP covers goodwill impairment separately.

104 *An impairment loss shall be recognized for a cash-generating unit (the smallest group of cash-generating units to which goodwill or a corporate asset has been allocated) if, and only if, the recoverable amount of the unit (group of units) is less than the carrying amount of the unit (group of units). The impairment loss shall be allocated to reduce the carrying amount of the assets of the unit (group of units) in the following order:*

> (a) *First, to reduce the carrying amount of any goodwill allocated to the cash-generating unit (group of units)*
> (b) *Then, to the other assets of the unit (group of units) pro rata on the basis of the carrying amount of each asset in the unit (group of units)*

These reductions in carrying amounts shall be treated as impairment losses on individual assets and recognized in accordance with paragraph 60.

105 *In allocating an impairment loss in accordance with paragraph 104: an entity shall not reduce the carrying amount of an asset below the highest of*

> (a) *Its fair value less costs to sell (if determinable);*
> (b) *Its value in use (if determinable); and*
> (c) *Zero.*

US GAAP does not include the reference to either goodwill or VIU/fair value since it does not contain the dual measurement basis that IAS 36 includes (the recoverable amount is the higher of the VIU or fair value less costs to sell).

ASC 360-10-35

Allocating Impairment Losses to an Asset Group

28 *An impairment loss for an asset group shall reduce only the carrying amounts of a long-lived asset or assets of the group. The loss shall be allocated to the long-lived assets of the group on a pro rata basis using the relative carrying amounts of those assets, except that the loss allocated to an individual long-lived asset of the group shall not reduce the carrying amount of that asset below its fair value*

whenever that fair value is determinable without undue cost and effort. *See Example 1 (paragraph 360-10-55-20) for an illustration of this guidance.*

Note that both IAS 36 and ASC 360-10 require that an asset is not to be reduced below the fair value (nor VIU for IFRS) if that amount is determinable.

REVERSAL OF IMPAIRMENTS

Because US GAAP explicitly prohibits the reversal of impairments, this section will cover only IFRS.

IAS 36 requires that in periods subsequent to one in which an impairment is recognized, an entity shall determine if circumstances that caused the impairment have turned favorable and thus warrant the reversal of an impairment.

IAS 36

> 110 *An entity shall assess at the end of each reporting period whether there is any indication that an impairment loss recognized in prior periods for an asset other than goodwill may no longer exist or may have decreased. If any such indication exists, the entity shall estimate the recoverable amount of that asset.*

1AS 36.111 covers the factors considered in impairment reversals, but they are essentially the same as the triggers that are assessed for an impairment:

> 112 *Indications of a potential decrease in an impairment loss in paragraph 111 mainly mirror the indications of a potential impairment loss in paragraph 12.*

IAS 36 requires that an entity reconsider the useful life of the asset after an impairment reversal, just as it does for impairment recognition:

> 113 *If there is an indication that an impairment loss recognized for an asset other than goodwill may no longer exist or may have decreased, this may indicate that the remaining useful life, the depreciation (amortization) method, or the residual value may need to be reviewed and adjusted in accordance with the IFRS applicable to the asset, even if no impairment loss is reversed for the asset.*

IAS 36 further stipulates, however, that a reversal should be based only on the factors that gave rise to the impairment:

> 114 *An impairment loss recognized in prior periods for an asset other than goodwill shall be reversed if, and only if, there has been a change in the estimates used to determine the asset's recoverable amount since the last impairment loss was recognized. If this is the case, the carrying amount of the asset shall, except as described in paragraph 117, be increased to its recoverable amount. That increase is a reversal of an impairment loss.*

IAS 36.115 refers to IAS 36.130 which covers disclosures for impairment reversals. The verbiage is dependent on whether the entity used fair value less costs to sell or VIU.

IAS 36 also prohibits an impairment reversal to create income. That is, the restored value cannot be higher than the carrying amount would have been if the impairment never occurred. Additionally, IAS 36 specifies that the increase in cash flows due to the passage of time (the unwinding of a discount) is not a basis for impairment reversal. This is in effect a limitation on the quantitative aspect of impairment reversal:

IAS 36

116 An asset's value in use may become greater than the asset's carrying amount simply because the present value of future cash inflows increases as they become closer. However, the service potential of the asset has not increased. Therefore, an impairment loss is not reversed just because of the passage of time (sometimes called the "unwinding" of the discount), even if the recoverable amount of the asset becomes higher than its carrying amount.

Reversing an Impairment Loss for an Individual Asset

117 The increased carrying amount of an asset other than goodwill attributable to a reversal of an impairment loss shall not exceed the carrying amount that would have been determined (net of amortization or depreciation) had no impairment loss been recognized for the asset in prior years.

Since IAS 16, *Property, Plant, and Equipment*, permits an entity to use the Revaluation Model (rather than the Cost Model), the following paragraph ties impairment reversal into that concept:

IAS 36

118 Any increase in the carrying amount of an asset other than goodwill above the carrying amount that would have been determined (net of amortization or depreciation) had no impairment loss been recognized for the asset in prior years is a revaluation. In accounting for such a revaluation, an entity applies the IFRS applicable to the asset.

NUMBER OF CASH-GENERATING UNITS

In practice, the number of CGUs in an entity is not voluminous. Costs benefit and materiality constraints limit them to a manageable number. However, since this is an area that requires a significant level of judgment, the granularity of CGUs will be a decision reached jointly between management and the external auditors. The less complex an entity is, the fewer CGUs it will have because it will have a tendency to have constituent parts that are in service of a few goals.

If an entity is composed of many relatively independent operations (i.e., a "roll-up" entity), the number of CGUs can be great. However, if an entity is run in this fashion, the information to assess impairment will be available (revenue and cost of goods for a store). Also, the paragraphs in IAS 36 that "override" the basic judgment of the existence of a CGU (e.g., IAS 36.70: if a part of entity produces goods that have a ready market), will cause an entity to "defend" fewer CGUs in the existence of these dynamics.

In practice, an entity, on average, will have more CGUs under IFRS than US GAAP.

GOODWILL

Goodwill is defined essentially the same under IFRS and US GAAP, although the inherent differences between IFRS and US GAAP may cause the carrying values to differ under identical circumstances (e.g., borrowing costs/capitalized interest, fair value measurement, etc.). Also, both standards prohibit the reversal of goodwill impairment.

As was covered in the previous section, under IFRS goodwill is allocated to the lowest level CGU, and thus is considered in impairment for asset groups (CGUs). US GAAP specifies that goodwill is only allocated to and tested for impairment at the operating segment level (ASC 280) or one unit below. Because of this, a company would mostly likely experience different frequency and amounts of goodwill impairments under IFRS versus US GAAP. Because US GAAP tests goodwill at a high level, the superior performance of an operation of an entity subsidizes the poor performance of another business unit.

There are differences in the incidence of impairment loss to the parts of a CGU or a US GAAP reporting unit. US GAAP requires that accounting for business combinations is essentially redone, allocating fair value to the existing assets. The remaining shortfall is then deducted from goodwill. Conversely, IAS 36 directs that the entire amount of the impairment loss is deducted from goodwill, with any loss in excess of the carrying value over goodwill being allocated based on carrying values (IAS 36.104).

Under IFRS, the lower level at which Goodwill is tested, and the apportionment of goodwill to the sale of an operation that is part of a CGU will result in a more volatile value of goodwill (it will decrease faster under IFRS than US GAAP, even though it is not amortized). This is because IFRS by its design does not allow as much subsidizing of operations with profits and losses.

CHAPTER SUMMARY

Both IFRS and US GAAP employ the concept of impairment. That is, when economic circumstances, both as a result of management actions and external economic effects, reduce the ability of an asset(s) to generate cash flows, these assets must be evaluated for impairment.

However, the standards have different thresholds for recognition of impairment (US GAAP uses a two-step process where impairments are recognized only if undiscounted cash flows exceed the carrying amount). They also differ with regard to amount to which an asset should be reduced (IFRS uses the higher of fair value or value in use), the level at which impairments are recognized (cash-generating units versus asset groups based on the connection of net cash flow), and composition of the asset groups (inclusion of liabilities). The most significant difference is, however, that IFRS requires reversals of impairments where circumstances indicate, whereas US GAAP prohibits them. This disparity regarding impairment reversal is emblematic of the tension between IFRS and US GAAP with regard to relevance and reliability.

INDEX

Printed and bound by CPI Group (UK) Ltd, Croydon, CR0 4YY

23/04/2025

14661015-0001